Current Trends on Digital Technologies and Gaming
for Teaching and Linguistics

Inmaculada Clotilde Santos Díaz /
Milagros Torrado Cespón /José María Díaz Lage /
Sidoní López Pérez (eds.)

Current Trends on
Digital Technologies and Gaming
for Teaching and Linguistics

PETER LANG

Lausanne - Berlin - Bruxelles - Chennai - New York – Oxford

Library of Congress Cataloging-in-Publication Data
A CIP catalog record for this book has been applied for at the
Library of Congress.

Bibliographic information published by the Deutsche Nationalbibliothek.
The German National Library lists this publication in the German National
Bibliography; detailed bibliographic data is available on the Internet
at http://dnb.d-nb.de.

This work was supported by the project e-LPHON4L: SOUNDS: teaching the sounds
of English to L2 and L3 learners in digital learning environments (RETOS 2019,
Programa Estatal de I+D+i, FEDER, 2020-2023, Ref. No. PID2019-105678RB-C21,
TED2021-130283B-C21, USC2022-RC031-2)

The cover image courtesy of Jorge Rodríguez Durán.

ISBN 978-3-631-88900-8 (Print)
E-ISBN 978-3-631-90431-2 (E-PDF)
E-ISBN 978-3-631-90432-9 (E-PUB)
10.3726/b20963

info@peterlang.com - www.peterlang.com

This publication has been peer reviewed.

Contents

6   Contents

Introduction

The emergence of new digital technologies over the last decades has significantly changed the experience of the teaching-learning process in education. In addition, the various benefits that digital games can bring to education, and specifically to foreign and second-language learning and teaching, have also received significant attention in recent years. Generally, both teachers and students are positive toward digital games in the classroom. However, their implementation continues to be far from expected and this is mainly due to different problems and obstacles, such as lack of knowledge and/or training, preparation time, and also instructional and technical barriers. In order to provide more insight into all these aspects, this volume includes different chapters that refer to digital technologies and gaming and their various applications and implications for language use, teaching and learning. These chapters are based on the research carried out by professors and researchers from different international universities, and they revolve around important aspects, such as the design, testing and evaluation of digital environments and literacies, including engineering, ICTs, learning, corpus linguistics, translation and language learning as well as educational policies, society, sustainability, internationalization, and the trends and challenges in gaming and video games.

The monographic volume opens with Adriana Gewerc Barujel's chapter on "Memes and Gender Stereotypes: A Study on Social Networking Practices among Adolescents in Mexico and Spain" in which she presents the results of the research project, "Digital environments and gender identity in adolescence" (EDIGA), which was funded by the Ministry of Science, Innovation and Universities (PID2019-108221RB-I00). Gewerc analyzes four common adolescent practices (selfies, video clips, profiles and memes), which are usually displayed in digital environments, especially in social networks, through both a quantitative and qualitative methodology. In the second chapter, whose title is "Using a Bilingual Concordancer to Promote Metalinguistic Reflection in the Learning of an Additional Language: The Case of B1 Learners of Catalan," Johannes Graën, Carme Bach and Daniel Cassany deal with the importance of using a bilingual concordancer in order to promote metalinguistic reflection in the learning of Catalan as an additional language. In the third chapter, titled "Improving Virtual Presence in Higher Education Hybrid Learning Digital Environments," Manuel Caeiro Rodríguez, María Lorenzo Rial, Manuel Fernández Iglesias, Fernando Mikic Fonte and Martín Llamas Nistal describe and analyze the features of said hybrid environments and the main functionalities that they include, while also considering the main issues still present and the new trends toward their solution. Mercedes González-Sanmamed, Iris Estévez and Alba Souto-Seijo approach the advantages and shortcomings of learning ecologies and digital literacy in their chapter, "Learning Ecologies and Digital Literacy: Opportunities and Challenges." Their study aims at analyzing the levels of digital competence of pre-service teachers of Early Childhood Education in the area of information and informational literacy.

The teaching and learning of English phonetics and pronunciation in digital and other learning environments is the focus of the next chapter by José María Díaz Lage, María de los Ángeles Gómez González and Inmaculada Clotilde Santos Díaz, whose title is "Teaching and Learning English Phonetics/Pronunciation in Digital and Other Learning Environments: Challenges and Perceptions of Spanish Instructors and Students." In this paper, they address phonetics and pronunciation as two of the most challenging areas for Spanish-speaking students of English as a foreign language and they also explore the reasons behind these challenging areas by looking at some of the answers to a survey addressed to a sample of 127 teachers and 494 students. The answers to these questions conform to the findings of prior research and highlight the need for special attention to be paid to phonetics and pronunciation in Spanish EFL classrooms. María de los Ángeles Gómez González and Alfonso Lago Ferreiro focus on serious games in their chapter entitled "Using a Serious Game for English Phonetics and Pronunciation Training: Foundations and Dynamics." They present *English Sounds on the Way* (e-SoundWay [0.0]), which is a serious game that has been devised for Spanish-speaking learners of English to improve their phonetic competence and pronunciation skills while walking the *Camino de Santiago* or the "Way of Saint James." The seventh chapter, titled "Evaluation of the *CleverCookie* Tool for Learning and Teaching English as a Foreign Language" by Milagros Torrado Cespón and Inmaculada Clotilde Santos Díaz deals with an online tool which is aimed at secondary school students, adults, and Internet users in general, which resulted from the research work done by ENTELEARN at the International University of La Rioja. The name of the tool is CleverCookie and in this chapter the authors explain the perception of voluntary undergraduate students who tested the tool based on an online questionnaire offered by the professor. Irene Doval Reixa presents and deals with parallel corpora in her chapter about "The English-Spanish Parallel Corpus PaEnS," which is part of a major ongoing project under the name of Spanish Parallel Corpora (PaCorES) that aims at collecting a series of bilingual parallel corpora with Spanish as the central language.

Gamification and learning are the focus of Carina Soledad González González's chapter entitled "Gamification and Immersive Learning in AR/VR Virtual Learning Environments." Her paper describes an educational experience which is based on the gamification of virtual environments using different tools and techniques that include virtual reality and augmented reality in higher education. In the next chapter, whose title is "Promoting Higher Education through Games," Flávio Costa and Carlos Vaz de Carvalho center on the specific field of the use of games for marketing, advertising and communication, which are also known as advergames. They specifically propose an advergame to promote the Instituto Superior de Engenharia do Porto (ISEP), which is a higher education institution in Portugal. Subsequently, José Carlos López Ardao's chapter, whose title is "Gamification in learning English as a second language (LESL)", proposes a gamification architecture through Moodle in which he defines and explains about the necessary gamification elements and the interrelationships between them, while focusing on the teaching of English as an L2. Last, but not least, Jonathan Reinhardt focuses on educational gaming and promotes its use in the teaching and learning of an L2 (second/foreign/additional language) in his chapter entitled "Researching gameful L2 teaching and learning: Challenges and potentials".

The result of all this effort lies in the fact that this monographic volume on digital technologies and gaming can be said to be one of the significant collections of literature and research devoted to the topic, while contributing to establishing Peter Lang as a leading international publisher according to the prestigious Scholarly Publishers Indicators (SPI). As such, Peter Lang excels in the Humanities and Social Sciences and it continues to offer top quality publishing services to higher education institutions and academics, allowing them to present their studies and research. For all these reasons, we would like to take this opportunity to express our sincere gratitude to both the publisher and the authors for their invaluable work, research and experience.

Adriana Gewerc (University of Santiago de Compostela)

Chapter I Memes and gender stereotypes. A study on social networking practices among adolescents in Mexico and Spain

I. Introduction

The influence of social networks in the daily lives of young people in recent years has been confirmed by extensive research (Boczkowski et al., 2018; Lasén Diaz, 2019). Social networks are used by 85 % of Internet users aged 16–70, with Instagram, Telegram, TikTok, Pinterest and Twitch standing out as the ones that are growing most significantly (IAB, 2021). Thus, it can be said that young people have found in cyberspace a suitable environment to develop discursive practices that allow them to take the floor, to narrate themselves and to position themselves before others. They are used to communicate, interact, entertain, etc., a use that is not innocuous, since the platforms on which this is done form an architecture that in some way suggests and orients the type of activities and practices that take place on them, which highlights the platformed nature of society (Srnicek, 2018; Van Dijck et al., 2018).

This digitalization of the processes of human interaction plays a fundamental role in the construction of youth subjectivities, as processes are generated through practices that, when repeated, help shape the subjects that negotiate in each power-knowledge relationship (Foucault, 1980). The way people present themselves in connection with others and the way they show themselves publicly are signs of identity. Surfing the network serves to validate the identity presented. When they create or share a meme, they validate a way of thinking and being, a discourse through which the subjects who carry out the action identify themselves (Ruiz Martínez, 2018), and in which gender is found.

This text is based on the EDIGA (Digital Environments and Gender Identities in Adolescence) research project, funded by the Spanish Ministry of Science, Innovation and Universities (PID2019-108221RB-I00), which aims to analyze and understand the role that digital environments play in the process of constructing gender identities at this stage of development, in different socio-cultural contexts. With this aim in mind, a sequential explanatory mixed design was used

(Creswell & Plano Clark, 2018), with a first quantitative phase, through a survey study, and a second qualitative case study phase.

The research focused on analyzing the knowledge, meanings and conditions of production of social practices (selfies, video clips, profiles and memes) that are deployed in digital environments, specifically in social networks. This paper presents survey results related to the production and distribution of memes, analyzing how they mobilize knowledge, meanings and strategies that lead to the reaffirmation of deeply rooted gender stereotypes among young people. In this historical moment, when gender equality is being questioned at the same time that macho attacks are taking place, with high popularity of sexting, and access to digital pornography, etc., it is extremely valuable to understand how the subjectivities and gender identities of adolescents are constructed in the digital environments in which they move.

1.1. Social practices and gender identity

Practices, as complex situated processes based on historically shaped cultural knowledge and habits, are always embedded in social processes (Klückmann, 2016). From this perspective, the social is a field of embodied practices, materially intertwined and centrally organized around shared understandings (Schatzki et al., 2001).

They are oriented by the know-how, the meanings attributed to them and the materialities in which they are produced (Bourdieu, 1991; Reckwitz, 2002; Schatzki et al., 2001). They are historically and socially situated, in such a way that it is only possible to explain the practices if they are related to the social conditions in which they have been constituted and the habitus (Bourdieu, 1991) that has engendered them. They are therefore understood as complex situated processes that emerge in a variety of contexts influenced by different factors.

From this perspective, social networking activities, insofar as they are repeated, are social practices that help construct subjectivity. Hence, research in this field must ask how they are generated, how people make sense of them and how they help construct subjects who negotiate certain power-knowledge relations (Foucault, 1980).

Social platforms and networks are places where the image is mobilized, experimented with and materialized in a system of circulation of social interaction (Lasén Díaz, 2019). Thus, the identity shown is constructed, taking into account not only the individual self-concept but also the collective self-concept. A process mediated by gender roles and conceptions of masculine and feminine, socially constructed and defining the ways in which adolescents present themselves to others (Acosta Valentín, 2021).

The resulting gender patterns become sources of identity, self-presentation and self-revelation to the world, in a circle of coexistence with the inequalities, stereotypes and prejudices that predominate in their normative constructions. Gender is constructed through these different practices, and social networks may become tools that influence people's behavior and roles, activating gender boundaries and establishing identity categories (Connell & Pearse, 2018).

These digital platforms seem to transmit a preconfigured framework linked to gender stereotypes, in which the perpetuation of the need to establish canons of beauty for them is visualized, in a permanent hegemony of what is normalized (Ferreiro Habrá, 2018). Thus, social networks have served to socialize and disseminate gender roles considered traditional, stereotyping them in the process, but also non-traditional ones, exposing sameness and difference at the same time.

Through the processes of socialization and the interactions that take place in these environments, patterns of relationships can be visualized that reproduce stereotypes linked to the canons and ideals of beauty, based on a conception of what is feminine and masculine.

Although at the same time as a commodification of gender discourses (Banet-Weiser, 2018), which favors the perpetuation and reproduction of power-knowledge relations (Foucault, 1980), opportunities are also mobilized for young people with dissident gender identities, women and men, from different territories, races and socio-economic classes (Miño-Puigcercós et al., 2019), agency and representation (Vera et al., 2020).

1.2. Memes

Memes can be defined as cultural units that are reproduced and disseminated through the network. They represent a very popular symbolic resource among adolescents. On the one hand, they bring together shared meanings and, on the other hand, give them a new meaning within the framework of the peer group. They are historically, culturally and linguistically situated, and thus relate to symbols, stereotypes and codes belonging to a particular place and time (Shifman, 2014).

The term meme comes from the Greek "mimema," meaning that which is imitated. In his book *The Selfish Gene*, Richard Dawkins (2002) introduced the term as a theoretical unit of cultural information disseminated from one person to another and transmissible from generation to generation. Generally, it is a combination of images and texts, of a humorous nature, presented in different formats (videos, gifs, comics, graphics, photographs, images, etc.) and susceptible to changes and transformations, causing diverse communicative effects in social networks (Vera, 2016). What characterizes a meme and defines it as such is: (1) the fidelity to the event to be highlighted, so that it is recognizable by citizens; (2) the fecundity or potential for transmission, usually of a viral nature, depending on the value that the community gives it; (3) the ease with which it remains in time and space on the network (Arango, 2015), and (4) its humorous nature (Cama et al., 2018).

Through the rapid transmission and ease of assimilation of content, memes "create and reinforce communities of meaning, guilds or social groups" (Alarcón Zayas, 2017, p. 144), thus reflecting the collective "imaginary" of a given spatial-temporal scenario. Specifically, adolescents' social values, which define their identity and sense of belonging, are reinforced by the multiplicity of information they handle on the Internet.

Far from becoming a mere process of production and reproduction of digital content, through memes, adolescents participate in processes of resignification and reinterpretation of reality, allowing realities to be implanted and social stereotypes to be normalized and presented through memes, which perpetuate patriarchal behaviors that have remained over time and have now transcended social networks. Through them, social representations of gender are being constructed, consciously and unconsciously, not only in a generalized way, but also virally and constantly (Ballesteros-Doncel, 2016). Thus, it is necessary to investigate the possible existence of the influence that visual pieces, called "memes," have on young people, due to the fact that memory practices contain gender discourses that are produced in the historical and cultural context of each person (Santos & Faure, 2018).

Although they can become a powerful tool to question, criticize and propose actions related to what is commonly represented as masculine and feminine, in many cases they consolidate and expand traditional imaginaries, and we are faced with the continuation of traditional patterns in which, with the same simple formulas of humor, many forms of violence are naturalized. For this reason, Alarcón Zayas (2017) argues that "memes form the intellectual basis of our culture, just as genes form the basis of our life" (p. 123). Thus, we begin to understand that we are not dealing with a superfluous and irrelevant phenomenon, but with a form of communication that deserves to be studied with its variations and different meanings, mainly because of the signs and the way of using the language that make it up.

Both in the making of a meme and in its reproduction, there is a reinterpretation or positioning with respect to a reality, given that, although the medium is digital, the act of communicating is the product of a social being who is traversed by a historical, social, cultural, economic and political context that influences his or her way of perceiving the world. So, while the creation of the meme reflects an individual perspective, its viralization reflects a more general perspective of society, making it an interesting phenomenon for learning about ideological perspectives, symbolic values, prejudices, etc.

In this way, the multiple meanings from which youth produce and exchange memes are shown. They use parodic images as a privileged language, through which they participate in the global media culture and in their local contexts of interaction.

Memes have traditionally belonged to popular culture, like myths, legends, jokes or oral stories, and their authorship is irrelevant (Alarcón Zayas, 2017), given that they are usually modified, replicated, copied, re-signified and appropriated (Hungtington, 2016) by the collective and are usually anonymous (Wiggins & Bowers, 2015). Therefore, they are closely related to the group in which they are framed and are essential to understand the new trends of digital participation, co-creation and dissemination among virtual audiences (Martínez-Rolán & Piñeiro-Otero, 2016). They also make it possible to question hegemonic power by exercising resistance and expressing alternative discourses.

II. Methodology

This study is framed within the research project Digital Environments and Gender Identities in Adolescence (EDIGA) (PID2019-108221RB-I00). In accordance with the objectives, the survey method was used, by means of an online questionnaire designed ad hoc on the Survio platform, with 71 questions distributed in six sections: two general sections—(I) Sociodemographic issues and (II) Use of social networks—and four specific sections, relating to the main activities carried out by young people on digital platforms identified in the literature (Boczkowski et al., 2018), (III) Media profile setting, (IV) Selfies, (V) Meme creation and (VI) Video clips. For this chapter, the questions related to the production and circulation of memes were taken into account.

The study was carried out in the Autonomous Community of Galicia (Spain) and the city of Puebla (Mexico), through public secondary schools in both regions. They were selected according to the population density of the areas in which they are located, through stratified proportional cluster sampling.

To ensure the validity of the instrument (Taherdoost, 2016), an expert judgment was carried out according to the literature (Escobar-Pérez & Cuervo-Martínez, 2008), with six specialists in educational technology, social research methodology and gender identity. The revision allowed for the inclusion of new response options, improvement and adaptation of wording and language.

A pilot study was then conducted with 46 adolescents from Galicia and Puebla with similar characteristics to the study population. As a result, additional response categories were incorporated, and attitudinal items were added. The final version was used in the 21–22 school year in selected schools.

The sample consisted of 6,654 adolescents: 1,020 living in Galicia (Spain) and 5,634 in Puebla (Mexico). The informants are mostly between 14 and 17 years old; more than half of the sample is composed of cis females (51.481 %), followed by 39.6 % of cis men and 9.42 % of people who identify themselves within identities that differ from the hegemonic norm (transgender, non-binary or other) (Table 1).

Table 1. Sociodemographic Characterization of the Sample

Variable	Category	N	%
Gender	Cis man	2,587	39.1 %
	Cis woman	3,419	51.48 %
	Trans Man	93	2.5 %
	Trans Woman	75	1.16 %
	Non-binary	311	4.6 %
	Other	75	1.16 %
	Total	**5,808**	**100.0 %**
Age	14	1,097	16.5 %
	15	2,018	30.3 %
	16	1,847	27.8 %
	17	1,511	22.7 %
	More than 17	181	2.7 %
	Total	**6,654**	**100.0 %**

Variable	Category	N	%
Territory	Galicia	1,020	15.3 %
	Mexico	5,634	84.7 %
	Total	**6,654**	**100.0 %**

The data collected were analyzed using IBM SPSS 25 statistical software. Univariate descriptive analyses (frequencies, percentages) were carried out for the sample as a whole and for each of the subsamples according to territory and gender, for the main variables.

III. Results

The definition of meme as *an image with a humorous phrase* is found in most responses (42.9 % in Galicia and 35.8 % in Mexico). The second place is divided between those who use a more simplified definition (*nonsense that circulates on the Internet*) (23 % in Galicia and 24.1 % in Puebla) and those who use a more elaborate definition that is closer to the OER definition: *A phrase, image, video or a more developed idea that goes viral, mainly through social networks* (26 % Galicia, 35.8 % Puebla). Only 5 % in Galicia and 4 % in Puebla chose to indicate the option that considers the communication of *values and opinions* as one of the defining characteristics of memes.

The adoption of specific terms in the digital environment (and by extension, in social networks) is a phenomenon that has been favored by the ability to bring people from different vernaculars into contact with each other. Mostly of Anglophone origin, these words permeate the lives of people who use social media to the extent that they are used outside their own sphere of origin.

The vast majority of adolescents in both cultural contexts create memes in Spanish (Puebla 83.9 %; Galicia 62 %), although a percentage do so in Spanglish (Puebla 12.1 %; Galicia 17.6 %). Fewer make creations in Galician (13 %) or in other languages in Mexico (1.1 %). Most are inspired by other viral phenomena, such as videos, current affairs, or elements of popular culture, such as series/movies or video games. One in four people also admit to having been inspired by personal experiences. Once again, political, gender or sexual orientation claims are almost anecdotal.

The creation of their own terminology in the sphere of social networks, adopting acronyms and complete words from the English language (some going through a process of Spanishization) is a sign of the influence of the

English-speaking world on the Hispanic world and of the knowledge that adolescents have of meme culture. Terms such as WTF (54.9 % Puebla and 81.3 % in
Galicia) or *Crush* (80.4 % Galicia and 58.9 % Puebla) are familiar to most of the
population studied, while those more related to the specific meme culture, such
as *dankmemes* (17.8 % Galicia and 9.5 % Puebla) or *memesphere* (7.7 % in Puebla
and 8.3 in Galicia), are only familiar to a small part.

Although the proportion is similar in the two cultural contexts, in the case of
the Galician population, the knowledge they show of this type of terminology is
remarkable, reaching over 80 %, showing the level of penetration in the usual vocabulary of the pupils. Other terms, more directly associated with meme culture,
such as Normies, Dankmemes or the Memesphere are less popular.

Despite this lower popularity of the specific "jargon," the dissemination of
memes is a majority activity for the population in both contexts. 83 % of the
Galician population and 84 % of the Puebla population have shared a meme at
some point. The frequency with which this type of content is shared is remarkable: 33.5 % (Galicia) and 12 % (Puebla) of the cases say they share memes at
least *many times* and one in five (20.1 % in Galicia; 27.1 % in Puebla) say they do
never or almost never.

35.45 % of respondents in Galicia and 26.6 % in Puebla started sharing memes
before the age of 13. 19.65 % in Galicia and 24.7 % in Puebla did not share a
meme until they were 15 or older.

A peak age for this practice can be seen at 13 years of age, which declines
until 17 years of age. Adolescents in Puebla tend to start sharing memes at an
older age.

81.4 % of respondents in Galicia and 81.7 % in Puebla said they share memes
to make their friends laugh. Ideological and critical motivations, such as *showing
my own ideas* (14.2 % in Galicia, 23 % in Puebla) or *Criticizing a situation* (Galicia 10.7 %, 3.6 % in Puebla) received timid responses, although they are in
second place in terms of importance. However, gender and sexual orientation
claims are the issues least present among the responses, behind issues such as
Getting followers or *Winning over the person I like*.

A very similar situation in the two cultural contexts, except for *Showing my
own ideas*, which doubles the percentage of Galician young people.

In the survey of the study population, the subject is asked to choose between
three images for the scenario in which the subject would share this choice (see
Figure 1): Image 1 shows three people, and a man, presumably heterosexual,
is seen having a slight toward his partner in favor of another woman. In the
second image, the situation is the same, but with the genders of the people involved reversed. The third, however, does not allow any reading of the sexual

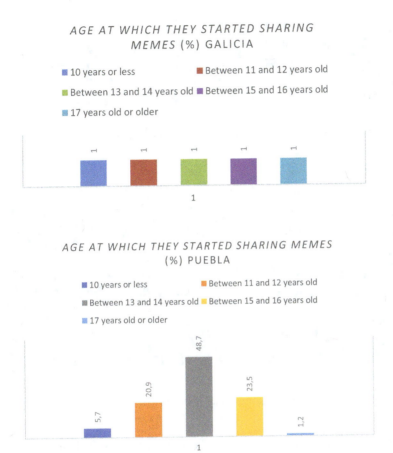

Figure 1. Age at which they started sharing memes (Galicia and Puebla). Own elaboration.

orientation of the participants, and does not address any related controversy: the gender identities of the people depicted are independent of the meme's message.

This is a meme that went viral shortly before the period in which the survey was taken. A quick search now generates over a million hits, it has become well known and a myriad of variations have been generated, as can be seen in Figure 4, which shows the screenshot of searches related to the meme.

The choice, in this case, is a majority (54 % Galicia: 47 % Puebla) in favor of Image 1. The next most supported is the one showing greater neutrality on

Figure 2. Meme selected for survey question. Own elaboration.

Figure 3. Screenshot of the selected meme's popularity search. Own elaboration.

gender and sexuality issues (28 % Galicia; 31 % Puebla), while Image 2, with a more feminine point of view or "protagonist," reaches 18 % in Galicia and 22 % in Puebla.

Despite the fact that the option most frequently chosen as the motivation for the choice is *I think it is funnier* (36.3 % Galicia; 42.4 % Puebla), in order to interpret this figure, it is essential to observe the percentages according to the choice made. Image 1 was chosen to a greater extent because *it seemed funnier*, while those who selected image 2 indicated in a higher proportion that they felt identified with it, that it represented them (40.1 % in Galicia, 23.5 % in Puebla). Image 2 clearly makes a shift in point of view to place a woman as the protagonist, possibly causing more people to use the justification of identification or sense of representativeness. The third image, which as noted, equalizes the gender factor to a large extent, sees an increase in people choosing it for reasons of gender

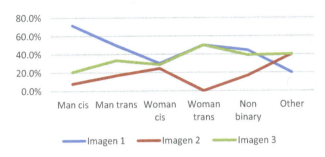

The meme I would share- Galicia

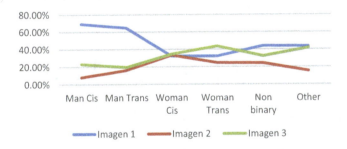

The meme I would share- Puebla

Figure 4. Which meme would you share (Galicia and Puebla). Own elaboration.

vindication, as well as opposition to sexist narratives and the perpetuation of gender stereotypes (30 % in Galicia and 29.5 in Puebla).

Image 1 was chosen mainly by cis men, while in the choice of image 2 and 3, cis women predominated (24.4 % Galicia and 33.3 % Puebla).

Despite these nuances, *I think it is funnier* is, in sum, the answer most frequently invoked by students in both Puebla and Galicia (Figure 6).

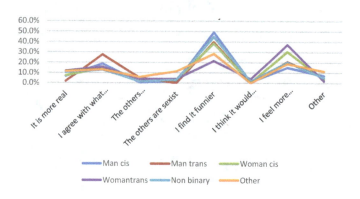

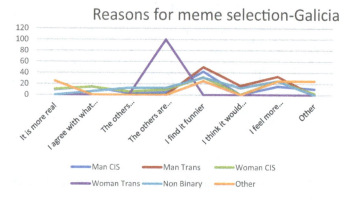

Figure 6. Reasons for meme selection by gender (Puebla-Galicia). Own elaboration.

IV. Discussion and conclusions

Digital platforms are key to understanding the latent changes in new contemporary lifestyles, generating new forms of interaction, relationships, connection and identity construction of subjects (Lasén Diaz, 2019). Through the processes of socialization and the interactions that take place in them, patterns of relationships can be visualized that reproduce stereotypes based on a conception of the feminine and masculine.

The results of the study carried out through the survey of young people between 12 and 17 years of age in Puebla (Mexico) and Galicia (Spain), show the forms of participation in the global media culture in their local contexts of interaction. Their knowledge of memes as a social practice that helps to construct a way of thinking and being becomes evident. The meaning they give in their definition, as well as their knowledge of slang, highlights the value of the meme as a popular symbolic resource among adolescents (Knobel & Lankshear, 2006). The majority of subjects in both cultural settings share memes "to make my friends laugh," giving humor a place of superficiality that it does not really have. This avoids reflection and critical awareness of the situations posed. Situations that "cause fun" and at the same time reproduce some stereotypes that give rise to different power relations (Foucault, 1980). By choosing/sharing the meme they are assuming values and way of thinking (Alarcón Zayas, 2017) and by doing so they learn gender rules (Connell & Pearse, 2018).

The question of which of the three images they would share opens the discussion to the gender stereotypes involved in the decisions that are made and, also to the way in which a cultural production such as memes is helping, through humor (Ballesteros-Doncel, 2016) to reproduce certain stereotypes, where reflection on the meaning of the shared image does not enter into the equation. The similarity of the results in both cultural contexts is striking, showing a globalized perspective of the situation, an issue that is also visualized in the generalization of the language that standardizes, through Spanglish or English and Spanish as dominant, without the languages themselves appearing as significant. It is worth exploring further in future works where small differences are evident that may perhaps account for some specific cultural diversity in these settings. Differences that suggest cracks in the platform models (Srnicek, 2018; Van Dijck et al., 2018).

References

Acosta Valentín, L. (2021). *Alfabetización digital con perspectiva de género: teoría y prácticas sobre el uso de Instagram como herramienta pedagógica en Educación Secundaria* [Tesis de doctorado, Universidad Complutense de Madrid]. https://eprints.ucm.es/id/eprint/65585/1/T42307.pdf

Alarcón Zayas, V. (2017). Humorismo como creación y fortalecimiento de los vínculos en la sociedad red: el caso de los memes sobre filósofos. *Revista de Comunicación, 16*(1), 122–146. http://orcid.org/0000-0002-1995-5769

Arango, L. (2015). Una aproximación al fenómeno de los memes en Internet: claves para su comprensión y su posible integración pedagógica.

Comunicação Mídia e Consumo, 12(33), 110–132. https://doi.org/10.18568/cmc.v12i33.677

Ballesteros-Doncel, E. (2016). Circulación de memes en Whatsapp: ambivalencias del humor desde la perspectiva de género. *Emipiria. Revista de Ciencias Sociales, 35*, 21–45. https://doi.org/10.5944/empiria.35.2016.17167

Banet-Weiser, Sarah (2018) Empowered: Popular Feminism and Popular Misogyny. New York: Duke University Press

Boczkowski, P., Matassi, M., & Mitchelstein, E. (2018). How Young Users Deal With Multiple Platforms: The Role of Meaning-Making in Social Media Repertoires. *Journal of Computer-Mediated Communication, 23*, 245–259 http://dx.doi.org/10.1093/jcmc/zmy012

Bourdieu, P. (1991). *El sentido práctico.* Taurus.

Cama, L., Valero, A., & Vendrell, M. (2018). "Hackeando memes": Cultura democrática, redes sociales y educación. *Espiral. Cuadernos del Profesorado, 11*(23), 120–129. http://dx.doi.org/10.25115/ecp.v12i23.2017

Connell, R., & Pearse, R. (2018). *Género: desde una perspectiva global.* Universitat de València.

Creswell, J. W., & Plano Clark, V. L. (2018). Designing and Conducting Mixed Methods Research (3rd ed.). SAGE.

Dawkins, R. (2002). *El gen egoísta. Las bases biológicas de nuestra conducta.* Salvat.

Escobar-Pérez, J., & Cuervo-Martínez, A. (2008). Validez de contenido y juicio de expertos: una aproximación a su utilización. *Avances en Medición, 6*, 27–36. https://tinyurl.com/y5l8edxr

Ferreiro Habra, A.C. (2018). Masculinidades en el discurso publicitario. *Question, 1*(58). https://doi.org/10.24215/16696581e053

Foucault, M. (1980). *Power/knowledge.* Pantheon.

Hungtington, H. (2016). Pepper spray cop and the American dream: Using synecdoche and metaphor to unlock Internet memes' visual political rhetoric. *Communication Studies, 67*(1), 77–93. http://dx.doi.org/10.5944/signa.vol27.2018.21856

IAB. (2021). Estudio de redes sociales 2021. IAB Spain. https://iabspain.es/estudio/estudio-de-redes-sociales-2021/

Klückmann, M. (2016). Practicing community: Outline of a praxeological approach to the feeling of We-ness. *Cultural Analysis, 15*(1), 28–56. https://www.ocf.berkeley.edu/~culturalanalysis/volume15/pdf/kluckmann.pdf

Knobel, M., & Lankshear, C. (2006). Online memes, affinities, and cultural production. In M. Knobel & C. Lankshear (Eds.), *A new literacies sampler* (pp. 199–227). Peter Lang.

Lasén Díaz, A. (2019). Lo ordinario digital: digitalización de la vida cotidiana como forma de trabajo. *Cuadernos de Relaciones Laborales, 37*(2), 313–330. ISSN 1131-8635.

Martínez-Rolán, X., & Piñeiro-Otero, T. (2016). Los memes en el discurso de los partidos políticos en Twitter: análisis del Debate sobre el Estado de la Nación de 2015. *Communication & Society, 29*(1), 145–160. http://dx.doi.org/10.15581/003.29.1.sp.145-160

Miño-Puigcercós, R., Vargas, P.R., & Alonso, C. (2019). Comunidades virtuales: dinámicas emergentes de participación social y aprendizaje entre los jóvenes. *Education in the Knowledge Society, 20*(22), 1–21. http://dx.doi.org/10.14201/eks2019_20_a21

Reckwitz, A. (2002). Toward a theory of social practices: A development in culturalist theorizing. *European Journal of Social Theory, 5*(2), 243–263. https://doi.org/10.1177/13684310222225432

Ruiz Martínez, J.M. (2018). Una aproximación retórica a los memes de Internet. *Revista Signa, 27*, 995–1021. https://doi.org/10.5944/signa.vol27.2018.21856

Santos, M., & Faure, A. (2018). Affordance is power: Contradictions between communicational and technical dimensions of WhatsApp's end-to-end encryption. *Social Media + Society, 4*(3). https://doi.org/10.1177/2056305118795876

Schatzki, T., Knorr Cetina, K., & von Savigny, E. (2001). *The practice turn in contemporary theory*. Routledge.

Shifman, L. (2014). *Memes in digital culture* [Kindle]. MIT University Press.

Srnicek, N. (2018). *Capitalismo de plataformas*. Caja Negra Editora.

Taherdoost, H. (2016). Sampling methods in research methodology; how to choose a sampling technique for Research. *International Journal of Academic Research in Management(IJARM), 5*(2), 18–27. http://dx.doi.org/10.2139/ssrn.3205035

Van Dijck, J., Poell, T., & De Waal, M. (2018). *The platform society: Public values in a connective world*. Oxford University Press.

Vera, E. (2016). El meme como nexo entre el sistema educativo y el nativo digital: tres propuestas para la enseñanza de Lenguaje y Comunicación. *Revista Educación y Tecnología, Año 5, 2*(8), 1–15. http://revistas.umce.cl/index.php/edytec/article/viewFile/525/522

Vera, Mª.T., Sánchez-Labella Martín, I., & Romo, C. (2020). Identidades digitales en WhatsApp: la representación del género entre la población universitaria.

Análisis: cuadernos de comunicación y cultura, 2020, 67–83. https://doi.org/
10.5565/rev/analisi.3244

Wiggins, B., & Bowers, B. (2015). Memes as genre: A structurationalanalysis of
the memescape. *New media & Society*, *17*(11), 1886–1906. https://doi.org/
10.1177/1461444814535194

Johannes Graën (Universität Zürich, Switzerland), Carme
Bach (Universitat Pompeu Fabra, Serra Húnter Fellow,
Spain), Daniel Cassany (Universitat Pompeu Fabra, Spain)

Chapter II   Using a bilingual concordancer to promote metalinguistic reflection in the learning of an additional language: The case of B1 learners of Catalan

I. Introduction

In this work we describe the experimental use of a bilingual concordancer in a learning class of Catalan as an additional language. The concordancer is fed with translated sentences for several language pairs from a freely available parallel corpus. Users of the application can use simple search terms or regular expressions on source and target language in order to filter the available corpus examples.

Information technology is omnipresent in modern Western lives. It comes as no surprise that information and communication technology (ICT) also plays an important role in today's language-learning settings, including learning a language as an additional language, as is the case of Catalan, a minority language next to Spanish or English. Proficiency in technology use is a prerequisite for the successful employment of ICT in settings and learner autonomy.

The objective of corpus exploration exercises on parallel texts is to encourage learners to develop hypotheses that serve to explain the examples they observe and evaluate them with further corpus queries. That process is designed to promote metalinguistic reflection and foster learner autonomy in line with the data-driven learning paradigm.

The bilingual concordancer PaCLE (Parallel Corpora for Learning Exercises) is part of a framework designed to let learners and teachers generate language-learning exercises from parallel corpus material (Graën, 2022). We evaluate its use qualitatively by analyzing screen recordings of a class of B1 learners of Catalan following the methodology established by Vázquez-Calvo (2016) for describing technology use in language learning.

II. Theoretical framework

Information technology can also be used to foster metalinguistic reflection of learners of additional languages at basic levels, such as the didactic experience we show in this chapter.

Since learners began to play an active role in learning in general a few years ago, leaving the teacher's role as a merely complementary one, technologies have also become essential for language learning and for promoting learner autonomy.

> Technology opens up several potentials for language learning: access to native speakers and language peers around the world, easy 24/7 access to a wide range of authentic and learning-supportive language teaching and learning materials, building and exposure to engaging learning experiences and environments, and facilitating the construction of positive learner identities. (Lai & Gu, 2011, p. 317)

In this context, Data-Driven Learning was born as an interesting and effective method for language learning and teaching. According to Vyatkina and Boulton (2017), the use of corpora for language learning brings a significant gain in learning at the same time that its use motivates students to learn a new language.

Specifically, for teaching Spanish as a foreign language Buyse (2011) states that the use of corpora in the ELE classroom helps to clearly improve the quality of students' written expression. For Cobb and Boulton (2015), working with corpora is a "generally constructivist and inductive approach to language learning."

> The basic idea is that massive but controlled exposure to authentic input is of major importance, as learners gradually respond to and reproduce the underlying lexical, grammatical, pragmatic, and other patterns implicit in the languages they encounter. (Cobb & Boulton, 2015, p. 481)

First of all, it is necessary to talk about metalinguistic awareness, known as the process of introspective or explicit thinking through which learners are able to reflect on the use of some linguistic structures in their own language or in other languages they are going to use. As noted in Joan-Casademont et al. (in press), the degree to which learners of an additional language develop metalinguistic awareness depends, to some extent, on the tools and environment used for their learning (Festman, 2021; Witney & Dewaele, 2018). Clearly, the process of enduring language learning is enhanced if metalinguistic reflection takes into account the learners' prior linguistic knowledge as learners of other languages, their own or additional languages.

III. Methodology

We use a bilingual concordancer for our experiment. The software allows users to perform flexible searches on sentence pairs extracted from parallel corpora. The exercises that students had to do as part of their classroom activities mainly focus on the comparison of Catalan with Spanish (Castilian) and French in one exercise. However, students were encouraged to explore correspondences for any other language pair involving Catalan and also to use other language assistance resources to better understand the use of some grammatical aspects in Catalan and the similarities between Catalan and other dominant languages such as Spanish or French.

3.1. The bilingual concordancer

The PaCLE tool[1] (Graën, 2022) is designed as a tool to turn parallel corpus data into language-learning exercises. Target user groups are language teachers and autonomous learners. The latter group can use the tool to automatically generate exercises or simply use the built-in concordancer to perform corpus searches. The early prototype used by our learners for this work comprises the parallel concordancer with sentence pairs from the OpenSubtitles corpus (see the following section) for any pair of the languages Catalan, English, French, German, Italian, Spanish and Swedish.

Corpus searches are performed on the whole sentences in one or both of the respective languages. We can specify one word, a fixed sequence of words or a pattern described by regular expressions. We expect that only a few (if any) of the envisaged users will be acquainted with regular expressions. To unlock the great potential that comes with such a versatile instrument, we would need to instruct users on how to use it, which is out of the scope of a regular language-learning class. Searching the corpus with regular corpus query tools is equally challenging for language learners without basic education in linguistics. We cannot expect them to be acquainted with concepts such as tokens, lemmas or morphological features and their values, although they will probably be familiar with their manifestations in the target language.

---

1   PaCLE stands for "Parallel Corpora for Language Exercises."

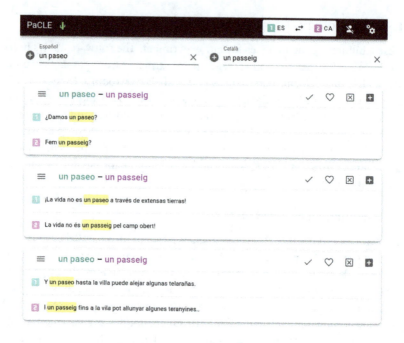

Figure 1. Excerpt of the PaCLE search results for sentence pairs Spanish-Catalan where the sequence "un paseo" can be found in Spanish and "un passeig" in Catalan translation.

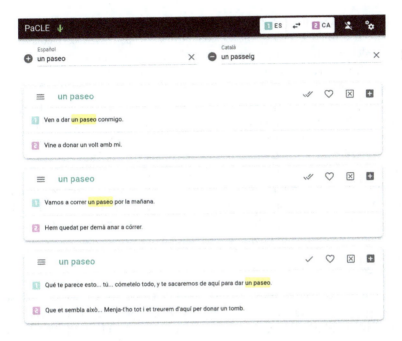

Figure 2. Excerpt of the PaCLE search results for sentence pairs Spanish-Catalan where the sequence "un paseo" can be found in Spanish, but "un passeig" not in the Catalan translation. Therefore, no text passage is marked on the Catalan translations.

A simple query that users can perform without any prerequisites is the search for a singular word or a continuous sequence of words in one or both languages. Figure 1 shows a query with some search results where the parallel occurrence of "un paseo" in Spanish and "un passeig" in Catalan is required. The search can be negated for each language, which means that the tool only shows sentence pairs where the negated search term or expression does not occur (as depicted in Figure 2). This function is particularly useful to search for example sentences with other translation variants than the default one.

3.2. The OpenSubtitles corpus

More and more parallel corpora have been made openly available in the past decades. The OPUS collection[2] (Tiedemann, 2009, 2012) comprises numerous

2   https://opus.nlpl.eu/.

parallel corpora from a variety of sources with different text types and domains. For our experiments, we use the OpenSubtitles corpus (Lison & Tiedemann, 2016) which comprises movie subtitles that have been, for the most part, translated to numerous other languages by volunteers or, alternatively, extracted from videos by means of OCR (Lison & Tiedemann, 2016).

Subtitles are limited in space and time; they need to be shown for a sufficiently long time for the reader to be able to process them. For the same reason, they cannot be overly long. Longer sentences that need to be displayed in chunks are often marked with ellipses and can thus be reconstructed. While shorter sentences are, in general, easier to comprehend than longer ones, the necessity of shortness can bring about phenomena that run counter to comprehension such as the omission of parts that an experienced reader can reconstruct. We describe other potential sources of parallel corpora and their utility for language-learning applications in Graën (submitted, sec. 2.1 and 7.1).

3.3. Classroom experiment

We used the PaCLE application in a course entitled "Comparative use of Catalan and Spanish" (Ús comparat català-castellà),[3] which consisted of 20 learners of Catalan as an additional language (L2) with the CEFR target level B1. The course took place during the academic year 2020–2021 and was conducted exclusively online via the Zoom video conferencing software due to sanitary measures taken against the spreading of COVID-19. Participants were either L1 speakers of Spanish or had a proven competence of at least C1 level in Spanish. As language students, they also had other additional languages. All of them knew English, 13 were studying French and five were studying German. Three participants had Italian as their L1. For the participants, learning takes place in an environment of immersion as Catalan is the main language used at their place of study.

One of the methodologies used in this course—as foreshadowed by its title— is the comparison of Catalan and Spanish, first and foremost with regard to syntactic aspects. That is why we considered the course setting ideal for the experimental use of PaCLE. The acquisition of one language by way of comparison with another language (be it L1 or a strong L2) and metalinguistic reflection about similarities and differences of the languages in question are central course objectives.

---

3 The course forms part of the degree in Translation and Interpreting and Applied Languages of Pompeu Fabra University.

The PaCLE application was presented to the students in week five (out of ten), after other helpful ICT resources had been introduced. The application was showcased by means of guided exercises via screen sharing by the lecturer to demonstrate its functionality and point out its utility. Afterward, the URL of the application was shared via the learning management system used in this course.

In week nine, the students were given an auto-reflexive exercise about three aspects of Catalan syntax, which had been part of the teaching and learning content of the course. As an incentive, those participants who did the exercise would earn extra credits for the final mark. The exercise consists of the following subtasks:

1. Explain the difference between the use of relative adjectives *cuyo, cuya, cuyos, cuyas* and the Catalan corresponding expressions *el qual, la qual, els quals, les quals*. Provide four useful examples obtained from searches in the PaCLE application, and explain the differences observed. Help yourself to any material you consider necessary.

2. Which are the syntactic functions provided by the weak pronoun *hi*? Remember to take into account both possible forms of the pronoun, *hi* and -*hi*. What happens in the Spanish texts?
   What if we make the comparison with French? What differences do you observe compared to Spanish? Provide four useful examples obtained from searches in the PaCLE application, and explain the differences observed between Catalan and Spanish, and Catalan and French. Help yourself to any material you consider necessary.

3. What type of conjunction is *perquè*? Does it only have one function? What are the differences with Spanish? Did you encounter any use of *perquè* in which it was not used as a conjunction? If so, what is it grammatically in that case? Provide four useful examples obtained from searches in the PaCLE application, and explain the differences observed. Help yourself to any material you consider necessary.

As can be seen in the exercise description, it was suggested from the teacher's side to resort to a number of resources, beyond performing searches in PaCLE, in order to explain the observed differences. Students were given complete freedom to use any of the resources they consider helpful to answer the exercise questions:

1. Dictionaries
   a. *DIEC2*,[4] dictionary of the Catalan language (diccionari de la llengua catalana), web portal for this normative monolingual dictionary of the Catalan language by the Institute for Catalan Studies (Institut d'Estudis Catalans).
   b. *DLE*,[5] dictionary of the Spanish language (diccionario de la lengua española), web portal for this normative monolingual dictionary of the Spanish language by the Royal Spanish Academy (Real Academia Española).
2. Grammars
   a. *GEIEC*,[6] Essential grammar of the Catalan language (Gramàtica essencial de la llengua catalana), scaled-down version adapted for online queries by the Institute for Catalan Studies (Institut d'Estudis Catalans)
3. Tools providing linguistic information
   a. *Optimot*,[7] a service for linguistic queries provided by the Directorate General for Language Policy (Direcció General de Política Lingüística) in collaboration with the Institute for Catalan Studies (Institut d'Estudis Catalans) and the Centre for Terminology TERMCAT (Centre de Terminologia TERMCAT).
   b. *esadir.cat*,[8] language portal of the Catalan Media Corporation (Corporació Catalana de Mitjans Audiovisuals [CCMA]), which is a serviceable tool for anyone working in the field of communication and teaching, students, and, in general, everyone interested in the use of the Catalan language.
   c. *Google Translate*,[9] machine translation service offered by Google, often used as a complementary tool for language learning.

---

4   Institut d'Estudis Catalans. Diccionari de la llengua catalana. 2a edició [DIEC2]. http://dlc.iec.cat/.
5   Real Academia Española. Diccionario de la lengua española, 23.ª ed. [versión 23.5 en línea]. https://dle.rae.es.
6   Institut d'Estudis Catalans (2018). Gramàtica essencial de la llengua catalana [GEIEC]. Barcelona: Institut d'Estudis Catalans. https://geiec.iec.cat/.
7   Generalitat de Catalunya. Optimot. Servei de consultes lingüístiques. https://aplicacions.llengua.gencat.cat/llc/AppJava/index.html.
8   Corporació Catalana de Mitjans Audiovisuals. esadir. https://esadir.cat/.
9   Google Translate. https://translate.google.com/.

d. *Diccionario Panhispánico de dudas*,[10] a website provided by the Royal Spanish Academy (Real Academia Española) addressing frequently asked questions concerning the use of the Spanish language.

3.4. Instruments

For evaluating the use of PaCLE in the course on "Comparative use of Catalan vs. Spanish," we considered two means:

1. The result of the auto-reflexive exercise that students were requested to do subsequent to performing searches in PaCLE in order to gain extra credits. We analyzed the degree of success students showed in response to the three exercise questions, the productive use of PaCLE, the capacity of metalinguistic reflection and the way other tools were employed to answer the questions, be it the aforementioned additional resources or other tools known to the students, independent of whether they are used as complementary or exclusive means.
2. The recordings of the students' desktops demonstrating how they used the respective tools, but also comprising their communication with the teacher in case of questions or doubts.[11]

For the analysis of the screen recordings, we used the schema proposed by Vázquez-Calvo (2016), which has been developed specifically for the description of technology use in language learning. This schema helps us study how digital resources are used by our language learners, in particular how each of the tasks has been solved, which techniques they carried out in order to solve the tasks, and how adequate the solutions they obtained from the respective resources have been.

We refrained from collecting feedback by means of a questionnaire as the number of participants was fairly low and we believed that a qualitative analysis of the students' activities would be considerably more adjuvant.

---

10 Real Academia Española, *Diccionario panhispánico de dudas* (Madrid: Santillana, 2005). https://www.rae.es/dpd/.
11 All screen recordings happened with the consent of the respective student encompassing their use for our research, always following the criteria of the Institutional Commission for Ethical Review of Research Project (Comissió Institucional de Revisió Ètica de Projectes [CIREP]) of the Pompeu Fabra University.

| | | Secuencia 5 | |
| | | Análisis | |
Mín.	Datos	Descripción	Interpretación
Tarea:	Composición escrita en EN. Resumen de un vídeo y continuación de la historia	El alumno: 1) Sin dilación, al abrir GT, el alumno comienza a usarlo. 2) La interfaz de GT está configurada de manera que la combinación lingüística es ES-CA.	El alumno: — Usa el RLL que tiene más accesible para solucionar la duda que tiene en mente. Prima la inmediatez por el resultado. (1) — No configura el RLL para su uso específico ante la duda que tiene en mente: configuración de
Duda lingüística:	Léxico	3) El texto que inserta es «La hsitoria*». 4) Cambia de lengua de salida a EN. 5) A continuación acude al texto y comienza la escritura en EN con «The history».	idioma, dirección de lenguas, etc., en este caso realiza esta configuración después de introducir la duda y no antes (2, 4). — Usa GT como un diccionario bilingüe unívoco, lo que le induce a calcos léxicos. (3) — Usa GT como un diccionario autocorrectivo, y descuida el texto de entrada a nivel ortográfico. (5)
Finalidad:	Producción en EN		
Recurso:	GT		
Solución:	No adecuada		

(Inicio: 08:00 — Fin: 08:10)

Figure 3. Schema proposed by Vázquez-Calvo (2016, p. 239) for analyzing how language learners make use of technology.

Figure 3 shows an example from Vázquez-Calvo (2016), where for a particular activity of a given task metadata has been annotated. Besides the timespan from the respective screen recording (on the left) and a running number assigned to each sequence as technical data (on top of the box), general information regarding the task is recorded in the first column, a description of which actions can be seen in the video in the second, and the interpretation of those actions in the third one.

As for general information, the schema stipulates five fields: (1) the task that the student is carrying out, which is typically a predefined one, (2) the type of linguistic doubt that the student tries to resolve, (3) the intended purpose of the task, (4) the resource or resources used, and 5) whether the selected solution is judged adequate, partially adequate or inadequate. The description lists sequentially all interactions that the student performs. The interpretation part refers to those actions while commenting on the presumable reasons why they led to an adequate, partially adequate or inadequate solution of the task set.

IV. Analysis

In order to carry out the analysis of the data that will allow us to evaluate the usefulness of the bilingual concordancer, we have triangulated the data from the recording of the students' desks, on the use of the tools proposed to promote learning based on the proposed metalinguistic reflection with the final task they have written, in which they explain the functioning of linguistic features of Catalan in comparison to similar features of other languages, in particular Spanish.

In the following, we provide details on some of the individual activities performed by the students to solve the tasks explained in the previous section. Tables 1–4 show different levels of adequacy as assessed by us.

Table 1. Example of the Analysis Schema Showing a Partially Adequate Solution for the Task in Question

Student 1—Sequence 7				
Analysis				
Min.	**Properties**		**Description**	**Interpretation**
67 — 76	Task	Writing down the solution found	After copying examples of *haver-hi* and *-hi* as adverbials of place, the student proceeds to answer the question. The student does not investigate the full list of examples provided by PaCLE but stick to the first two pages (each comprising 10 examples) and does not realize that *hi* can be used regardless of the verb *haver-hi* in proclitic position, as an adverbial pronoun as "L'Anna estudia a la seva habitació? Sí *hi* estudia" or as a verb phrase complement, as in the example below "Ja penses en la teva mare? Sí *hi* penso."	This student is ignorant of how to use regular expressions and does not try to find *hi* independent of *haver-hi* in a proclitic position. The comparison with French could have led to more fruitful results as a proclitic position *il y a* is not lexicalized as are *hay* and *hi ha*. Since he/she does not know how to talk about lexicalization or grammaticalization, he/she uses the word *partícula* (particle) to refer to the lexicalized *hi* in *hi ha / il y a* and *-hi*. He/she could have
	Linguistic doubt	Differences in the way *hi/-hi* works in Catalan compared to Spanish and French		
	Objective	Solve the second task		
	Resource	PaCLE, MS Word		
	Solution	Partially adequate (very little)		

Student 1—Sequence 7			
Analysis			
Min.	Properties	Description	Interpretation
		Using a different regular expression in order to exclude cases of *haver-hi* could have been worth trying out, but he/she apparently does not know how to do that and does not ask for support, which he/she would have received if such a question had been raised.	referred to it as weak pronoun (*pronom feble*) which was the term used in the task description, but he/she did not use that term. He/she talks about interpretation, unable to syntactically analyze the pronoun. The student does not find cases of verb phrase complements, only one of an adverbial of place, in enclitic position. He/She does comprehend the typographic markers of metalinguistic uses of the words, which the student finds entertaining to format in italics.

Table 2. Example of the Analysis Schema Showing an Adequate Solution for the Task in Question

Student 14—Sequence 4				
Analysis				
Min.	**Properties**		**Description**	**Interpretation**
7 — 15	Task	Consult PaCLE	The student copies the search expressions provided in the task description to PaCLE, skims the results and quickly starts copying them to Word. Interestingly, he/she chooses examples that do not coincide in gender and number. Very important: he/she picks examples that are not complete, which we would have removed from the corpus examples in the first place, if we had seen them, but the student does not assess them, as he/she has already selected sufficient examples. The student walks through examples until reaching the ninth page (each comprising 10 examples). He/she does not copy example pairs as other students do, but copies them one by one.	Very good selection of examples that do not coincide in gender and number between Catalan and Spanish. Pragmatic when choosing examples; he/she only focuses on differences between Catalan and Spanish, namely gender and number and the concordance between the possessor and its possessive in each language. The examples that we would consider deficient are not necessarily bad, all depends on the intention behind the corpus search.
	Linguistic doubt	Differences in the use of possessive relative pronouns in Catalan and Spanish		
	Objective	Solve the first task		
	Resource	PaCLE, MS Word		
	Solution	Adequate		

Table 3. Example of the Analysis Schema Showing a Perfectly Adequate Solution for the Task in Question

Student 11—Sequence 13			
Analysis			
Min.	**Properties**	**Description**	**Interpretation**
76	Task — Consult PaCLE	The student opens PaCLE and knows how to search by modifying the search expression successfully. He/she might have previous knowledge of regular expressions. Already on the first page (each comprising 10 examples), the student finds all required examples, and even more. He/she copies one example that serves him/her well and explains it in Word. Then, the student copies and pastes the example from PaCLE. The student does not provide four different examples as there are actually no four distinguishable cases to explain.	The student is probably familiar with regular expressions; as a matter of fact, all of the students should have come in contact with them as part of the lecture "ICT resources" (recursos TIC). This student is even aware that there are fewer than four different functions of *perquè* and therefore does not provide four different examples, but only three very appropriate ones.
	Linguistic doubt — Functions of *perquè*		
	Objective — Solve the third task		
	Resource — PaCLE, MS Word		
	Solution — Very adequate		

Table 4. Example of the Analysis Schema Showing an Inadequate Solution for the Task in Question

Student 15—Sequence 12				
Analysis				
Min.	**Properties**		**Description**	**Interpretation**
56	Task	Consult Optimot	The student opens the Optimot application to find out how to translate the Spanish word *nombre* to Catalan. He/she searches for *número* instead and since the same word exists in Catalan, the student does not corroborate or look up any further information but accepts the result as it is. What is more, this student chooses Catalan-Spanish in the application and the correct result is shown on the first page, but he/she ignores it or does not pay attention to it.	The student looks up *número*. Even if that word has a different meaning in Catalan, he/she takes it for granted. He/she uses *Optimot* only for corroborating what he/she thinks should be the translation, without actually revising the results obtained, even though he/she performs the right search for Catalan-Spanish translation and the result comprises the information he/she was looking for.
	Linguistic doubt	Differences in the use of possessive relative pronouns in Catalan and Spanish		
	Objective	Find out how to say *nombre* in Catalan		
	Resource	Optimot		
	Solution	Inadequate		

The respective analyses can be aggregated in two dimensions. First, we look at the individual student's activity records, which allows us to draw conclusions about their respective capabilities concerning metalinguistic reflection as well as technical proficiency, and second, we aggregate analyses over all participants regarding individual task in order to assess the technical resources used, in particular our bilingual concordancer.

The triangulation of the data, both from the recordings of the students' use of the tool and from the results observed in the final work they handed in, allowed us to establish three student profiles, according to the degree of use of the bilingual concordancer provided and of the other resources consulted:

A. The student who does not know how to take advantage of PaCLE: they look at the results, but do not know how to interpret them, nor do the additional linguistic resources provided seem to be of any help to them.
B. The student who is able to partially interpret the data without the need to consult any other type of linguistic resource, given that their knowledge of Spanish and their reasoning ability are good and allow them to comprehend how the grammatical element in question works in Catalan.
C. The student who not only draws good conclusions from the use of PaCLE but also attempts to seek further explanations in complementary linguistic tools provided and in other ones.

We classified 26.7 % of the participants as type A, 33.3 % as type B and 40 % as type C students. No generalizations can be made from this observation as many factors potentially play a role with regard to a student's ability to draw conclusions from language samples obtained (such as linguistic background, previous experience with using such resources, and the assistance provided by the respective teacher). Nonetheless, we are convinced of the potential of parallel corpora for comparative language-learning classes. Overall, a majority of the students who participated in our experiment were able to solve the tasks autonomously with as little preparation as one introductory session.

As for the concordancer PaCLE, we observed several issues on more than one occasion. Most notably are difficulties in understanding regular expressions, which is why we provided search expressions for each task (which the students could manipulate but did not need to in order to solve the tasks). In theory, the participants should know the concept from a previous lecture (see Table 4, Interpretation), but expecting them to write regular expressions from scratch seemed to us very challenging when conceiving the exercises.

Since only a small subset of the features provided by regular expressions is needed for corpus searches in general (namely alternatives as in "cuyo|cuya|cuyos|cuyas," word boundaries as in "\yhi\y" or variable suffixes as in "$cuy\w+$," which we did avoid by explicitly listing the alternatives instead), one potential improvement could be the use of a query language with a reduced feature set. The downside of this, however, would be that more technically experienced users would not be able to make use of the full potential of regular expressions and the features of that new query language would still need to be explained to users.

A potential improvement of the PaCLE application that we derived from the analysis of the screen recordings concerns the way in which results are presented. Currently, we show all matching sentence pairs in an aleatory order and only highlight the matching parts in both languages. The idea behind not ordering the results is that users would go through the list of results and select those that they consider useful. In some cases, we observed exactly this behavior; in other cases, students were browsing through a large number of examples but were apparently unable to judge them.

Two improvements to the interface that we had sketched out but have not implemented to date would potentially improve use experience. First, we designed the visual presentation of the individual examples to allow for interactive presentation of linguistic features such as the part of speech, syntactic relations and morphological features. Enhanced with this feature, we expect users to spend more time on exploring the respective examples and facilitate the selection of good examples. Second, we planned to provide options for ordering results, for example, by conflating similar sentence pairs to one that is most representative, deriving readability and proficiency level measures on sentence pairs, and list corresponding translation equivalents and their frequencies.

V. Final reflections

We have described how we employed a bilingual concordancer in a language-learning class to foster learner autonomy and promote metalinguistic reflection. Students were given three exercises about Catalan syntax and we provided them with links to the concordancer PaCLE and several other language resources on the Internet. The concordancer had already been introduced in a previous class.

For evaluating the use of the concordancer and other technical resources, we analyzed screen recordings provided by the participants using an already established schema and also consulted the written answers to the exercise questions. We classified the students into three groups by their ability to interpret the results obtained from the concordancer and draw the right conclusions with regard to the properties of Catalan syntax.

We could see that the majority of the students were able to use the tool in a beneficial way, the capability of metalinguistic reflection is key for their success. Our analysis revealed several minor problems concerning the use of our tool, some of which were not unique to an individual student. Those are of the utmost interest for us, as one of our goals is to address them in future versions of the concordancer and thus improve its usability.

We would have liked to provide feedback to the participants who provided their screen recordings to us. Unfortunately, the shift from a physical to an online format required additional time that we were lacking in the end.

Acknowledgments

This research is partly supported by the Swiss National Science Foundation under grant P2ZHP1 184212 through the project "From parallel corpora to multilingual exercises: Making use of large text collections and crowdsourcing techniques for innovative autonomous language learning applications," conducted at Pompeu Fabra University in Barcelona (with Grael, Grup de Recerca en Aprenentatge I Ensenyament de Llengües) and at the University of Gothenburg (with Språkbanken Text).

References

Buyse, K. (2011). ¿Qué corpus en línea utilizar y para qué fines en la clase de ELE? Del texto a la lengua. *La aplicación de los textos a la enseñanza-aprendizaje del español L2-LE, 37*, 277–288.Cobb, T., & Boulton, A. (2015). Classroom applications of corpus analysis. In D. Biber & R.

Reppen (Eds.), *The Cambridge handbook of English corpus linguistics* (pp. 478–497). Cambridge University Press.

Festman, J. (2021). Learning and processing multiple languages: The more the easier? *Language Learning, 71*, 121–162.

Graën, J. (2022). Learning languages from parallel corpora: a blueprint for turning corpus examples into language learning exercises. *Slovenščina 2.0*, 10(2): 101 -131.

Joan-Casademont, A, Bach, C., & Viladrich, È. (in press). Analysis of training needs in coherence and cohesion based on corpora: Some online didactic proposals for Catalan as an additional language (AL). In H. Tyne & S. Spina (Eds.), *Applying corpora in teaching and learning Romance languages*. John Benjamins.

Lai, C., & Gu, M. (2011). Self-regulated out-of-class language learning with technology. *Computer Assisted Language Learning, 24*(4), 317–335. https://doi.org/10.1080/09588221.2011.568417

Lison, P., & Tiedemann, J. (2016, May). *OpenSubtitles2016: Extracting large parallel corpora from movie and TV subtitles*. Proceedings of the 10th International Conference on Language Resources and Evaluation (LREC), Portorož, Slovenia.

Tiedemann, J. (2009). News from OPUS—a collection of multilingual parallel corpora with tools and interfaces. *Proceedings of Recent Advances in Natural Language Processing (RANLP), 5*, 237–248.

Tiedemann, J. (2012, May). *Parallel data, tools and interfaces in OPUS*. Proceedings of the 8th International Conference on Language Resources and Evaluation (LREC), Istanbul, Turkey.

Vázquez-Calvo, B. (2016). *Digital language learning from a multilingual perspective: The use of online language resources in the one-to-one classroom* [PhD thesis, Universitat Pompeu Fabra].

Vyatkina, N., & Boulton, A. (2017). Corpora in Language learning and teaching. *Language Learning & Technology, 21*(3), 1–8.

Witney, J., & Dewaele, J.M. (2018). Learning two or more languages. In A. Burns & J.C. Richards (Eds.), *The Cambridge guide to learning English as a second language* (pp. 43–52). Cambridge University Press.

Manuel Caeiro Rodríguez, María Lorenzo Rial, Manuel
Fernández Iglesias, Fernando Mikic Fonte, and Martín
Llamas Nistal (Universidade de Vigo, Spain)

Chapter III Improving virtual presence in higher education hybrid learning digital environments

I. Distance learning

Distance learning origin can be situated at the beginning of the eighteenth century, when Caleb Phillips from Boston (USA) decided to offer education via lessons provided weekly by US mail (Clark, 2020). This was the beginning of "correspondence" courses. Since the adoption of this basic "communication technology" to support education, society witnessed how all the advances in the electronic telecommunications field were used to support distance learning, from radio broadcasts in the 1920s, going through the television, until the adoption of computer networks and the Internet.

The contemporary concept of distance learning has been defined by Greenberg (1998) as "a planned teaching/learning experience that uses a wide spectrum of technologies to reach learners at a distance and is designed to encourage learner interaction and certification of learning." This involves much more than the communication of information among teachers and learners. The adoption of the Internet to support distance learning increased the chances to share information in the form of "web pages" where text, pictures and even video could be delivered. In addition, it also facilitated the communication through services such as email, instant messaging, bulletin boards and videoconference; and even enabled the distance interaction with remote labs or user experiences in virtual worlds. The key word is "digitalization," referred not just to tools that enable activities to be performed at a distance, but also to the support of educational processes and, as in many other areas nowadays, the capture of data about what is happening along educational processes.

Nowadays, learning at higher education is commonly supported by electronic tools. According to (Dumford & Miller, 2018), prior to the COVID-19 pandemic almost 70 % of higher education institutions provided some form of distance learning supported by technology. Nevertheless, this support is not just for distance learning, but traditional face-to-face learning is also being extended and facilitated with technology in the so-called hybrid learning digital environments. In this paper we analyze the features of these environments and the main functionalities included. We also consider the main issues still present and the new trends toward their solution.

II. Technology to support learning from a distance

Distance learning over the Internet can exist in two primary modes (Awoke et al., 2021, Clark, 2020):

a. *Synchronous*. It refers to sessions where teacher and learners are together at the same time, and they can communicate and collaborate all together. Face-to-face courses involve a synchronous model, with students and instructors meeting for teaching sessions, tests, etc. Online meetings, instant messaging or shared whiteboards are examples of synchronous tools.

b. *Asynchronous*. This involves students interacting with materials, quizzes, exams, and other activities at their own pace. Although students could still have to follow some schedules, such as deadlines for the submission of tasks, the timing to perform learning activities is flexible. These courses offer maximum time flexibility for learning 24x7. For example, this model is adopted when a teacher posts all lecture material and class assignments at the beginning of a course. Document annotation, video-recorded lectures, wikis or shared workspaces are examples of asynchronous tools, where the students can work at their own pace.

A variety of digital tools are commonly available to support learning at higher education, both in the synchronous and asynchronous models. Two of the most popular ones are *Learning Management Systems (LMS)*, mainly used to support the logistics of entire courses, enabling *asynchronous* access to information and learning materials, assessments and communications; and *Virtual Classrooms*, which are the natural replacement for the *synchronous* physical space of a classroom. These tools enable real-time interaction during the performance of learning activities, allowing students to communicate with the teacher or other students through text, video and voice messaging.

While LMS can be clearly recognized as tools on their own in the educational field, the concept of Virtual Classroom is many times provided using general-purpose videoconference and collaboration tools. In addition, there are other more specific educational tools such as remote and virtual labs, or assessment and feedback tools, also important to support remote learning.

2.1. Learning management systems

Acoording to Kasim and Khalid (2016), a "Learning Management System (LMS) is a web-based software application that is designed to handle learning content, student interaction, assessment tools and reports of learning progress and student activities." Its basic functionalities are (i) users management; (ii) course management; and (iii) monitorization of students' progress. Among the most outstanding characteristics of a LMS are interactivity, scalability, flexibility or usability. Most LMS include the ability to:

a. Define the educational activities to be carried out for different environments (including blended learning).
b. Enable participants to collaborate on certain activities: forum, wiki, etc.
c. Prepare, deliver and manage score tests.
d. Provide reports for students, teachers, and administrators.

Some of the most used LMS today are listed below, along with a brief description of their main characteristics to support distance learning.

a. *Moodle* (moodle.org) is an *open-source* learning platform providing an integrated system with many features with a simple interface for educators, administrators, and students. Moodle includes drag-and-drop features that facilitate the management of courses, and an active development community of users and developers offering well-documented resources. Moddle has a modular configuration and interoperable design enabling developers to create plugins and integrate external applications to achieve specific functionalities. With a default interface compatible with mobile devices and cross compatibility with different Internet browsers, the content on the Moodle courses is easily accessible from different browsers and devices.
b. *ATutor* (atutor.github.io) is another *open-source* LMS solution enabling us to develop and manage online courses. ATutor provides functionalities enabling educators to organize, package, and provide educational content to conduct online courses. It is also possible to import pre-packaged content. ATutor users can use functionalities to create a network of contacts, manage interest groups, communicate with other users through private messages, setup a network profile, and link remote gadget applications into their networking environment. ATutor also provides some analytics features, such as used statistics that can be used to identify gaps in content coverage, learning tendencies for specific learners, etc.
c. *Dokeos* (www.dokeos.com) has an approach based on learning through interaction, so it has *virtual classrooms* and tools that facilitate collaborative

Manuel Caeiro Rodríguez et al.

learning. It allows you to create, edit and configure courses. It allows users to create custom training modules, create exams using quizzes, place multimedia content, surveys and assessment, agendas, calendars, forums, chats, new surveys, and wikis (all of this with SCORM content support).

d. *".LRN"* (dotlrn.org) is an *open-source* initiative from the MIT focused on enabling not just e-learning, but also the operation of digital communities. This platform provides functionalities to administer "classes" or "communities." It also enables users customizing the portal layout, choosing the language, setting the time zone for their class, or including portlets with specific functionalities. The platform supports different roles such as students, professors, and administrative staff.. LRN also provides a variety of default applications such as: attachments, bulk-mail, calendar, FAQ, file-storage, forums, general-comments and news.

e. *Sakai* (www.sakailms.org) is another fully *open-source* platform, created by and for educators. It can be used to support face-to-face sessions or online learning. As previous platforms it includes several synchronous and asynchronous tools for messaging, discussions, social connections, and collaborative work. A special feature of this platform is the availability of an API that can be used by developers to create native integrations with third-party applications. It provides high-stakes testing, formative assessment, online assignments, and rubric-based scoring.

f. *Chamilo LMS* (chamilo.org) is another open-source *virtual campus* available under the GNU/GPLv3 license. It offers a complete suite of teaching and administrative tools, providing a very simple interface for teachers and students while maintaining a dynamic structure for those developers who want to make modifications to the code. Chamilo has a large number of tools aimed at facilitating learning, such as wikis, *spaces for group work* with collaborative group resources, classroom blogs with assignable tasks, scoring forums, internal social network for promotion of the informal exchange of knowledge, and a mixed grading system (virtual and face-to-face). All these tools are provided along additional tools such as instant messaging, glossaries, links, announcements, etc. It also offers student files with detailed monitoring and the possibility of controlling absences, online assessment, and assignment of scores.

g. *Blackboard* (www.blackboard.com) is a *proprietary* virtual learning ecosystem, which offers an intuitive way of interacting with courses, content, teachers and other students, which can also be personalized according to what each educational community needs. Some of the functions it offers are the create of spaces for each course, with its modules, contents and units;

preview elements, activities and exams; participate in discussions, send announcements, interact with members of a class; manage tasks; attach and download study material (images, text, video, audio); grade activities; change the configuration of elements for assessments and other content; and access classes by videoconference. *Blackboard Collaborate* is a kind of *virtual classroom* tool which allows meetings to be held synchronously with multiple users, as well as to develop activities such as online tutorial supervision, research meetings, class development, development of collaborative activities, etc.

h. *Canvas LMS* (www.instructure.com/en-gb) is an open-source e-learning platform that integrates several basic modules for the administration of users and courses, with a set of complementary functionalities. Teachers can create courses, add all kinds of content, and students are able to consume them. Canvas LMS can integrate with various types of cloud applications and has an open API that makes it easy to add different modules. In addition, administrators can control the students who access the courses, their attendance, progress, evaluation, etc.

As a summary, we can see that all the LMS presented herein have a set of tools and characteristics oriented for the most part to asynchronous e-learning (forums, activities, tasks, exams, etc.). In addition, most LMS are also integrating tools to support synchronous e-learning, either explicitly, as is the case of Sakai, or by including certain tools normally used for it, such as videoconferencing or virtual classes, as in the cases of Blackboard and Dokeos, see Figure 1. Other trends are the development of interfaces for mobile devices and the integration of learning analytics features.

2.2. Videoconferencing tools

In higher education, videoconferencing is considered one of the most used tools to facilitate students' use of technology in a synchronous mode, supporting the Virtual Classroom concept (Fischer et al., 2017). Currently, some of the most widely used videoconferencing tools are Google Meet, Zoom, Microsoft Teams, Cisco WebEx Teams, GoTo Meetings, Skype, and WhatsApp (Singh, & Awasthi, 2020), which are described below.

a. *Zoom* was created by Eric Yuan in 2011. This videoconferencing facility can handle up to 1,000 users at the same time. Moreover, it is possible to have up to 49 users working together and showing their screens simultaneously. This

Figure 1. Screen capture of the Blackboard Collaborate tool.

tool is also available on mobile platforms and has many functionalities, such as screen sharing, recording, team conferencing, and many history features.

b. *Google Meet* is another online meeting tool that was introduced by Google in 2017. Nowadays, it is being used by millions of organizations around the world. It has the capacity to facilitate up to a hundred participants simultaneously. It also has many features like screen sharing, conference calling, meeting recording and conference room equipment.

c. *Microsoft Teams* is an online meeting tool developed and deployed by Microsoft. Nowadays, it is a popular tool widely used by different organizations for work meetings, training courses, etc.

d. *Skype* is a Microsoft-owned software (integrates the former Windows Live Messenger) that allows text, voice and video communications using the Internet. Skype users can talk to each other for free.

e. *Cisco WebEx Teams* is a video conferencing and web conferencing solution. It enables users to communicate online according with schedule meetings, but also to start and join meetings on the fly, without any previous arrangements. A specific feature of this solution is that users can create virtual workplaces to work on short-term projects. It provides native support for external video as up to 200 video users can join the team meeting.

f. *WhatsApp*, currently owned by Facebook, is an instant messaging application originally available on smartphones, but now also on computers. Messages are sent and received via the Internet, as well as images, videos, audio, audio recordings (voice memos), documents, locations, contacts, gifs, stickers, as well as calls and video calls with several participants at the same time, among other functions. Similar tools are Telegram and Discord, very popular nowadays.

A recent study on the impact evaluation of some of these videoconferencing systems as tools to support learning identified a series of didactic potentialities of these systems (Correia, Liu, & Xu, 2020), such as their high reliability in protecting the real identity of participants, interactivity, integration of audio and video features of social media, incorporation of augmented video applications (filters, image manipulation, high-quality photographs and animated virtual backgrounds) and the possibility of fast and reliable technical customer support.

Their increasingly widespread use motivated different studies in the last year, mainly in relation to the didactic potential that each of the systems offers as a communication platform and support for teaching in times of COVID-19. The research conducted by Correia, Liu and Xu (2020) shows that Skype is the best in terms of usability, navigability, efficiency, learnability, security, and satisfaction, followed by Zoom, Teams and WhatsApp. The biggest differences seem to be related to the efficiency, effectiveness, safety, satisfaction, and usefulness and usability factors.

2.3. Collaboration tools

Collaboration tools in education enable individuals, both teachers and students, to work together to achieve a defined and common educational purpose. Typically, they exist in two forms, synchronous and asynchronous. Cloud services became the foundation of most state-of-the-art educational collaboration solutions. Information stored in the cloud is accessed quicker and easier, which in turn promotes the generation of knowledge through joint authorship. By providing concurrent remote access to educational tools, mobility and flexibility is provided, as access is supported from any device in real time. Next, the most popular collaboration tools used to support distance learning nowadays are described:

a. *Microsoft's Office 365 platform* (https://www.office.com) is one of the most comprehensive suites to support collaborative work in general, and more specifically collaborative learning. It provides, under a single system, the popular Office package (i.e., Microsoft Word, PowerPoint, Excel, Outlook and One-Note) together with a complete portfolio of additional services such as shared file storage (OneDrive), collaborative presentations (Sway), a tool to build surveys and other questionnaire-based projects (Forms), a video streaming service (Stream) and a collaborative workflow tool (Flow). Besides, Office 365 also provides a digital center where the conversations, calls, content, the applications above and other collaboration-supporting features are integrated (Teams). This platform is free for students, and it provides a wide portfolio of educational plans for institutions and educators, with options including computing devices for remote and hybrid learning. Microsoft also hosts the Educator Center, with a huge repository of educational resources.

b. *Google Suite for Education* (https://edu.google.com) is the Google's proposal for an integrated collaborative environment. This is a collection of cloud-based Google suite services that allow collaborative document editing and instant communication from any device, anywhere. Apart from the popular Google Workspace (formerly Google Suite) applications, Gmail, Calendar, Meet, Chat, Drive, Docs, Spreadsheets, Presentations, Forms and Sites being the most popular, it supports both online and offline collaboration working individually or with the whole class. Thanks to applications like Google Classroom, teachers can also manage programs, assignments and grades from one place. Google Classroom is a free service that can be used by schools, non-profit organizations, or even any user with a personal Google account. Classroom facilitates communication between students and teachers, both inside and outside the educational centers.

c. *Padlet* (padlet.com) is a software tool designed to allow people to make and share content with others. Content can be managed collaboratively and may have many different forms (cf. Figure 2), such as a bulletin board, a blog, or a portfolio. Content creators can invite others to work together on shared projects, assignments, and activities. Besides, content management is flexible, as Padlet supports most types of files and formats, content can be organized in many different ways, and made public or private at any time. Padlet includes the Padlet Backpack, an exclusive workspace for schools, designed to help teachers and students collaborate easily in a private environment. Members are added to ensure private access. Student accounts can be also added without an email address. Padlet supports integration with popular LMS such as Moodle.

d. *Popplet* (www.popplet.com) is a web-based tool, also available as an app, where users create mind maps on a board in a dynamic and interactive way. Students can use text, drawings, images, or video to build their maps, named Popplets. Popplets can be connected among them, forming an interactive outline of related ideas. There's a library of public Popplets and a tab to view maps shared by other users. In an educational setting, Popplet may be used to build organizational skills for reviewing and note-taking; to teach paragraph structure, supporting an argument, creating an outline; and more.

e. *Mural* (www.mural.co) is a tool to support collaborative working or learning based on an easy-to-use digital canvas. This tool includes advanced facilitation features, guided methods, and features to support teamwork independently of the organization. Mural brings many conventional whiteboard tools in a digital workspace for ideation and teamwork (cf. Figure 3), such as clickable sticky notes to easily add ideas, suggestions, feedback, and thoughts; different types of text, comment and title boxes; a rich set of shapes, connectors and frameworks to map complex workflows while collaborating through the workspace; visual tools like icons and drawings for teams to freely describe ideas and thoughts, or graphical content.

f. *Wakelet* (wakelet.com) is a digital curation tool, that is, it can be used to organize and oversee digital content and present it in an attractive way. It supports the collection of online resources in one place, called a wake. These wakes can then be shared to be accessed online. Teachers can create wakes as a way to pool resources, allowing students to explore references and other sources of information to prepare for an upcoming lesson or classroom session.

Collaboration tools gained in popularity within educational settings, changing the way e-learning is conceived and implemented today. Applications like Padlet allow class members to share content anywhere anytime. Mural creates a space for learning based on an easy-to-use digital canvas, and cloud-based office tools similar to Google or Microsoft's offerings which facilitates collaborative development of educational content. With these, students and teachers can work remotely, or even when traveling, offering educational institutions and families the potential for significant cost savings.

2.4. Virtual and remote labs

Labs and hands-on environments are fundamental to the learning process since they allow students to put into practice and experience the knowledge acquired in classroom lectures. Computers and the network were long used to support laboratory experiences at a distance (Anido et al., 2000), either to carry out simulations using computer programs or to distribute the laboratories themselves through the Internet. In Anido et al. (2001), one of the first approaches to the concept of Internet-based laboratory is described as well as one of the first classifications of the so-called virtual laboratories, differentiating the simulations from the laboratories that use real equipment, either locally or remotely.

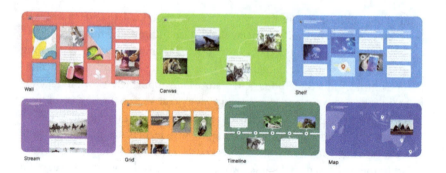

Figure 2. Padlet features different kinds of representations.

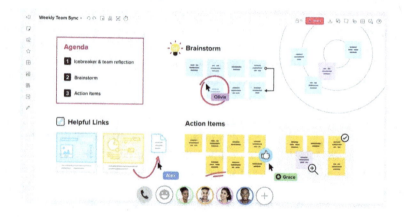

Figure 3. Mural teamwork software.

Over the years, terms such as remote, virtual or online laboratories gained in popularity, many of which were implemented globally to support distance learning. Bencomo (2004) proposes a classification of laboratories according to their local or remote character, and to real equipment or simulations:

a. *Local access-real resource.* This represents the traditional scenario where the student sits in front of an experimentation station with the needed resources to perform some task.

b. *Local access-simulated resource.* In this case, there is no real resources, but the environment is simulated by software running on a computer. The user interacts with a simulated interface, virtual and physically non-existent re-source, which together with the interface is part of the computer. This config-uration is also defined as a mono-user virtual laboratory where a single user interacts with the simulated resource on an individual basics.

c. *Remote access-real resource.* This configuration represents users getting ac-cess to a real-equipment laboratory available on the Internet. Working re-motely through an experimentation interface, the user operates and controls a real equipment. This approach is named remote laboratory, telelaboratory or teleoperation through WWW.

d. *Remote access-simulated resource.* This is like the one above configuration, but in this case a simulated resource replaces the physical system. Getting ac-cess through an experimentation interface, the student operates on a virtual system accessible through the Internet. Notice a main difference, as in this case several users may interact simultaneously with the same virtual system. As it is a simulated process, it can be instantiated to serve any person who asks for it. Therefore, this is a kind of multi-user virtual laboratory or WBS environment.

Saliah-Hassane et al. (2019) stated the following definitions for remote laboratories:

a. *Laboratory.* This refers to hardware or software (or both) elements that are integrated to enable the performance of scientific experiments.

b. *Remote laboratory.* This involves a set of network-connected physical devices to the components real laboratory that can be observed and controlled at distance.

c. *Virtual laboratory.* In this case, an interactive simulation of physical phe-nomena supported by mathematical models or experimental datasets is pro-vided to simulate real experiences.

d. *Online laboratory.* This kind of laboratory is accessible online through a com-puter network, such as the Internet. It can either be remote, accessing to a real laboratory, but also virtual when the lab is simulated, or a hybrid of both.

The main advantages of online, remote and virtual laboratories are the reduced costs, the anywhere and anytime availability, accessibility for people with disabil-ities and the safety for dangerous experimentations.

There are currently several examples of such laboratories. In Potkonjak et al. (2016), there are several examples of virtual labs in the field of science, tech-nology, and engineering. Within the field of engineering, the *VISIR project* (Gus-tavsson et al., 2007) is one of the most outstanding ones. More recently, it is remarkable the *LabsLand initiative*, focused on providing a platform that promotes educational remote laboratories maintainability, sustainability and adoption (Orduña et al., 2016).

2.5. Assessment and feedback tools

Quality and timely feedback for students about their performance on assignments of their participation in forums is a main factor to support student learning (Steele & Holbeck, 2018). In a similar way, the answers, reactions, and comments provided by students during the performance of proposed learning activities are important for improving pedagogical approaches and educational resources provided. First, students' learning behavior can be analyzed to provide the basics for personalized services and content via recommender systems. Second, general difficulties of the students with specific resources or the proposed learning path can also be identified. This monitoring of the students' behavior and performance helps to improve the interaction between teachers and students, and frequent input from students aids in the development of a better learning environment.

In a traditional face-to-face classroom, teachers get a lot of clues from characteristics such as students' gaze, faces and gestures. This provides important information that allow to evaluate the performance, behavior and sentiment of the students (Pireva et al., 2015). When we move to an online scenario, teachers can get a direct communication with students via videoconferencing tools, but that kind of student and assessment is a challenging and almost impossible task without further support.

It is important to recognize two different purposes on student evaluation: summative and formative. Summative assessment is focused providing a certain mark for the student. This has a specific value for the final academic performance and as a result, students usually pay a lot of attention to achieve a good result. The majority of standardized examinations are in the form of a summative assessment. Nevertheless, these assessments are not designed to give teachers and students quick, contextualized feedback during the learning process. They are a final check at the end of an instructional stage. On the contrary, formative assessment main goal is to provide students feedback to support their learning. It occurs not at the end of an instructional stage, but in the middle or even at the beginning. The point is to make learners motivate and engage students, making them aware of their actual knowledge and capabilities. In this way, students can engage in a comparable, self-reflective process (Taras, 2005). Nevertheless, as students do not get a direct result for their academic goals, many times they don't devote as much effort as in the case of summative assessments.

Considering these challenges, new technologies are being explored to support student engagement and motivation, mainly on online environments but also on face-to-face settings. For example, student response systems, such as Socrative, Mentimeter, Plickers, GoSoapBox and Poll Everywhere, have become very popular as a way to get rapid responses from students and check their understanding. The anonymity of this tools and their high interactivity boost the participation of students. Moreover, in recent years these tools have integrated gamification features, such as Kahoot!, making them very popular at all educational levels. Although the concept is not new, its application in the classroom in the context of a play or competition has a direct impact on various aspects, such as classroom participation and encouragement to the development of the activity, perception of the learning, commitment to the subject, and interest in deepening theoretical concepts (Pireva et al., 2015). In online educational scenarios these tools are also available and can be used without many efforts. In addition, at these scenarios learning analytics solutions are being developed to provide further insights from user activities and performance using available data (traces) that comes from students' online interactions.

III. New technologies to support learning from a distance

This section covers new technologies that are not yet a reality in higher education, but that were under research during many years and experienced to some extent. We refer specially to virtual and augmented reality (VR and AR) technologies that provide new spaces where teaching and learning can be performed (Carbonell Carrera & Bermejo Asensio, 2017). For example, these technologies can be used to create virtual worlds, namely, computer-based simulated environments that may be populated by users, each one with a personal avatar. In this way, users can explore the virtual world, participate in its activities and communicate with others.

3.1. Virtual and augmented reality

Virtual Reality (VR) technologies can be used to provide completely simulated scenarios or immersive experiences, integrating computer-generated elements in the real world. In this way, they fully replace or augment a user's perception of the spatial world. Milgram and Kishino (1994) defined the Milgram's Mixed Reality (MR) continuum, considering the ratio of real to digital objects in the user's view, representing the amount of digital augmentation. When a real to digital ratio of 1:0 is considered, at the beginning of the spectrum, the user is operating on the real world. From that point and moving to the right, digital content can be added and superimposed onto the user's senses. The position on the MR continuum is determined by the amount of digital content superimposed. At the other extreme of the continuum, when the real to digital ratio is 0:1, the experience of the user is completely virtual, namely, VR. With VR, the user has no view of the real world and can only see a computer-generated world that exists in the same spatial area as the real world.

Figure 4. Milgram's MR continuum.

VR ideas and concepts have been around from several decades. Nevertheless, they have not been generally accessible until recently thanks to the development of new technological devices such as mobile platforms (e.g., iOS and Android), head-mounted displays (HMDs), or game consoles. The most advanced solutions include high-resolution screens, earpieces like noise-cancelling headphones to control the user's auditory field, and handheld controllers which increase the methods of input for the immersive experience. These new devices allow the user to experience authentic VR scenarios at an affordable cost.

In addition to immersive solutions, during the last years there have appeared non-immersive devices specially focused on AR experiences. These include handheld displays such as a smartphone or tablet. In this kind of scenario the user can move around freely, and while he gets a view of the real world through a screen, all of the digital content is superimposed over it. The AR experience can also take advantage of the data provided by the camera, gyroscope, and/or accelerometer available on the device to enhance an immersive experience. Non-Immersive devices that can provide AR experiences have been used more prevalently education.

VR and AR technologies can be used to tackle some problems in existing distance learning education (Awoke et al., 2021), such as a lack of social interaction, student engagement and or focus, comprehension and information retention. Nevertheless, the development of quality educational AR or VR resources is still too complex and demanding to be utilized by regular teachers. Of course, there exist many studies demonstrating the viability of using AR and VR for educational purposes, but they used pre-developed content for instructors that involved a high amount of specialized technical development. Creating AR and VR content requires advanced skills in technology and the use of advanced frameworks and devices. This is not at the hands of regular teachers and instructors. Moreover, the chances to adapt or personalize existing contents to specific contexts are also very limited. This makes it very difficult to integrate these advanced resources into lesson plans with the same fluidity as with traditional learning materials.

3.2. Virtual worlds and avatars

Very related to VR and AR it is the concept of virtual world. This is a kind of immersive 3D online environment that users can explore autonomously and independently, represented by avatars. They can move through the spaces and interact with other users and objects. Users are provided with a sense of being there. In this way, virtual worlds have been explored to support new learning experiences where the student is situated on specific conditions.

The concept of virtual world has been defined by Girvan (2018) as "shared, simulated spaces which are inhabited and shaped by their inhabitants who are represented as avatars. These avatars mediate our experience of this space as we move, interact with objects and interact with others, with whom we construct a shared understanding of the world at that time" (p. 1099). "What makes [virtual worlds] distinct from the material or physical world are the types of experience available for the user afforded by the combination of different technical features, most notably the avatar" (Girvan, 2018, p. 1093).

According to Gregory et al. (2015), "virtual worlds provide synchronous collaborative social spaces that can be utilized for a range of authentic learning experiences and cater for a range of learners." In the higher education context, virtual worlds have been applied in virtual lectures, virtual laboratories, virtual field trips, simulations, in-world creations, gaming, assessment and socialization (Ghanbarzadeh & Ghapanchi, 2018).

IV. Issues

Recent studies stress that digital technologies, such as the ones described in the previous sections, are being adopted and used widely in higher education contexts to support the academic learning processes (Pinto & Leite, 2020). This is happening both on face-to-face settings and distance learning scenarios, contributing to blurring the traditional borders between learning spaces and time, between formal and informal learning environments.

Nevertheless, although current technology offers many opportunities to improve higher education and solve existing needs, mainly on distance learning scenarios, some disadvantages remain (Sadeghi, 2019):

a. *High chances of distraction.* Without face-to-face interaction, direct presence of teachers, and no classmates who can help with constant reminders about pending assignments, distance learning scenarios involve high chances for students of getting distracted and losing track of deadlines.

b. *Complicated technology.* There is an overdependence on technology. This involves a great level of stress for teachers. Any software or hardware problem implies that the class session must be suspended, something that can interrupt the learning process.

c. *No social interaction.* When learners are studying alone they may feel isolated and miss the social and physical interaction that comes with attending a traditional classroom. Issues such as motivation based on peers' interaction, or the ability "to ask to other people," can be very hard in distance contexts.

d. *Difficulty staying in contact with instructors.* In a traditional classroom, when learners have trouble with assignments or questions about a lecture is generally simple to ask to the instructor. This happens usually before or after the class session, or on scheduled meetings that can be arranged at any time. At distance learning, students have more difficulty getting in touch with their instructor and arranging meetings to solve this kind of problems.

V. Conclusions

The COVID-19 pandemic forced teachers to face a completely new situation. At first the students cannot go to classroom. Later, in different stages, the activities in the classroom were resumed, in some cases in a completely face-to-face manner as before the pandemic, but in the majority on hybrid settings, with some students in class and other students remotely, or alternating time in class and time at a distance for the same students. Moreover, this situation involved a great uncertainty, as teachers did not know what could happen in the following weeks. In this scenario, the need to develop alternative hybrid educational models that facilitate virtual interaction to complement the physical presence became evident.

Previously, blended learning models had been explored, in which face-to-face teaching was mixed with online education. Educational activities could include formal instruction sessions, online access to educational content, group collaboration in class, home projects delivered through the LMS, receiving effective feedback, maintaining open lines of communication with educators and peers, etc. Existing technologies, in particular LMS, enabled the delivery of multimedia content, including text, images and video, the completion of quizzes or exercises, and the presentation and grading of projects. However, these systems were not enough to support education during the different pandemic scenarios, including all the activities that require a quality higher education. Specifically, existing solutions showed difficulties to involve students in highly interactive teamwork that simulates the group collaboration that can occur and develop in a physical classroom environment. The need for collaboration is driving demand for platforms that simulate as realistically as possible team communication taking place in a single room. Educators need to create meaningful and effective learning experiences in adapting practices to address evolving student needs in the fluid pandemic environment. More specifically, the need to flexibly adjust the exposure of students to combinations of virtual and face-to-face activities. Technology can significantly support these needs in distance learning settings, but users still need to adopt these innovations.

Acknowledgement

This work is supported by the VIE project funded by the Erasmus+ program (project code 2020-1-EE01-KA226-HE-093367). The European Commission's support for the production of this publication does not constitute an endorsement of the contents, which reflect the views only of the authors, and the Commission cannot be held responsible for any use which may be made of the information contained therein."

References

Anido, L., Llamas, M., & Fernández, M.J. (2000). Labware for the Internet. *Computer Applications in Engineering Education, 8*(3–4), 201–208.

Anido, L., Llamas, M., & Fernández, M.J. (2001). Internet-based learning by doing. *IEEE Transactions on Education, 44*(2), 18pp.

Awoke, A., Burbelo, H., Childs, E., Mohammad, F., Stevens, L., Rewkowski, N., & Manocha, D. (2021). An overview of enhancing distance learning through augmented and virtual reality technologies. *arXiv preprint* arXiv:2101.11000.

Bencomo, S.D. (2004). Control learning: Present and future. *Annual Reviews in Control, 28*(1), 115–136.

64 Manuel Caeiro Rodríguez et al.

Carbonell Carrera, C., & Bermejo Asensio, L.A. (2017). Augmented reality as a digital teaching environment to develop spatial thinking. *Cartography and Geographic Information Science, 44*(3), 259–270.

Clark, J.T. (2020). Distance education. In *Clinical engineering handbook* (pp. 410–415). Academic Press.

Correia, A.P., Liu, C., & Xu, F. (2020). Evaluating videoconferencing systems for the quality of the educational experience. *Distance Education, 41*(4), 429–452.

Dumford, A.D., & Miller, A.L. (2018). Online learning in higher education: Exploring advantages and disadvantages for engagement. *Journal of Computing in Higher Education, 30*(3), 452–465.

Fischer, A.J., Collier-Meek, M.A., Bloomfield, B., Erchul, W.P., & Gresham, F.M. (2017). A comparison of problem identification interviews conducted face-to-face and via videoconferencing using the consultation analysis record. *Journal of School Psychology, 63*, 63–76.

Ghanbarzadeh, R., & Ghapanchi, A.H. (2018). Investigating various application areas of three-dimensional virtual worlds for higher education. *British Journal of Educational Technology, 49*(3), 370–384.

Girvan, C. (2018). What is a virtual world? Definition and classification. *Educational Technology Research and Development, 66*(5), 1087–1100.

Greenberg, G. (1998). Distance education technologies: Best practices for K-12 settings. *IEEE Technology and Society Magazine, 17*(4), 36–40.

Gregory, S., Scutter, S., Jacka, L., McDonald, M., Farley, H., & Newman, C. (2015). Barriers and enablers to the use of virtual worlds in higher education: An exploration of educator perceptions, attitudes and experiences. *Journal of Educational Technology & Society, 18*(1), 3–12.

Gustavsson, I., Zackrisson, J., Håkansson, L., Claesson, I., & Lagö, T.L. (2007). The visir project—an open-source software initiative for distributed online laboratories. In Proceedings of the REV 2007, Conference, Porto, Portugal.

Kasim, N.N.M., & Khalid, F. (2016). Choosing the right learning management system (LMS) for the higher education institution context: A systematic review. *International Journal of Emerging Technologies in Learning, 11*(6), 55–61.

Milgram, P., & Kishino, F. (1994). A taxonomy of mixed reality visual displays. *IEICE TRANSACTIONS on Information and Systems, 77*(12), 1321–1329.

Orduña, P., Rodriguez-Gil, L., Garcia-Zubia, J., Angulo, I., Hernandez, U., & Azcuenaga, E. (2016). October. LabsLand: A sharing economy platform to promote educational remote laboratories maintainability, sustainability and adoption. In *2016 IEEE Frontiers in Education Conference (FIE)* (pp. 1–6). IEEE.

Pinto, M., & Leite, C. (2020). Digital technologies in support of students learning in Higher Education: Literature review. *Digital Education Review, 37*, 343–360.

Pireva, K., Imran, A.S., & Dalipi, F. (2015). User behaviour analysis on LMS and MOOC. In *2015 IEEE Conference on e-Learning, e-Management and e-Services* (IC3e) (pp. 21–26). IEEE.

Potkonjak, V., Gardner, M., Callaghan, V., Mattila, P., Guetl, C., Petrović, V.M., & Jovanović, K. (2016). Virtual laboratories for education in science, technology, and engineering: A review. *Computers & Education, 95*, 309–327.

Sadeghi, M. (2019). A shift from classroom to distance learning: Advantages and limitations. *International Journal of Research in English Education, 4*(1), 80–88.

Saliah-Hassane, H., Zapata Rivera, L.F., Rodriguez Artacho, M., Zalewski, J., Shockley, J., Gillet, D., Aguas, R., Arenas, E., Berqia, A., Bhimavaram, K.R., & Bueno-Pizarro, N.A. (2019). *1876-2019: IEEE standard for networked smart learning objects for online laboratories.* http://dx.doi.org/10.1109/IEEE STD.2019.8723446

Singh, R., & Awasthi, S. (2020). *Updated comparative analysis on video conferencing platforms—Zoom, Google Meet, Microsoft Teams, WebEx Teams and GoToMeetings* (pp. 1–9). EasyChair: The World for Scientists.

Steele, J., & Holbeck, R. (2018). Five elements that impact quality feedback in the online asynchronous classroom. *Journal of Educators Online, 15*(3), n.3.

Taras, M. (2005). Assessment—summative and formative—some theoretical reflections. *British Journal of Educational Studies, 53*(4), 466–478.

Mercedes González-Sanmamed (University of A Coruña),
Iris Estévez (University of Santiago de Compostela), Alba
Souto-Seijo (University of Santiago de Compostela)

Chapter IV Learning ecologies and digital literacy: Opportunities and challenges

I. Introduction

Technology plays a fundamental role in the modern world. It is present in all aspects of human life, and so digital transformation has an impact in all of them (Báez & Clunie, 2019; Bates, 2019). It is affecting how we live, how we interact with others, our access to work, and how we produce new knowledge. Facing these new challenges calls for digital literacy (Cope & Kalantzis, 2009) which is realized through digital competencies that everyone should develop (Iordache et al., 2017).

The ubiquity of digital technology is both a challenge and an opportunity (UNESCO, 2014). On the one hand, there is far more information available nowadays than people can process (Brey, 2009). This information overload (Cornella, 2000; Toffler, 1970) is characteristic of our age and means that many people find it difficult to convert information into knowledge. On the other hand, digital technologies open up countless possibilities for learning anywhere at any time, and it is worth highlighting that these new formats have become generalized due to the spread of mobile devices in daily life. These learning environments to be created can be accessed in various contexts and situations, providing limitless learning experiences (Alexander et al., 2019).

This new social paradigm has led to new analysis frameworks for knowledge development and people's education. This included the emergence of the idea of Learning Ecologies (LEs), defined as "the processes [created] in a particular context, for a particular purpose, which provide [...] opportunities, relationships, and resources for learning, development, and achievement" (Jackson, 2013, p. 14).

This construct has been operationalized grouping together the components that make up people's LEs in two main dimensions: the personal dimension and the contextual dimension. It is worth noting that within the contextual dimension—which is essentially social, interpersonal, and environmental in nature—there is a key element related to using digital resources in the continual process of learning and everyone's personal, academic, and professional development (González-Sanmamed et al., 2020).

Mastery of digital technologies lies in the acquisition of a set of competencies that allow a person to continue learning throughout their life and to perform effectively in a complex society. According to the European Commission (2018), digital competence is one of the eight key competences that everyone needs to be able to adapt to changes in society. The competency is defined as follows:

> Digital competence involves the confident, critical and responsible use of, and engagement with, digital technologies for learning, at work, and for participation in society. It includes information and data literacy, communication and collaboration, media literacy, digital content creation (including programming), safety (including digital wellbeing and competences related to cybersecurity), intellectual property related questions, problem solving and critical thinking. (European Commission, 2018, p. 9)

In addition to the needs teachers share with the rest of the population to be digitally competent in their personal activity, their professional work is linked to developing and promoting the present and future knowledge society. Nowadays, this requires them to attain excellent digital teaching competence, something that is specifically covered in Spanish education legislation (Organic Law 3/2020, 29 December, which modifies Organic Law 2/2006, 3 May, on Education [LOMLOE]). Furthermore, this legislative framework requires teachers to contribute to their students' development of digital competency both through specific content and transversally (LOMLOE, 2020).

In fact, according to Royal Decree 95/2022, 1 February, which establishes the order and minimum teaching requirements for infant education, it is in this educational stage where students should begin acquiring these skills. More specifically, the area of "Communication and Representation of Reality" lays out the basic content related to digital literacy: (a) Applications and digital tools for different purposes—creation, communication, learning, and enjoyment; (b) Healthy, responsible use of digital technologies; (c) Critical reading and interpretation of images and information received through digital media; and (d) The educational function of technological devices and elements in students' surroundings.

In this regard, one of the—presumably—surprising aspects is that, despite students nowadays being considered "digital natives" (Prensky, 2001), some research has shown that they do not demonstrate excellent mastery of technological tools (Gallardo, 2012), particularly in relation to educational purposes. Therefore, it is in formal education settings (schools) where these needs must be explicitly addressed and remedied, without ignoring or devaluing actions that may be taken in non-formal and informal settings.

This idea puts the teacher at the center of the issue as the person with the professional responsibility and duty to educate and promote the acquisition of these digital skills. Lázaro and Gisbert (2015) define it as "the need for teachers to have a level of digital competence that allows them to effectively and properly use technology in a manner that is appropriate for their students and the learning they need to achieve" (p. 325).

Over recent years, various models for analyzing teachers' digital competence have been developed. These include the Information and Communication Technology (ITC) Competency Standards for Teachers (UNESCO, 2008, 2019), the National Educational Technology Standards for Teachers (International Society for Technology in Education [ISTE], 2008), and DIGCOMP (Ferrari, 2013). Various national schemes have also been proposed, such as those from the Chilean Ministry of Education and Enlaces (2008) and the Colombian Ministry of Education (2013).

The Spanish context has seen the creation of the Common Digital Competence Framework for Teachers (MCCDD) [*Marco Común de Competencia Digital Docente*] (INTEF, 2017), comprising 5 areas of competency and 21 specific competencies (see Figure 1). This was designed with the aim of improving diagnosis and development of teachers' digital skills, considering knowledge as well as capabilities and attitudes (INTEF, 2017).

In this study we focus specifically on the first of the areas, called *Information and data literacy*. This area is linked to identifying, locating, obtaining, storing, organizing, and analyzing information (INTEF, 2017). Figure 2 shows the three competency dimensions making up this area.

The Common Framework of Digital Teaching Competence (INTEF, 2017) arose as a precursor for the recognition of professional development for both active and trainee teachers. This implies that the study plans for the degree courses that future teachers will study must provide sufficient education in subjects related to digital competence (Girón-Escudero et al., 2019; Moreno Rodríguez et al., 2018). However, studies such as Gutiérrez and Cabero (2015) have shown that university students doing degrees in infant and primary education have moderately low levels of digital competence.

This study was performed in order to analyze future infant education teachers' levels of digital competence in the area of information and informational literacy.

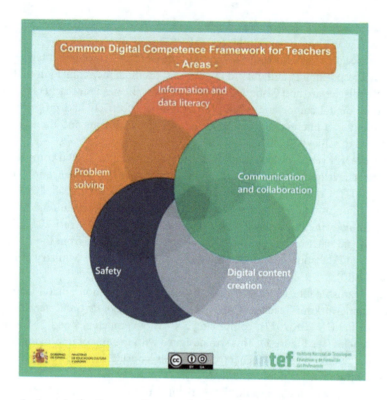

Figure 1. Areas in the Common Framework of Digital Teaching Competence.
Source: INTEF (2017, p. 13)

II. Method

This quantitative, empirical-analytical study used a non-experimental descriptive design via survey. It was transversal, as the data were collected at a single timepoint.

2.1. Participants

The participants in the study were 72 final-year students doing the degree in Infant Education at the University of A Coruña. They were selected via convenience sampling. Almost all of the participants, 66 (91.7 %), were women, while 6 (8.3 %) were men. The youngest participant was 21 years old, the oldest was 35, the mean age was 22.9 years (see Figure 3).

Figure 2. Competency dimensions in the area of *Information and data literacy*.
Source: authors' own work based on INTEF (2017)

2.2. Instrument

The instrument used for the study was designed and created based on the standards established by the MCCDD (INTEF, 2017). The questionnaire was tailored to the target group (final-year students doing an infant education degree), with the wording being modified but leaving the structure proposed by INTEF (2017) unchanged.

To assess validity criteria, the instrument was subject to expert review by teachers at the University of A Coruña. The final version has four dimensions. The first dimension is related to participants' sociodemographic characteristics (sex, age, university where they study, training and level of knowledge about ICT for teaching). The remaining items cover the three dimensions making up the area of *Information and data literacy*. The scale contains 30 items (10 per dimension) which adhere to the mean competency levels established in the MCCDD. The first dimension is *Browsing, searching and filtering data, information and*

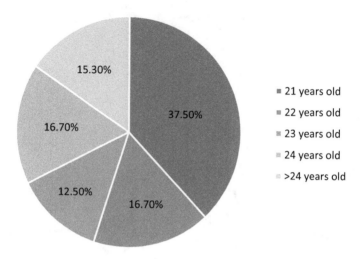

Figure 3. Age of study participants.

digital content (e.g., I use tools to identify and tag relevant information). The second dimension is *Evaluating data, information and digital content* (e.g., I assess the usefulness, accuracy, and trustworthiness of the information I seek). The final dimension is *Managing and retrieval of data, information and digital content* (e.g., I create copies of the files I need before storing content of interest, whether privately or publicly). The item responses are given on a Likert-type scale from 1 to 4 (where 1 is completely disagree/not at all/never, and 4 is completely agree/a lot/always).

The reliability of the scale was determined via Cronbach's coefficient. In this case, the overall coefficient for the instrument was 0.86. The reliability indices for the three dimensions were 0.78, 0.74, and 0.75, which confirms the questionnaire's reliability.

2.3. Procedure

The instrument was administered online using the Google Forms platform. It included an introductory section explaining the study objective, and assuring participants of the anonymity and confidentiality of their responses and data. The application was open for 40 days. On average, it took about 9 minutes to complete the questionnaire.

2.4. Data analysis

The first step in analyzing the data was to assess its quality, looking at the distribution (asymmetry and kurtosis), determining the summary measures (mean) and calculating dispersion (standard deviation). Once it was determined that the data were within the parameters for normality, descriptive and frequency analyses were performed in response to the objectives. In addition, the variables linked to the three dimensions were constructed (from the items associated with each one) along with a global variable linked to the competency area of *Information and data literacy* (from all of the items in the scale). A descriptive analysis was also applied to those new variables. Data analysis was performed using SPSS 25.0 software.

III. Result

3.1. Preliminary results

Table 1 shows the results of the descriptive analysis, confirming that the data fell within the parameters of normality, allowing them to be interpreted.

3.2. Overall competency level for area 1: Information and data literacy

There was a moderately high overall level of competence (see Figure 4) in *Information and data literacy* (M = 2.67; SD = 0.39). There was a moderately high mean score for Dimension 1 (*Browsing, searching and filtering data, information and digital content*) of M = 2.67 (SD = 0.48). Dimension 2 (*Evaluating data, information and digital content*) had a mean score of M = 2.74 (SD = 0.39), which was the highest score out of the three dimensions making up *Information and data literacy*. The participants' most well-developed digital skills were related to evaluating, testing, and incorporating information in the digital landscape. Dimension 3 (*Managing and retrieval of data, information and digital content*) had a mean score of M = 2.59 (SD = 0.57), which although moderate was the lowest of the three dimensions. This may suggest that participants had relatively more difficulty in processes of storing and recovering digital information and data (see Figure 4).

Table 1. Descriptive Analysis, Frequencies and Percentages for the Observed Variables

Descriptive analysis

	Min.	Max.	M	DT	Asym.	Kurt.	n 1	2	3	4	1	2	3	4
D1. Browsing, searching and filtering data, information and digital content														
D1_1	1.00	4.00	2.59	0.78	-0.24	-0.24	6	24	35	7	8.3	33.3	48.6	9.7
D1_2	1.00	4.00	2.69	0.83	-0.27	-0.37	6	21	34	11	8.3	29.2	47.2	15.3
D1_3	1.00	4.00	2.91	0.72	-0.32	0.03	2	16	40	14	2.8	22.2	55.6	19.4
D1_4	1.00	4.00	2.38	0.95	0.12	-0.88	14	26	22	10	19.4	36.1	30.6	13.9
D1_5	2.00	4.00	2.97	0.67	0.03	-0.71	0	17	40	15	0	23.6	55.6	20.8
D1_6	1.00	4.00	2.81	0.87	-0.53	-0.22	7	14	36	15	9.7	19.4	50.0	20.8
D1_7	1.00	4.00	2.51	0.85	0.16	-0.58	7	31	24	10	9.7	43.1	33.3	13.9
D1_8	1.00	4.00	2.55	0.80	-0.01	-0.41	6	28	30	8	8.3	38.9	41.7	11.1
D1_9	1.00	4.00	2.95	0.79	-0.44	-0.14	3	15	36	18	4.2	20.8	50.0	25.0
D1_10	1.00	4.00	2.37	1.04	0.03	-1.18	19	18	24	11	26.4	25.0	33.3	15.3
D2. Evaluating data, information and digital content														
D2_1	1.00	4.00	3.11	0.72	-0.40	-0.22	1	12	37	22	1.4	16.7	51.4	30.6
D2_2	1.00	4.00	2.79	0.67	-0.31	0.30	2	19	43	8	2.8	26.4	59.7	11.1

Descriptive analysis

	Min.	Max.	M	DT	Asym.	Kurt.	n 1	2	3	4	1	2	3	4
D2_3	2.00	4.00	3.11	0.64	−0.09	−0.52	0	11	42	19	0	15.3	58.3	26.4
D2_4	1.00	4.00	2.77	0.75	−0.00	−0.50	2	24	34	12	2.8	33.3	47.2	16.7
D2_5	2.00	4.00	3.00	0.58	0.00	0.08	0	12	48	12	0	16.7	66.7	16.7
D2_6	1.00	4.00	2.97	0.69	−0.22	−0.09	1	15	41	15	1.4	20.8	56.9	20.8
D2_7	1.00	4.00	2.98	0.74	−0.40	−0.03	2	14	39	17	2.8	19.4	54.2	23.6
D2_8	1.00	4.00	2.16	0.83	0.11	−0.76	17	29	23	3	23.6	40.3	31.9	4.2
D2_9	1.00	4.00	2.70	0.70	−0.02	−0.21	2	25	37	8	2.8	34.7	51.4	11.1
D2_10	1.00	4.00	1.81	0.84	0.64	−0.52	31	25	14	2	43.1	34.7	19.4	2.8
D3. Managing and retrieval of data, information and digital content														
D3_1	1.00	4.00	2.44	0.87	−0.22	−0.69	12	22	32	6	16.7	30.6	44.4	8.3
D3_2	1.00	4.00	2.40	1.04	−0.11	−1.23	20	13	29	10	27.8	18.1	40.3	13.9
D3_3	1.00	4.00	2.81	0.99	−0.32	−0.98	8	19	23	22	11.1	26.4	31.9	30.6
D3_4	1.00	4.00	2.83	0.97	−0.48	−0.70	9	14	29	20	12.5	19.4	40.3	27.8
D3_5	1.00	4.00	2.33	1.21	0.20	−1.53	26	14	14	18	36.1	19.4	19.4	25

(continued)

Descriptive analysis

	Min.	Max.	M	DT	Asym.	Kurt.	n							
							1	2	3	4	1	2	3	4
D3_6	1.00	4.00	2.18	1.06	0.41	−1.06	24	22	15	11	33.3	30.6	20.8	15.3
D3_7	1.00	4.00	2.86	1.03	−0.56	−0.80	11	11	27	23	15.3	15.3	37.5	31.9
D3_8	1.00	4.00	3.18	0.89	−0.85	−0.09	4	11	25	32	5.6	15.3	34.7	44.4
D3_9	1.00	4.00	2.59	1.09	−0.05	−1.30	14	21	17	20	19.4	29.2	23.6	27.8
D3_10	1.00	4.00	2.29	1.01	0.13	−1.12	20	20	23	9	27.8	27.8	31.9	12.5

Note: the frequencies and percentages are described based on the Likert-type scale from 1 to 4 (where 1 is completely disagree/not at all/never and 4 is completely agree/a lot/always).

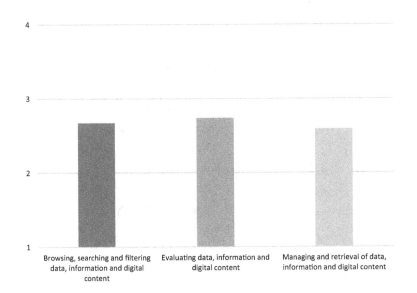

Figure 4. Mean scores for the dimensions making up the area of *Information and data literacy*.

The results of examining each of the dimensions and their constituent descriptors are given below.

3.2.1. Dimension 1: Browsing, searching and filtering data, information and digital content

The overall mean score for this dimension was M = 2.67 (SD = 0.48). As Figure 5 shows, the item with the highest mean score was Item D1_5 with a mean of M = 2.97 (SD = 0.67). This item refers to participants' ability to navigate the Internet to find information and teaching resources in various formats and from various sources. There was a similar score for Item 9, with a mean of M = 2.95 (SD = 0.79). This item is about searching for information using key words to limit the number of hits. These were the two highest-scored items in Dimension 1, identifying the competencies in which the participants exhibited the best levels of competency.

One of the lowest-scoring items in Dimension 1, with a mean of M = 2.38 (DT = 0.95), was Item D1_4. This item refers to skills in using RSS feeds and subscriptions to access information more easily. On similar lines, Item D1_10 had the lowest mean score (M = 2.37; DT = 1.04). This item refers to entering

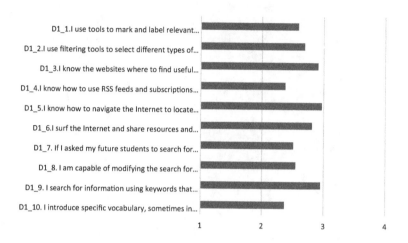

Figure 5. Descriptors for Dimension 1.

specific vocabulary, sometimes in English, and combinations of letters and symbols to find relevant information in various digital search tools. Thus, we can conclude that, despite the moderately high levels of competencies, these items were comparatively lower scoring, and indicate the actions in which participants demonstrated slightly lower levels of competency.

3.2.2. Dimension 2: Evaluating data, information and digital content

The overall mean score for dimension 2 was M = 2.74 (SD = 0.39). More specifically, Item D2_1 had a mean score of M = 3.11 (SD = 0.72) (see Figure 6). This item refers to maintaining a critical attitude to information and teaching or educational resources found on the Internet before implementing them in practice. Item D2_3 also had a mean score of M = 3.11 (SD = 0.64). This item is about the ability to choose the most suitable sources from various options, considering future professional needs. Here we establish that these closely related variables are identified with actions in which students exhibit higher levels of competency.

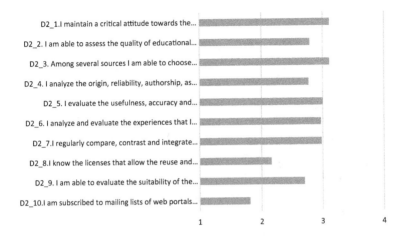

Figure 6. Descriptors for Dimension 2.

Now we look at the lowest-scoring items within this dimension. Item D2_8 had a mean score of M = 2.16 (SD = 0.83). It refers to knowledge of the licenses that allow resources on the Internet to be re-used or shared. The lowest scoring item in this dimension was D2_10, with a mean of M = 1.81 (SD = 0.84), indicating a low level of competency. This item refers to mailing lists for websites to keep up to date or to obtain useful resources for future teaching activity. These two items represent the lowest scores in Dimension 2 and describe digital activities in which the participants reported more limitations.

3.2.3. Dimension 3: Managing and retrieval of data, information and digital content

The overall mean score for Dimension 3 was M = 2.59 (SD = 0.57), which was the lowest of the three dimensions. Item D3_7 had a mean score of M = 2.86 (SD = 1.03), indicating moderately high skills in using portable devices and external storage to transfer files from one device to another if the Internet is not available. Item D3_8 had a mean score of M = 3.18 (SD = 0.89). This indicates that the participants had high levels of digital competency in terms of storing what they had produced or downloaded onto external devices, if working with devices at school or university. As these were the highest scored items in the dimension, they indicate the digital activities in which the students were most competent.

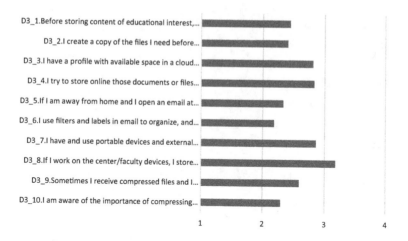

Figure 7. Descriptors for Dimension 3.

The low-scoring items included Item D3_6, with a mean score of $M = 2.18$ (SD = 1.06). This item refers to the specific digital competency of using filters and tags for email and to organize and recover required information more effectively. Item D3_10 had a mean score of $M = 2.29$ (SD = 1.01). It refers to the belief that it is important to compress files and optimize storage space. As these were the lowest-scoring items in the dimension, the conclusion is that they are the two descriptors where the students are least competent.

IV. Discussion and conclusions

Digital competency, and particularly digital competency in teaching, together with technological literacy as an unavoidable requirement of twenty-first-century citizens (Avni & Rotem, 2016), are enormously interesting topics in public policy, especially in educational policy (which can be confirmed by noting the various proposals from the European Union, supranational bodies such as UNESCO, and various national governments). That interest is also notable for the arguments it produces (Azoulay, 2018; Bokova, 2017), the thoughts and questions it raises (Castañeda et al., 2018; Gee, 2010; Selwyn, 2016), and the research it encourages, indicated by the review articles in the literature on the topic (Pinto et al., 2020; Puglia et al., 2020).

Pinto et al. (2020) established 4 classification categories for the 102 articles they reviewed. They found that 50.98 % presented results of self-perception or self-evaluation questionnaires, like the results presented in this chapter. In effect, one's own perception of one's level of technological literacy or mastery is an important indicator in measuring digital competency. This form of examination has other benefits, such as the person becoming aware of other potential for the technology. In addition, it encourages each subject's awareness of the topic and so opens up the possibility of improvements in the process of developing technological skills.

The results from this study do not support a hugely optimistic picture, whether about the level of university students' digital literacy—particularly in primary and infant education degrees—or about how well prepared they will be for their future teaching work. As in other studies (González-Calatayud et al., 2018), the three dimensions we analyzed had moderate scores which, once again, calls into question the idea that young people, having been born into and grown up in a digital context, will have high levels of technological skills (Prendes & Román, 2017). It is consistent with the perceptions young people themselves exhibit about their underuse of ICT technology due to a lack of instrumental, strategic, and emotional training (Sanmartín & Megías, 2020). It is also somewhat concerning that there has been no improvement over the results found in similar studies in previous years (Prendes, Castañeda & Gutiérrez, 2010; Raposo et al., 2006; Roblizo & Cózar, 2015).

It is more encouraging that, along with competencies related to external storage of information (highest mean score M = 3.18), the highest scores were in the two items related to the ability to apply a critical attitude to information and the selection of educational resources on the Internet (M = 3.11) and the selection of the most suitable sources of information for the best professional use (M = 3.11). It is precisely this critical perspective of ICT in general, and especially educational technology resources, that must be prioritized in teachers' personal activity and their work. The education and training aimed at improving teachers' technological skills must ensure it goes beyond the merely instrumental and move toward the integration of technical, pedagogical and content perspectives as indicated by the TPACK model (Koehler & Mishra, 2009).

These findings unarguably and urgently indicate the need to pay better attention to improving university students' technological skills, and the need for that to also address the demands of their future professional lives. This must have an impact at the level of educational policy, specifically on the definition and implementation of higher education courses, which need the inclusion of institutionalized technology education. But the findings also indicate the need to widen the picture and look at opportunities for learning outside of formal education. In this regard, it is essential to widen our view, and from the perspective of learning ecologies, allow for spaces, resources, and interactions that will contribute to expanding and enriching opportunities for personal and professional development and education (González-Sanmamed, Muñoz et al., 2021; González-Sanmamed, Tejada et al., 2021).

This study does have some limitations. Although it responded to the objectives established at the beginning, the results must be interpreted with caution, as the sample size does not allow generalization. It is also important to note that the sample selection criteria was by convenience, which can produce various biases that need to be considered, as they may affect the representativeness of the results.

Future lines of research could include larger, global studies that may allow us to identify the underlying reasons behind these modest results for digital skills in students doing degrees in infant or primary education, results which raise doubts about these future teachers' technological mastery in their professional performance. It would be interesting to design a sequential, qualitative study to look at this issue. In addition, the very recent update to the Common Framework for Digital Teaching Competency—from the Resolution on May 4, 2022, on General Management of Evaluation and Territorial Cooperation, published in the Agreement of the Sectorial Education Conference—calls for a review and subsequent incorporation of current standards in future work along these lines.

This is, without doubt, a very changeable issue which is continually evolving, and the models that are proposed must address the dual challenge of how to best represent the digital context we are in and try to predict new needs and requirements for a future that is marked by uncertainty, bafflement, and obsolescence. All the more reason, therefore, for education to ensure people's literacy and capabilities.

Acknowledgments

This chapter was produced within the framework of the research project: "How the best university teachers learn in the digital age: The impact of learning ecologies on teaching quality" (Reference EDU2015-67907-R) and "Learning ecologies in the digital age: new opportunities for teacher training in secondary education" (Reference RTI2018-095690-B-I00), partly funded by the Ministerio de Economía y Competitividad, and the Ministerio de Ciencia, Innovación y Universidades de España.

References

Alexander, B., Ashford-Rowe, K., Barajas-Murphy, N., Dobbin, G., Knott, J., Mc-Cormack, M., Pomerantz, J., Seilhamer, R., & Weber, N. (2019). *EDUCAUSE 2019 Horizon Report Preview*. https://bit.ly/37P5upS

Avni, E., & Rotem, A. (2016). Digital competence: A net of literacies. In Y. Rosen, S. Ferrara, & M. Mosharraf (Eds.), *Handbook of research on technology tools for real-world skill development* (pp. 13–41). IGI Global. https://10.4018/978-1-4666-9441-5.ch002

Azoulay, A. (2018). *Alfabetización y desarrollo de competencias*. Mensaje de la Sra. Aurey Azoulay, Directora General de la UNESCO, con motivo del Día Internacional de la Alfabetización [carta oficial]. https://en.unesco.org/commemorations/literacyday

Báez, C.I., & Clunie, C.E. (2019). Una mirada a la Educación Ubicua. *RIED. Revista Iberoamericana de Educación a Distancia, 22*(1), 325–344. https://doi.org/10.5944/ried.22.1.22422

Bates, A.W. (2019). *Teaching in a Digital Age. Guidelines for designing teaching and learning* (2nd ed.). Tony Bates Associates.

Bokova, I. (2017). *La alfabetización en un mundo digital*. Mensaje de la Sra. Irina Bokova, Directora General de la UNESCO, con motivo del Día Internacional de la Alfabetización [carta oficial]. http://unesdoc.unesco.org/images/0025/002578/257808s.pdf

Brey, A. (2009). La Sociedad de la Ignorancia. In A. Brey, D. Innerariry, & G. Mayos (Eds.), *La Sociedad de la Ignorancia y otros ensayos* (pp. 17–42). Infonomia.

Castañeda, L., Esteve, F., & Adell, J. (2018). ¿Por qué es necesario repensar la competencia docente para el mundo digital? *RED. Revista de Educación a Distancia, 56*, 1–20. http://dx.doi.org/10.6018/red/56/6

Cope, B., & Kalantzis, M. (2009). *Ubiquitous learning*. University of Illinois Press. https://bit.ly/2B10Skz

Cornella, A. (2000). Cómo sobrevivir a la infoxicación. *Infonomia, 8*.

European Commission. (2018). *Council recommendation of 22 May 2018 on key competences for lifelong learning*. https://bit.ly/2LynE44

Ferrari, A. (2013). *DIGCOMP: A framework for developing and understanding digital competence in Europe*. Publications Office of the European Union. https://doi.org/10.2788/52966

Gallardo, E.E. (2012). Hablemos de estudiantes digitales y no de nativos digitales. *UT. Revista de Ciències de l'Educació, 2012*, 7–21. https://revistes.urv.cat/index.php/ute/article/view/595/574

Gee, J.P. (2010). A situated-sociocultural approach to literacy and technology. In E.A. Baker (Ed.), *The new literacies: Multiple perspectives on research and practice* (pp. 165–193). Guilford Press. http://www.jamespaulgee.com/pubd isp.php?id=0&scateg=Linguistics

Girón-Escudero, V., Cózar-Gutiérrez, R., & González-Calero Somoza, J.A. (2019). Análisis de la autopercepción sobre el nivel de competencia digital docente en la formación inicial de maestros/as. *Revista Electrónica Interuniversitaria de Formación del Profesorado, 22*(3), 193–218. http://dx.doi.org/10.6018/reifop.22.3.373421

González-Calatayud, V.R., Román, M., & Prendes, M.P. (2018). Formación en competencias digitales para estudiantes universitarios basada en el modelo DigComp. *Edutec. Revista Electrónica de Tecnología Educativa, 65*, 1–15. https://doi.org/10.21556/edutec.2018.65.1119

González-Sanmamed, M., Estévez, I., Souto-Seijo, A., & Muñoz-Carril, P.C. (2020). Digital learning ecologies and professional development of university professors. *Comunicar, 28*(62), 9–18. https://doi.org/10.3916/C62-2020-01

González-Sanmamed, M., Muñoz-Carril, P.C., & Estévez, I. (2021). Ecologías Digitales en tiempos de COVID-19. *Publicaciones, 51*(3), 7–16. https://bit.ly/3tgnTbe

González-Sanmamed, M., Tejada, P., & Fernández-Cruz, M. (2021). Ecologías de aprendizaje: oportunidades para la formación en red. *Revista Educatio Siglo XXI, 39*(2), 13–18 https://revistas.um.es/educatio/article/view/483471

Gutiérrez, J., & Cabero, J. (2015). Estudio de caso sobre la autopercepción de la competencia digital del estudiante universitario de las titulaciones de Grado de Educación Infantil y Primaria. *Profesorado. Revista de Currículum y Formación del Profesorado, 20*(2), 180–199. Recuperado de http://recyt.fecyt.es/index.php/profesorado/article/view/52098

INTEF. (2017). *Common digital competence framework for teachers.* https://bit.ly/2Errprc

Iordache, C., Mariën, I., & Baelden, D. (2017). Developing digital skills and competences: A QuickScan analysis of 13 digital literacy models. *Italian Journal of Sociology of Education, 9*(1), 6–30. https://10.14658/pupj-ijse-2017-1-2

ISTE. (2008). *National educational technology standards for teachers.*

Jackson, N. (2013). The concept of learning ecologies. In N. Jackson & G.B. Cooper (Eds.), *Lifewide learning education and personal development* (pp. 1–21). https://bit.ly/2Bujbi1

Koehler, M., & Mishra, P. (2009). What is technological pedagogical content knowledge?. *Contemporary Issues in Technology and Teacher Education, 9*(1), 60–70.

Lázaro, J., & Gisbert, M. (2015). El desarrollo de la competencia digital docente a partir de una experiencia piloto de formación en alternancia en el Grado de Educación. *Educar, 51*(2), 321–248. http://dx.doi.org/10.5565/rev/educar.725

Ley Orgánica 3/2020, de 29 de diciembre, por la que se modifica la Ley Orgánica 2/2006, de 3 de mayo, de Educación. *Boletín Oficial del Estado,* 340, de 30 de diciembre de 2020. https://www.boe.es/diario_boe/txt. php?id=BOE-A-2020-17264

Ministerio de Educación Chile y Enlaces. (2008). *ICT standards for initial teacher education: A proposal in the Chilean context.* https://bit.ly/3Q6TSEe

Ministerio de Educación de Colombia. (2013). *ICT skills for teaching professional development.* https://bit.ly/3xdKN3U

Moreno Rodríguez, M.D., Gabarda Méndez, V., & Rodríguez Martín, A.M. (2018). Alfabetización informacional y competencia digital en estudiantes de magisterio. *Profesorado. Revista de Currículum y Formación de Profesorado, 22*(3), 253–270. http://dx.doi.org/10.30827/profesorado.v22i3.8001

Pinto, A.R., Pérez, A., & Darder, A. (2020). Revisión sistemática de la literatura sobre competencia digital docente en la formación inicial del profesorado. In E. Colomo, E. Sánchez, J. Ruiz, & J. Sánchez (Coord.), *La tecnología como eje del cambio metodológico* (pp. 513–517). https://bit.ly/39cNRWb

Puglia, E., Ferreira, A., & Piñeiro, R. (2020). La competencia digital docente de docentes de formación docente en América Latina, una revisión sistemática sobre el estado de la literatura. In E. Colomo, E. Sánchez, J. Ruiz, & J. Sánchez (Coord.), *La tecnología como eje del cambio metodológico* (pp. 1406–1410). https://bit.ly/39cNRWb

Prendes, M.P., Castañeda, L., & Gutiérrez, I. (2010). Competencias para el uso de TIC de los futuros maestros. *Comunicar, 35* (18), 175–182. http://10.3916/ C35-2010-03-11

Prendes, M.P., & Román, M.M. (2017). *Entornos Personales de Aprendizaje. Una visión actual de cómo aprender con tecnologías.* Octaedro.

Prensky, M. (2001). Digital natives, digital immigrants. *On the Horizon, 9*(5), 1–6. http://dx.doi.org/10.1108/10748120110424816

Raposo, M., Fuentes, E., & González, M. (2006). Desarrollo de competencias tecnológicas en la formación inicial de maestros. *Revista Latinoamericana de Tecnología Educativa, 5*(2), 525–537.

Real Decreto 95/2022, de 1 de febrero, por el que se establece la ordenación y las enseñanzas mínimas de la Educación Infantil. *Boletín Oficial del Estado,* 28, de 2 de febrero de 2022. https://www.boe.es/buscar/act.php?id=BOE-A-2022-1654

Resolución de 4 de mayo de 2022, de la Dirección General de Evaluación y Cooperación Territorial, por la que se publica el Acuerdo de la Conferencia

Sectorial de Educación, sobre la actualización del marco de referencia de la competencia digital docente.

Roblizo, M., & Cózar, R. (2015). Usos y competencias en TIC en los futuros maestros de educación infantil y primaria: hacia una alfabetización tecnológica real para docentes. *Píxel-Bit. Revista de Medios y Educación, 47*, 23–39.

Sanmartín, A., & Megías, I. (2020). *Jóvenes, futuro y expectativa tecnológica.* Centro Reina Sofía sobre Adolescencia y Juventud, Fad. https://doi.org/ 10.5281/zenodo.3629108

Selwyn, N. (2016). Profesores y tecnología: repensar la digitalización de la labor docente. *Boletín de la Institución Libre de Enseñanza, 104*, 27–36.

Toffler, A. (1970). *El shock del futuro.* Plaza & Janes.

UNESCO. (2008). *Estándares de competencias en TIC para docentes.* https://bit. ly/31Uqj16

UNESCO. (2014). *Enfoques estratégicos sobre las TICS en educación en América Latina y El Caribe.* https://bit.ly/3fQLTbc

UNESCO. (2019). *Marco de competencias de los docentes en materia de TIC UNESCO.* https://bit.ly/3GWrQY6

José María Díaz Lage (Universidad Nacional de Educación a Distancia, Spain), María de los Ángeles Gómez González (Universidade de Santiago de Compostela, Spain), Inmaculada Clotilde Santos Díaz (Universidad de Málaga, Spain)

Chapter V Teaching and learning English phonetics/pronunciation in digital and other learning environments: Challenges and perceptions of Spanish instructors and students

I. Introduction and theoretical framework

At this point in history, it is probably unnecessary to justify the importance of communication in English, but it is salutary to remember that, in order to communicate efficiently in this language, speakers—native and non-native alike—must possess an adequate command of English phonological awareness skills, currently better known as phonological control, as stated in the *Common European Framework of Reference for Languages* (CEFR, 2001, p. 107; 2020, p. 133). Furthermore, CEFR states that phonological competence refers to the knowledge of, and skill in the perception and production of sounds and prosodic features such as stress, rhythm and intonation, including such related features as accentedness (that is, accent and deviation from a "norm"), intelligibility (i.e., the accessibility of meaning for interlocutors, as well as their perceived difficulty in understanding or "comprehensibility") and phonetic accuracy or precision (CEFR, 2020, pp. 134, 261). Foreign language phonetic competence, on the other hand, refers to the phonetic organization of speech that basically determines the success or failure of verbal interaction in the context of intercultural communication. It is a multidimensional concept that involves declarative knowledge and awareness of specific phonetic and phonological aspects of language(s) (L2 or any other language, including the L1), as well as phonetic skills such as the perception, production and transcription of speech (Borysko, 2011; Gurova et al., 2020).

If we think specifically of English as a foreign language, factors of phonetic and phonological competence not only affect the main language skills (Underhill, 2011; Walker, 2014), but they also constitute an essential part of intelligible speech (Underhill, 2013). While interacting with non-native speakers, native speakers can understand their interlocutors as long as their utterances are pronounced correctly, even if they feature incorrect grammar and vocabulary (Levis, 2018; Pourhosein Gilakjani, 2016). If, on the other hand, those utterances are mispronounced, they can distract or even annoy their addressees (Fayer & Krasinski, 1987) or make them judge the utterers negatively (Anderson-Hsieh et al., 1992). Poor pronunciation can also deprive speakers of credibility (Lev-Ari & Keysar, 2010), give rise to negative stereotypes about them (Seidlhofer, 2001; Szpyra-Kozłowska, 2015), or simply lead native speakers to avoid conversation (Singleton, 1995).

The reasons for these phenomena are manifold, but we may mention the following: first of all, the existence of minimal pairs such as, for example, *seat—sit*; second, words whose stress might convey grammatical information, as in the case of *content* (/ˈkɒntent/ n—/kənˈtent/ a); third, semantic information encoded in pronunciation, as in the case of *row* (/raʊ/—/rəʊ/); fourth, the existence of inflectional endings, which contain grammatical information, as in the case of *intend—intended* (see, among others, Alcaraz & Moody, 1999; Baker, 2007; Cabrera-Abreu & Vizcaíno-Ortega, 2009; Collins & Mees, 2009; Estebas Vilaplana, 2009; Finch & Lira, 1982; Gimson, 1989; Gómez González & Sánchez-Roura, 2016; Monroy Casas, 2012; Mott, 2011; Roach, 2009; Sánchez Benedito, 1980). As to intonation, it must be borne in mind that different intonation patterns can attach different implications to the same utterance, even inadvertently.

The above suggests that the development of phonetic and phonological competence is of the utmost importance in the acquisition of a foreign language and that, therefore, instruction in English phonetics must be one of the underlying principles of teaching English as a Foreign Language (EFL).

However, the phonetics and pronunciation of English have proved to be particularly difficult for native speakers of Spanish and Galician, either in secondary or in higher education. The results of the PISA reports and the *European survey on language competences* are unambiguous in this respect. This should not come as a surprise: English pronunciation has long been established as one of the most challenging domains for speakers of Galician or Spanish (Alonso, 2014; Martínez-Flor et al., 2006; Szpyra-Kozłowska, 2015). Indeed, their difficulties are higher than those encountered by learners from other European countries: "European Spanish speakers, in particular, probably find English pronunciation harder than speakers of any other European language" (Coe, 2001, p. 91).

Quite a few, not mutually exclusive, reasons have been posited for this. Derwing and Munro (2005), for instance, mention the accent variation in the target language. Probably more relevant are the differences between the sounds and prosody of English and those of Spanish and Galician (and Catalan and Basque), as suggested by sundry scholars (Alcaraz & Moody, 1999; Cabrera-Abreu & Vizcaíno-Ortega, 2009; Estebas Vilaplana, 2009; Finch & Lira, 1982; Gómez González & Sánchez-Roura, 2016; Monroy Casas, 2012; Sánchez Benedito, 1980). Furthermore, attention is often paid to the use of inappropriate approaches to teaching and learning (Calvo Benzies, 2016).

Indeed, research seems to suggest that EFL classes see less time devoted to training in phonetics and pronunciation than to grammar, reading, writing and vocabulary (Cruttenden, 2014; Kelly, 1969; Chun, 1988; Rossiter et al. (2010); Underhill, 2013). There does not seem to be a univocal explanation for this: it has been suggested that students find phonetics far too difficult (Bakla & Demirezen, 2018; Stevick et al., 1975) and, for this reason, it is not targeted until upper levels, so that students are underexposed to phonetics and pronunciation until late—too late—in their training (Ducate & Lomicka, 2009). Teacher training, too, has been said to be an influence: their lack of proficiency in certain areas might make them ignore them or treat them inappropriately (Derwing & Munro, 2005; Gregory, 2005; Hismanoglu, 2012; Szpyra-Kozłowska, 2015). Even when the intention exists to address those areas, class time may not be enough, or the available materials may not be appropriate for the students (Henderson et al., 2015; MacDonald, 2002; Munro & Derwing, 2007).

Methodological questions can also have an impact: it has been argued (Baker & Burri, 2016; Foote et al., 2016; Levis, 2018) that EFL classes that follow the communicative approach are likely to neglect phonetic accuracy in favor of fluency and intelligibility. The recent abandonment of the "native speaker model," that is, the idea that the goal of EFL phonetic training is to achieve native-like pronunciation, and the acceptance of accentedness that goes with it (Piccardo, 2016), are not likely to improve matters in this respect.

Dialects and varieties are also aspects to take into consideration. Research tends to refer to standard varieties, either Standard Southern British English (SSBE), often conflated with Received Pronunciation (RP), or General American (GA) (see, for instance, Bradlow et al., 1999; Gómez González & Sánchez Roura, 2016; Iverson & Evans, 2009; Roach, 2009). However, studies suggest that accent variation and awareness of it are also crucial for native and non-native speakers alike. To focus on the case of native speakers, recent research has found that accent information is an important factor for speakers to recognize talk, to such an extent that a familiar accent can be more intelligible (Adank et al., 2009) and can allow for faster recognition of words (Nygaard et al., 1994). Accent can also be an influence on the understanding of vowel sounds (Evans & Iverson, 2004; Iverson & Evans, 2007).

If we shift our focus to the teaching and learning of EFL, specifically in the Spanish context, we find that the surveys carried out by scholars such as García-Lecumberri (1999) have rated pronunciation as extremely important. In the survey carried out by Calvo Benzies (2016), around a third of the participants believed that intelligibility was the sole important factor, but another third answered that achieving native-like pronunciation is the appropriate goal. Furthermore, 65 % of the teachers taking part in the survey stated that students should try to achieve native-like pronunciation.

Still, studies such as those by Alonso (2014), Calvo Benzies (2016), Derwing (2010), Fouz and Mompean (2021), Griffiths (2004), Lear et al. (2015), Rubio and Tamayo (2012), Szpyra-Kozłowska (2015), Underhill (2011) or Wei (2006) have invariably concluded that less work is conducted on oral skills than on writing skills and grammar. In one case, for instance, Walker (1999) found that only 37 % of the teachers who took part in the survey taught pronunciation regularly; 45 % did so occasionally. Unsurprisingly, this entails that students typically fare better in reading, writing, vocabulary and grammar than in listening, speaking and pronunciation (Bartolí, 2005; Chela, 2008; Martínez-Adrián & Gallardo, 2011; Szpyra-Kozłowska, 2015).

Most of the students and teachers surveyed by Calvo Benzies (2016) agreed that whatever pronunciation activities were included in the textbooks that they used were not conducive to improvement and that, despite this opinion, most teachers used exclusively those textbooks to introduce pronunciation, typically while they addressed reading, vocabulary or grammar.

With the above considerations in mind and with the aim of improving the phonetic and phonological competence of Spanish speakers in English, the authors in collaboration with other team members from different research groups (Scimitar, ENTELEARN) conducted the publicly funded research project entitled *Teaching the sounds of English to L2 and L3 learners in digital learning environments* (https://scimitar.es/index.php/research-projects/). We will not be concerned here with the main objective of this project, which was the design and development of the multi-platform app e-SoundWay, devised as a *serious game*, that is, a game with an educational purpose (Caballero-Hernández et al., 2017; Moizer et al., 2019), in this case to facilitate the teaching and learning of English phonetics by Spanish learners, as it has been discussed elsewhere at some length and depth (Lago Ferreiro et al., 2022; Gómez González et al. 2023 in this volume). Prior research has shown that key elements of game-based methodologies are that they can provide fun and challenging scenarios in which students can engage with practice task-based language instruction—including phonetic and pronunciation learning—(Pennington & Rogerson-Revell, 2019), fostering learning autonomy and nullifying the negative affective factors of anxiety and stress that have been related to lower levels of linguistic performance in face-to-face class instruction (Teimouri et al., 2019). Instead, in what follows we will be reporting on the results of two preliminary surveys that were carried out with the purpose of assessing the needs and perceptions of both instructors and learners toward EFL phonetics/pronunciation teaching and learning in digital and other learning environments.

II. Methodology

In order to ascertain the features that the new app should have, two surveys were conducted: one was addressed to students (n = 494) and the other to teachers of EFL (n = 127). In both cases, participants could be involved in pre-university (PU) or in university education (UN). Regarding students, 160 of them belonged to PU levels, and the remaining 334 belonged to UN levels. In the case of teachers, 51 taught at PU levels and 76 at UN levels.

Following guidelines proposed by Robles and Rojas (2015), a committee of experts in the field—EFL teachers from different stages—validated both questionnaires. Its members received them along with a letter introducing the project, and they were asked to assess each question using a Likert-type scale. Their feedback was incorporated into the questionnaires before they were sent out on a pilot phase, following the procedure designed by Dörnyei and Taguchi (2010).

The questionnaires were made available via Google Forms and specified their goals and a form to provide informed consent. Teachers were contacted and provided with both questionnaires so that they could answer the teacher questionnaire and distribute the student questionnaire among their pupils. This process took place in the spring of 2021. Once the members of the research project had received the answers, they grouped them in two databases: teachers and students. A descriptive analysis took place at this stage. Later, both databases were segmented according to educational stage.

This paper reports on the results obtained regarding nine questions of the launched questionnaires as the rest are exploited in other studies (see, for instance, Castillo et al. (2023)). More specifically, we shall be looking at the following items from the student questionnaire:

1. Do you think that the time devoted to pronunciation in class is enough with regard to other content?
2. Do you think that Spanish speakers (as first or second language) have problems with English phonetics/pronunciation?
3. Do you find it appropriate to learn issues related to the pronunciation of varieties of English beyond British English and American English?
4. Have you received specific training in English phonetics/pronunciation?

As to the teacher questionnaire, we shall be looking at the following items:

5. Have you received training to teach English phonetics?
6. What accent do you take as a reference in your English phonetics/pronunciation classes?
7. Why have you chosen that accent?
8. Do you use other accents in your phonetics/English pronunciation classes?
9. Do you think it is pertinent to explain and study non-native pronunciations/varieties?

III. Results and discussion

3.1. Students' answers

Asked whether they think that enough time is devoted to pronunciation in their EFL classes, most of the students who took part in the survey (68 %, n = 336) answered that it is not. Figure 1 depicts the relative frequency of each of the possible answers to this question.

Do you think that the time devoted to pronunciation in class is enough with regard to other content?

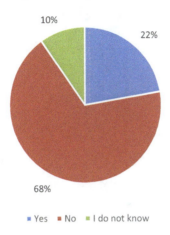

10%

22%

68%

▪ Yes ▪ No ▪ I do not know

Figure 1. Students' answers to Q1.

In keeping with the findings in scholarly literature (see section I), the participants tend to agree that Spanish-speaking students of English have problems with phonetics and pronunciation. In the case of this question, there are three possible affirmative answers: "yes, with sounds"; "yes, with intonation, rhythm and accent"; "yes, in both areas." Taking all three together reveals an impressive consensus: 96 % of the participants (n = 475) believe that students do have those problems. Interestingly, most (66 %, n = 329) of those participants believe that the problems appear in the production of individual sounds and in the realms of intonation, rhythm and accent. This is in line with the many studies that have highlighted these areas as particularly challenging for Spanish-speaking students of EFL (Alonso, 2014; Coe, 2001; Lago Ferreiro et al., 2022; Martínez-Flor et al., 2006; Szpyra-Kozłowska, 2015).

In marked contrast, relatively few participants locate the difficulty specifically on individual sounds (12 %, n = 59) or on intonation, rhythm and accent (18 %, n = 87). Finally, a very small percentage (4 %, n = 19) answered that no particular difficulties exist. Since participants were not given the option to expand on their answers, we cannot know whether they believe that Spanish learners master pronunciation or—which is more likely—that all students of EFL, regardless of their nationality, have problems with the pronunciation of English. Figure 2 presents the relative frequency of each possible answer.

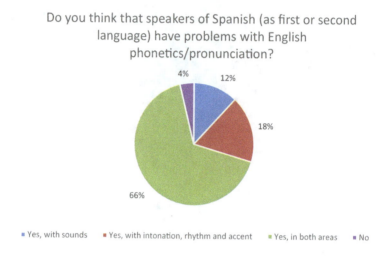

Do you think that speakers of Spanish (as first or second language) have problems with English phonetics/pronunciation?

■ Yes, with sounds   ■ Yes, with intonation, rhythm and accent   ■ Yes, in both areas   ■ No

Figure 2. Students' answers to Q2.

As we can see from the above results, a majority of the participants agree that the phonetics and pronunciation of English pose significant difficulties to Spanish-speaking students of EFL and, not unsurprisingly, they also agree that not enough time is devoted to those aspects in the classroom. Both issues go hand in hand: for, if pronunciation is perceived as being particularly difficult, it is only natural that students feel that more attention should be paid to it in the classroom. It seems that they feel more concerned about accuracy than could be expected given the basic tenets of the communicative approach to the teaching and learning of a foreign language. This is in keeping with the findings of Derwing and Munro (2009).

The third question whose results we will be discussing here is related to the different accents of English. Asked whether they thought that it is important to grow familiar with the pronunciation of other varieties of English than SSBE and GA, most participants (64 %, n = 316) answered in the affirmative. Figure 3 illustrates the frequency of each possible answer.

Do you think it is adequate to learn pronunciation issues related to other English varieties beyond BrE or AmE?

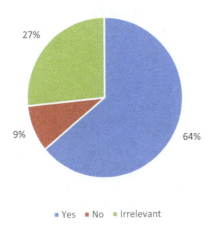

27%

9%   64%

■ Yes   ■ No   ■ Irrelevant

Figure 3. Students' answers to Q3.

As can be seen, therefore, there is a clear interest in exposure to other varieties of English, although it must be acknowledged that if we group together those participants who answered "no" (9 %, n = 47) and those who answered that it is irrelevant (27 %, n = 131), we can see that there is a significant percentage (36 %) who feel no interest in such exposure. Given the current interest in the status of English as a lingua franca of nigh-global scope, this can come as a surprise. We may surmise that this is not unrelated to the answers to questions 1 and 2: for, if more classroom time should be devoted to an area, English pronunciation, which poses significant challenges, exposure to other varieties of the language can be seen as an unnecessary waste of time. However, since we have no data that allow us to ascertain how true this is, it must remain a mere conjecture.

The final item that we will examine here is related to the answers that students gave to question 4, "have you received specific training in English phonetics/ pronunciation?" Since participants were given a range of options, of which they could choose more than one, their answers provide a wealth of information. Table 1 depicts answers to this question.

Table 1. Students' Answers to Q4

Variable	Frequency	Percentage
Yes, through specialized courses	67	13.5
Yes, during my daily sessions with the textbook	186	37.6
Yes, during my daily sessions with supplementary materials	145	29.3
Yes: other training: private sessions	7	1.42
Yes: other training: university	8	1.6
Yes: other training: self-training	1	0.2
I have not received specific training	93	18.8
I do not know whether I have received specific training	61	12.2

Starting with negative answers, 18.8 % (n = 93) of the respondents answered that they had never received specific training on English pronunciation or pho-netics, while 12.2 % (n = 61) answered that they did not know whether they had received it. In other words, slightly over two thirds of the participants did receive specific training of some kind.

Let us look at the figures for the different kinds of training. A significant mi-nority (13.5 %, n = 67) of participants answered that they had attended special-ized courses; a much greater number received training during regular classes, using either their habitual textbook (37.6 %, n = 186) or supplementary materi-als (29.3 %, n = 145). These two options are by far the most frequent. Among the seldom chosen ones, we can find 1.6 % (n = 7) who received specific training in private sessions: at an official language school, an academy or with a private tutor. A few of the respondents (1.62 %, n = 8) received their training at university. At this point, it is important to recall that our sample comprised pre-university and university students. It goes without saying that these eight participants belonged to the latter group. Finally, we can find a single respondent (0.2 %) who under-went self-training. The very possibility of training oneself in the pronunciation of English has been convincingly put forward by Estebas Vilaplana (2009): it is, therefore, fitting to find this result in our survey, even if it is limited to one participant.

3.2. Teachers' answers

Despite the title of this section, it must be borne in mind that our sample com-prises not only pre-university teachers, but also university lecturers: indeed, the latter are the majority. Of the 127 participants, 51 are pre-university teachers and 76 are university teaching staff. This accounts for some of the diversity of the answers with which we will now concern ourselves. Table 2 compiles the participants' answers to question 5, "have you received training to teach English phonetics?"

Table 2. Teachers' Answers to Q15

Variable	Frequency	Percentage
Yes, during my degree	104	81.9
Yes, during my master's degree in education/CAP	8	6.3
Yes, with specific courses after my degree	37	29.1
Yes, through studying manuals after my degree	49	38.6
Yes, through self-training	63	49.6
Yes, I have an MA/PhD in phonetics	6	4.7
I have not received specific training	5	4

There is, as could be expected, an overwhelming majority of respondents who have received specific training of some kind: roughly 96 % of the sample (n = 122) have answered affirmatively. Indeed, what is surprising is to find that 4 % of the participants (n = 5) have answered negatively. We cannot surmise the reason for these five answers since some degree of specific training in phonetics or pronunciation is surely included in any degree that an instructor in EFL may have undertaken.

There are a few participants (4.7 %, n = 6) who took either an MA or a PhD in English phonetics: they represent the most highly qualified fraction of our sample. A small percentage of the respondents (6.3 %, n = 8) answered that they received specific training during their master's degree in teaching or its predecessor, the CAP (postgraduate certificate in education). Given the features of these programs, this training was probably concerned with the pedagogy of English phonetics rather than with the discipline itself.

Percentages grow much higher for the following options. Thus, 29.1 % of the respondents (n = 37) answered that they had taken specialized courses after finishing their degrees. 49.6 % (n = 63) of the participants stated that they had undergone self-training; 38.6 % (n = 49) answered that they had received training by reading manuals after their degree, which amounts to a form of self-training too.

Finally, the great majority of the respondents (81.9 %, n = 104) stated that their training had taken place during their degree. There is nothing unexpected here, since the possible degrees that can lead an individual to the professional path of teaching EFL (e.g., English, Translation, Education) all include training in English phonetics to some extent.

If we move on to those parts of the questionnaire that concern the accents of English, the first question concerns the accent that EFL teachers use for their classes. Figure 4 includes the relative frequency of possible answers.

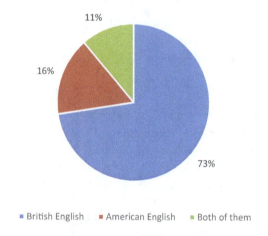

What accent do you take as a reference in your English phonetics / pronunciation classes?

11%

16%

73%

■ British English   ■ American English   ■ Both of them

Figure 4. Teachers' answers to Q6.

A great majority (73 %, n = 90) of the participants in the survey claim to use a British accent in their classes. American English, by contrast, proves to be much less popular (16 %, n = 20), even though it still seems rather high. As to those respondents who claim to use both accents, their number is the lowest (11 %, n = 14). The following question asked them to select the reason why they chose the accent that they use: their answers are displayed in Table 3.

Table 3. Teachers' Answers to Q7

Variable		Frequency	Percentage
Identification	a. Yes	b. 13	c. 10.2
	d. No	e. 114	f. 89.8
It sounds better	g. Yes	h. 1	i. 0.8
	j. No	k. 126	l. 99.2
The educational system recommends it	m. Yes	n. 11	o. 8.6
	p. No	q. 116	r. 91.4

Variable		Frequency	Percentage
I learned that accent	s. Yes	t. 74	u. 58.2
	v. No	w. 53	x. 41.8

The reasons for these choices are hardly surprising: by far the most frequent answer is simply "I learnt that accent" (58.2 %, n = 74). Taken together with the popularity of British English, we can hypothesize that the traditional emphasis on British English in the Spanish educational system is transmitted by teachers who teach the variety that they learned while training. All the other possible reasons proved to be much less popular: 10.2 % (n = 13) of the participants gave "identification" as the reason for their choice, and 8.6 % (n = 11) stated that they taught the variety that is recommended by the educational system.

A single participant (0.8 %) chose the option "it sounds better." This is an interesting choice because it is rather explicit: we may surmise that those participants who chose "I learnt that accent" also believe that it sounds better than other varieties; however, they did not choose that answer. This leads us to wonder whether this respondent learned that accent originally or she/he adopted it later because it seemed more euphonious to him/her.

The following question in the survey asked respondents whether they ever use other accents in their English pronunciation classes. Figure 5 presents the answers to this question.

Do you use other accents in your phonetics / English pronunciation classes?

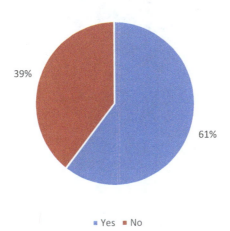

Figure 5. Teachers' answers to Q8.

This being an "either/or" type of question, the answers are unambiguous: 61 % (n = 77) of the participants answered that they do, while 39 % (n = 50) answered that they do not. However, here the unambiguity ends; for the notion of using other accents can mean different things. For instance, it would be quite one-sided to teach English phonetics without—assuming a British standard is chosen—reference to American pronunciation, or to non-SSBE varieties of British English. That would indeed be a case of using other accents to teach English pronunciation. On the other hand, "using a different accent" could be, but should not, be understood to mean "putting on an accent for a while": it is not likely that many EFL teachers do this. Although, regrettably, we do not have more specific data on this aspect, it would be interesting to know more about it. Use of audio material featuring different varieties of English is in all likelihood the most frequent teaching strategy.

While Q6 and Q7 explicitly refer to native varieties of English, and Q8 does so implicitly because the question would make no sense if it concerned non-native varieties, the survey also included questions about non-native varieties of English. The last item at which we will be looking concerns those. Asked whether they thought it appropriate to present non-native varieties, respondents answered as can be seen in Figure 6.

Do you think that it is important to explain and study non-native pronunciations/varieties?

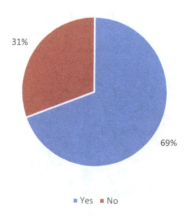

Figure 6. Teachers' answers to Q9.

As we can see on the table, a majority of teachers (69 %, n = 88) answered affirmatively, whereas only 31 % (n = 39) answered negatively. They were given no option to answer, "I do not know," which otherwise would have probably been a very popular response. For, while it is undeniable that addressing other native varieties of English can make a huge contribution to English phonetics classes, matters are not quite as clear-cut in the case of non-native varieties. That is probably the rationale behind the negative answers that we have found.

IV. Conclusions

By and large, the results that we have been analyzing were not unexpected. If we recapitulate the answers provided by students, we will find that most of them believe that Spanish-speaking learners of EFL find English phonetics and pronunciation difficult, either in the production of individual sounds, in intonation, rhythm and accent or (the prevailing view) in all these areas simultaneously. The great majority of participants stated that they had received specific training on these areas, but nevertheless they feel that the time devoted to them in the classroom is nowhere near enough. Since the most frequent approach taken during that training simply used the textbook as source material, we may hypothesize that this time could be employed more productively using a different approach.

As far as accents are concerned, more than half the respondents felt that exposure to different varieties of English other than British English (specifically, SSBE) and American English (specifically, General American) was an important part of learning English phonetics and pronunciation. Here we must stress that no other specific varieties were mentioned, so that we cannot really tell which of them seemed most necessary to students.

Turning now to the answers supplied by teachers, the issue of training to teach English phonetics and pronunciation yields predictable results: although we find the opposite ends of the spectrum, that is, participants who received postgraduate training in phonetics and pronunciation (MA or PhD) and participants who received no training at all, an overwhelming majority received their training during their degree. As was to be expected, most of the respondents use British English in their classes, the most frequent reason being that this is the variety of English that they learned. However, most of them stated that they do refer to other varieties of English when teaching phonetics and pronunciation. Again, as stated in the previous section, this seems the only plausible approach for a comprehensive overview of the sounds and intonation of English.

Finally, for a majority of teachers it is pertinent to address non-native varieties of the language. This result should be taken with a grain of salt, since the questionnaire does not go into further detail as to what these varieties might be or how they could be used in the classroom.

It remains for us to specify how these results have had an impact on the design of our multi-platform app. The research team behind this project has tried to address the concerns voiced by the students and the teachers who participated in its survey. The most influential consideration has been, of course, that there is an objective difficulty, indicated by both prior research and our survey, for speakers of Spanish to master English phonetics and pronunciation: hence the creation of the app itself. Only one of the students who answered our questionnaire stated that he/she self-trained in English phonetics: this seems to us an area where there is room for much improvement, especially since there is also a perception that not enough time is devoted to phonetics and pronunciation in the classroom. As a consequence, the app was designed so that learners can use it individually at their own convenience.

Additionally, since most teachers stated that their variety of choice is British English, we have also adopted it as the basis for the app, as it would be potentially counterproductive for students used to that variety to encounter a different one—e.g., GA—used in the app. However, our results have also highlighted that accent variation is valued by both teachers and students. Because we do wholeheartedly concur that encountering a diversity of varieties is a crucial part of learning English phonetics and pronunciation, the app also features different accents, such as Scottish English, Irish English, Yorkshire English, West Country English, General American or Australian English. An attempt has been made to give a cultural significance to these varieties, which is why they are associated to different historical characters.

Before closing, it is worth mentioning that, aware of the needs and expectations of students and teachers to optimize the teaching and learning of English phonetics and pronunciation by Spanish speakers, members of the above-mentioned project in collaboration with other colleagues and instructors have also developed the freely accessible interactive website EPSSML (English Pronunciation for Speakers of Spanish Multimedia Lab, https://www.usc.gal/multimlab/) (Gómez González et al., 2017, 2021). EPSSML adopts a contrastive English-Spanish perspective, illustrates accent variation (contextual and accent specific), and allows the affordances of *blended* instruction, combining face-to-face (synchronous) class-based methods, distance-learning (both synchronous and asynchronous) approaches and self-directed learning, in order to overcome the time constraints and other limitations that characterize more traditional teacher-centered learning (Means et al., 2009; Vernadakis et al., 2011).

It is our hope that both EPSSML and e-SoundWay will fill a gap in teaching and learning English phonetics and pronunciation targeting speakers of Spanish (or other languages): the results discussed here make it clear that such a gap exists, which in turn can be interpreted as an indicator of the necessity for a paradigm shift in EFL language (phonetic) learning toward other methodologies such as blended instruction and/or serious games training.

References

Adank, P., Evans, B.G., Stuart-Smith, J., & Scott, S.K. (2009). Comprehension of familiar and unfamiliar native accents under adverse listening conditions. *Journal of Experimental Psychology: Human Perception and Performance*, 35(2), 520.

Alcaraz, E., & Moody, B. (1999). *Fonética inglesa para españoles*. Editorial Marfil.

Alonso, R. (2014). Teaching speaking: An exploratory study in two academic contexts. *Porta Linguarum, 22*, 145–160.

Anderson-Hsieh, J., Johnson, R., & Koehler, K. (1992). The relationship between native speaker judgments of nonnative pronunciation and deviance in segmentals, prosody, and syllable structure. *Language Learning, 42*, 529–555.

Baker, A. (2007). *Ship or sheep? An intermediate pronunciation course*. Cambridge University Press.

Baker, A., & Burri, M. (2016). Feedback on second language pronunciation: A case study of EAP teachers' beliefs and practices. *Australian Journal of Teacher Education, 41*(6). Accessed December 9, 2022. http://ro.ecu.edu.au/ajte/vol41/iss6/1

Bakla, A., & Demirezen, M. (2018). An overview of the ins and outs of L2 pronunciation: A clash of methodologies. *Journal of Mother Tongue Education, 6*(2), 477–497.

Bartolí Rigol, M. (2005). La pronunciación en las clases de lenguas extranjeras. *Phonica, 1*, 1–27.

Borysko, N.F. (2011). Methods of forming foreign phonetic competence. *Foreign Languages, 3*(67), 3–14.

Bradlow, A.R., Nygaard, L.C., & Pisoni, D.B. (1999). Effects of talker, rate, and amplitude variation on recognition memory for spoken words. *Perception & Psychophysics, 61*(2), 206–219.

Caballero-Hernández, J.A., Palomo-Duarte, M., & Dorero, J.M. (2017). Skill assessment in learning experiences based on serious games: A Systematic Mapping Study. *Computers & Education, 113*, 42–60.

104   José María Díaz Lage et al.

Cabrera Abreu, M., & Ortega, V. (2009). *English phonetics and phonology for Spanish speakers*. Universidad de las Palmas de Gran Canaria University Press.

Calvo Benzies, Y. (2016). *The teaching and learning of English pronunciation in Spain. An analysis and appraisal of students' and teachers' views and teaching materials* [Unpublished PhD dissertation]. University of Santiago de Compostela.

Castillo Rodríguez, C.; Torrado Cespón, M.; Ferreiro Lago, A. (2023). The ideal English pronunciation resource: non-native teachers' beliefs. *Opción, 39*(100), 131-154.

CEFR. (2001). *Common European framework of reference for languages: Learning, teaching, assessment*. Accessed December 20, 2022, from https://rm.coe.int/16802fc1bf

CEFR. (2020). *Common European framework of reference for languages: Learning, teaching, assessment. Companion volume*. Accessed December 9, 2022, from https://rm.coe.int/common-european-framework-of-reference-for-languages-learning-teaching/16809ea0d4

Chela, B. (2008). Hacia la optimización de la enseñanza de la pronunciación de un segundo idioma. In R. Monroy & A. Sánchez-Pérez (Eds.), *25 años de Lingüística en España: Hitos y retos* (pp. 285–293). Editum, Servicio de Publicaciones de la Universidad de Murcia.

Chun, D.M. (1988). The neglected role of intonation in communicative competence and proficiency. *The modern language journal, 72*(3), 295–303.

Coe, N. (2001). Speakers of Spanish and Catalan. In M. Swan & B. Smith (Eds.), *Learner English: A teacher's guide to interference and other problems* (pp. 90–112). Cambridge University Press.

Collins, B., & Mees, I.M. (2009). *Practical phonetics and phonology: A resource book for students*. Routledge.

Cruttenden, A. (2014). *Gimson's pronunciation of English*. Routledge.

Derwing, T.M. (2010). Utopian goals for pronunciation teaching. In *Proceedings of the 1st pronunciation in second language learning and teaching conference* (pp. 24–37). Iowa State University.

Derwing, T.M., & Munro, M.J. (2005). Second language accent and pronunciation teaching: A research-based approach. *TESOL Quarterly, 39*(3), 379–397.

Derwing, T.M., & Munro, M.J. (2009). Putting accent in its place: Rethinking obstacles to communication. *Language Teaching, 42*(4), 476–490. http://dx.doi.org/10.1017/S026144480800551X

Ducate, L. & Lomicka, L. (2009). Podcasting: An effective tool for honing language students' pronunciation? *Language Learning & Technology, 13*(3), 66-86.

Dörnyei, Z., & Taguchi, T. (2010). *Questionnaires in second language research: Construction, administration and processing* (2nd ed.). Routledge.

Estebas Vilaplana, E. (2009). *Teach yourself English pronunciation*. Netbiblo.

Evans, B.G., & Iverson, P. (2004). Vowel normalization for accent: An investigation of best exemplar locations in northern and southern British English sentences. *The Journal of the Acoustical Society of America, 115*(1), 352–361.

Fayer, J.M., & Krasinski, E. (1987). Native and nonnative judgments of intelligibility and irritation. *Language Learning, 37*(3), 313–326.

Finch, D.F., & Lira, H.O. (1982). *A course in English phonetics for Spanish speakers*. Heinemann Educational Books.

Foote, J.A., Trofimovich, P., Collins, L., & Soler Urzua, F. (2016). Pronunciation teaching practices in communicative second language classes. *The Language Learning Journal, 44*(2), 181–196.

Fouz-González, J., & Mompeán, J.A. (2021). Phonetic symbols vs keywords in perceptual training: The learners' views. *ELT Journal, 75*(4), 460–470. https://doi.org/10.1093/elt/ccab037

García Lecumberri, M.L. (1999, July 12). Foreign language English sounds in young learners of three different age groups. In *VIII conference of the International Association of Child Language*. Donostia-San Sebastián.

Gimson, A.C. (1989). *An introduction to the pronunciation of English*. Edward Arnold.

Gómez González, M.A., & Sánchez Roura, M.T. (2016). *English pronunciation for speakers of Spanish. From theory to practice*. Mouton de Gruyter.

Gómez González, M.Á., Sánchez Roura, M.T., & Torrado Cespón, M. (2021). *English pronunciation for speakers of Spanish. A practical course toolkit*. Santiago de Compostela University Press. ISBN 978-84-18445-47-7. https://www.usc.gal/libros/en/categories/1040-english-pronunciation-for-speakers-of-spanish-.html

Gómez González, M.Á., Sánchez Roura, M.T., Torrado Cespón, M., Rollings, A., & Gómez Penas, M.D. (2017). *English pronunciation for speakers of Spanish (EPSS): DVD toolkit. Interactive multimedia DVD*. Santiago de Compostela University Press. ISBN 978-84-16954-20-9.

Gregory, A.E. (2005). What's phonetics got to do with language teaching. In N. Bartels (Ed.), *Applied linguistics and future teachers' education* (pp. 201–220). Springer Science & Business Media.

Griffiths, C. (2004). *Studying in English: Language skills development*. AIS St. Helens, Centre for Research in International Education.

Gurova, T., Riabukha, T., Zinenko, N., & Gostishcheva, N. (2020). Mobile learning in developing phonetic competence of future interpreters. *Advanced Education*, *14*, 66–74. https://doi.org/10.20535/2410-8286.155398

Henderson, A., Curnick, L., Frost, D., Kautzsch, A., Kirkova-Naskova, A., Levey, D., Tergujeff, E., & Waniek-Klimczak, E. (2015). The English pronunciation teaching in Europe survey: Factors inside and outside the classroom. In J.A. Mompeán & J. Fouz-González (Eds.), *Investigating English pronunciation* (pp. 260–292). Palgrave Macmillan.

Hismanoglu, M. (2012). An investigation of phonological awareness of prospective EFL teachers. *Procedia—Social and Behavioral Sciences*, *31*, 639–645.

Iverson, P., & Evans, B.G. (2007). Auditory training of English vowels for first-language speakers of Spanish and German. In *Proceedings of the 16th international congress of phonetic sciences* (pp. 1625–1628). Universität des Saarlandes.

Iverson, P. & Evans B. (2009). Learning English vowels with different first-language vowel systems II: Auditory training for native Spanish and German speakers. *The Journal of the Acoustical Society of America*, *126*(2), 866-77.

Kelly, L. (1969). *25 centuries of language teaching*. Newbury House.

Lago Ferreiro, A., Gómez González, M.Á., Fragueiro Agrelo, A., & Llamas Nistal, M. (2022). Multiplatform application for learning English phonetics: Serious game. *XV Technologies Applied to Electronics Teaching Conference*. 978-1-6654-2161-4/22. IEEE Xplore. https://ieeexplore.ieee.org/document/9840541

Lear, E., Carey, M., & Couper, G. (2015). Introduction to special issue: New directions in pronunciation theory and practice. *Journal of Academic Language and Learning*, *9*(1), E1–E3.

Lev-Ari, S., & Keysar, B. (2010). Why don't we believe non-native speakers? The influence of accent on credibility. *Journal of Experimental Social Psychology*, *46*(6), 1093–1096.

Levis, J.M. (2018). *Intelligibility, oral communication, and the teaching of pronunciation*. Cambridge University Press.

Macdonald, S. (2002). Pronunciation—views and practices of reluctant teachers. *Prospect*, *17*(3), 3–18.

Martínez-Adrián, M., & Gallardo, F. (2011). Hacia la mejora de la exposición oral en inglés en ámbito universitario. *GRETA Journal*, *19*, 45–55.

Martínez-Flor, A., Usó, E., & Alcón, E. (2006). Towards acquiring communicative competence through speaking. In E. Usó & A. Martínez-Flor (Eds.), *Current trends in the development and teaching of the four language skills* (pp. 139–157). Mouton de Gruyter.

Means, B., Toyama, Y., Murphy, R., Bakia, M., & Jones, J. (2009). Evidence of evaluation based practices in online learning: A meta-analysis and review of online learning studies. Retrieved November 17, from https://www.cu.edu/doc/student-experiences-online-classesqual-study.pdf

Moizer, J., Lean, J., Dell'Aquila, E., Walsh, P., Keary, A., & O'Byrne, D. (2019). An approach to evaluating the user experience of serious games. *Computers & Education, 136*, 141–151.

Monroy Casas, R. (2012). *La pronunciación del inglés británico simplificada.* Editum, Servicio de Publicaciones de la Universidad de Murcia.

Mott, B. (2011). *English phonetics and phonology for Spanish speakers.* Servicio de Publicaciones de la Universidad de Barcelona.

Munro, M.J., & Derwing, T.M. (2007). The functional load principle in ESL pronunciation instruction: An exploratory study. *System, 34*(4), 520–531.

Nygaard, L.C., Sommers, M.S., & Pisoni, D.B. (1994). Speech perception as a talker-contingent process. *Psychological Science, 5*(1), 42–46.

Pennington, M.C., & Rogerson-Revell, P. (2019). *English pronunciation teaching and research: Contemporary perspectives.* Palgrave Macmillan.

Piccardo, E. (2016). *Phonological scale revision process report.* Accessed December 9, 2022, from https://rm.coe.int/168073fff9

Pourhosein Gilakjani, A. (2016). English pronunciation instruction: A literature review. *International Journal of Research in English Education, 1*(1), 1–6.

Roach, P. (2009). *English phonetics and phonology. A practical course.* Cambridge University Press.

Robles, P., & Rojas, M.C. (2015). La validación por juicio de expertos: dos investigaciones cualitativas en Lingüística aplicada. *Revista Nebrija de Lingüística aplicada, 18.* Accessed December 20, 2022, from https://www.nebrija.com/revista-linguistica/files/articulosPDF/articulo_55002aca89c37.pdf

Rossiter, M.J., Derwing, T.M., Manimtim, L.G., & Thomson, R.I. (2010). Oral fluency: The neglected component in the communicative language classroom. *Canadian Modern Language Review, 66*(4), 583–606.

Rubio Alcalá, F.D., & Tamayo Rodríguez, L. (2012). Estudio sobre prácticas docentes en evaluación de la lengua inglesa en la ESO. *Profesorado: revista de curriculum y formación del profesorado, 16*(1). 295–316.

Sánchez Benedito, F. (1980). *Manual de pronunciación inglesa comparada con la española.* Editorial Alhambra.

Seidlhofer, B. (2001). Pronunciation. In R. Carter & D. Nunan (Eds.), *The Cambridge guide to teaching English to speakers of other languages* (pp. 56–65). Cambridge University Press.

Singleton, D. (1995). Introduction: A critical look at the critical period hypothesis in second language acquisition research. In D. Singleton & Z. Lengyel

(Eds.), *The age factor in second language acquisition* (pp. 1–29). Multilingual Matters.

Stevick, E., Morley, J., & Wallace Robinett, B. (1975). Round Robin on the teaching of pronunciation. *TESOL Quarterly, 9*(1), 81–88.

Szpyra-Kozłowska, J. (2015). *Pronunciation in EFL instruction. A research-based approach.* Multilingual Matters.

Teimouri, Y., Goetze, J., & Plonsky, L. (2019). Second language anxiety and achievement. A meta-analysis. *Studies in Second Language Acquisition, 41*(2), 363–387.

Underhill, A. (2011). Pronunciation: The Cinderella of language teaching. *Humanizing Language Teaching, 13*(5).

Underhill, A. (2013). Cinderella, integration and the pronunciation turn. *Speak Out!, 49*, 4–8.

Vernadakis, N., Antoniou, P., Giannousi, M., Zetou, E., & Kioumourtzoglou, E. (2011). Comparing hybrid learning with traditional approaches on learning the Microsoft Office Power Point 2003 program in tertiary education. *Computers & Education, 56*, 188–199.

Walker, R. (1999). Proclaimed and perceived wants and needs among Spanish teachers of English. *Speak Out!, 24*, 25-32.

---- (2014). Technology for pronunciation. *English Teaching Professional, 95*, 29–31.

Wei, M. (2006). *A literature review on strategies for teaching pronunciation.* ERIC Institute of Education Sciences. Accessed December 20, 2022, from https://files.eric.ed.gov/fulltext/ED491566.pdf

María de los Ángeles Gómez González and Anxel Fragueiro
Agrelo (University of Santiago de Compostela, Spain),
Alfonso Lago Ferreiro (University of Vigo, Spain)

Chapter VI   Using a serious game for English phonetics and pronunciation training: Foundations and dynamics

I. Introduction

The importance of English in today's context is evident since it is spoken by more than 1.35 billion people worldwide and is often used a lingua franca in the era of globalization (i.e., *World English(es)*, *English as an International Language [EIL]*) (Crystal, 2003). One of the essential factors for effective communication in English (and in any other language) is to have an adequate command of productive and receptive phonological skills, both by native and non-native speakers, as highlighted in the *Common European Framework of Reference for Languages: Learning, Teaching, Assessment* (Council of Europe, 2018).

Nevertheless, investigations have found that phonetic training is often neglected in EFL classes, as compared to the efforts devoted to the development of other skills such as reading, writing, grammar or vocabulary. Among the factors mentioned to explain this situation are that fluency and intelligibility are prioritized over phonetic accuracy, particularly in communicative second-language classes (Baker & Burri, 2016; Foote et al., 2016; Levis, 2018), or that phonetic contents are difficult for students (Bakla, 2018). Pronunciation, phonology, or phonetics are issues normally targeted in the upper-level specialized courses, so learners may not be exposed to systematic phonetic and pronunciation training until late in their language-learning process (Lara & Lara, 2009). In addition, other reasons adduced include that EFL teachers often lack enough phonetic training in certain areas that consequently are either not taught or not effectively taught (Szpyra, 2015), alongside the lack of class time or the dearth of suitable materials for phonetic training (Henderson et al., 2015; MacDonald, 2002; Munro & Derwing, 2007).

Similarly, in Spain, despite the importance attributed to EFL phonetic training by both teachers and students (e.g., Calvo Benzies, 2016; Cenoz & García-Lecumberri, 1999; Walker, 1999), numerous reports (e.g., PISA, EF EPI, ESLC, PIRLS) and empirical studies highlight the insufficient communicative skills of English language learners (Alonso, 2014; Martínez-Flor et al., 2006; Szprya, 2015 among others). Pronunciation and phonological competence, two essential factors for comprehension and understanding (Huensch & Thompson, 2017; Rossiter et al., 2010), are reported to be particularly cumbersome for secondary and university Spanish-speaking learners of English (SSLE) for different reasons. In addition to individual personal, perceptual, cognitive, affective and acculturation variables (i.e., degree of social/psychological interaction with the target group) (Gallardo del Puerto et al., 2009), other frequently used explanations are the disparities existing between the sound, spelling and prosody of English, on the one hand, and Spanish (or Galician, Catalan and Basque), on the other, as well as the challenges involved in handling accent variation (Derwing & Munro, 2005; Estebas Vilaplana, 2009; Finch & Lira, 1982) or the application of allegedly inadequate methodologies (Calvo Benzies, 2016; Chela, 2008). A combination of these factors reportedly justifies the fact that SSLE perform better in grammar, vocabulary, reading or writing than in phonetic skills (Bartolí Rigol, 2005; Martínez-Adrián & Gallardo, 2011).

To contribute to reversing this situation, this chapter presents *English Sounds on the Way* (e-SoundWay [0.0]), a *serious game* that has been devised for SSLE to improve their phonetic competence and pronunciation skills while walking the *Camino de Santiago* or the "Way of Saint James" (Gómez González & Lago Ferreiro, Forthcoming; Lago Ferreiro et al., 2022). Prior studies have shown that the use of so-called "serious games" designed for educational purposes are strategies that motivate students to become involved in the learning process and improve their results (Filella et al., 2017; Fraga-Varela et al., 2021). Likewise, previous research has shown that the employment of digital technologies such as *Computer-Assisted Language Learning* (CALL) or *Computer-Assisted Pronunciation Training* (CAPT) (Levy, 2007; Setter, 2008) are effective tools to enhance the perceptual and productive skills of students of (supra)segmental phonetic content, while favoring lifelong learning, collaboration, innovation and the acquisition of digital competences (Gómez González & Lago Ferreiro, Forthcoming; Kim, 2012; Luo, 2016; Mompeán & Fouz-González, 2016).

The remainder of this contribution is structured as follows. Section II provides details for the design of e-SoundWay (0.0), describing its linguistic foundations (2.1), geographic and socio-cultural context (2.2) and technical architecture

(2.3). Finally, examples of use are presented in section III, followed by the main conclusions.

II. DESIGN OF e-SoundWay (0.0)

2.1. Linguistic foundations

As already noted, e-SoundWay (0.0) aims at enhancing SSLE's *phonetic competence* which includes the focus areas of *phonological competence*, that is, knowledge of, and skill in the perception (*receptive*) and production (*productive*) of sounds and prosodic features like stress, rhythm and intonation, including such related features as accentedness (i.e., accent and deviation from a "norm"), intelligibility (i.e., the accessibility of meaning for interlocutors, as well as their perceived difficulty in understanding or "comprehensibility") and phonetic accuracy or precision (Common European Framework of Reference for Languages [CEFR], 2020, pp. 134, 261). In addition, phonetic competence also considers the capability of individuals to accomplish speech activity based on their existing knowledge, skills and abilities that are the main features of any competence based on prior work (Gurova et al., 2020).

To enhance SSLE's phonetic competence, the contents of e-SoundWay (0.0) are based on the EPSS (*English Pronunciation for Speakers of Spanish*) method consisting of Gómez González and Sánchez Roura (2016) and *EPSS Multimedia Lab* (EPSSML) (Gómez González et al., 2019), an e-book and an open-access website, respectively. The EPSS method addresses the goals associated to a second-year English Phonetics and Phonology course at the University of Santiago de Compostela (USC) in Spain: to grasp key concepts on English phonetics and phonology, as well as the perception, production and transcription of the sound system of *Standard Southern British English* (SSBE), the accent of reference in most EFL textbooks and materials, especially in Europe, that is contrasted with European Spanish (ES).[12]

Following the EPSS method, e-SoundWay (0.0) offers a journey through 49 SSBE phonemes assembled in 12 categories. It begins with 12 vowels divided into five groups to be contrasted with those of ES: /iː ɪ/ (Group 1), /e ɜː ə/ (Group 2), /ʌ æ ɑː/ (Group 3), /ɔː ɒ/ (Group 4), /uː ʊ/ (Group 5). After this, 13 vowel series or glides are presented, including closing /eɪ aɪ ɔɪ əʊ aʊ/ and centring /ɪə eə ʊə/

---

12 Other labels assigned to SSBE or closely associated with it are *Received Pronunciation* (*RP*), *General Received Pronunciation* (GRP) or *General British or BBC English* (Cruttenden, 2014; Gómez González & Sánchez Roura, 2016).

diphthongs (Group 6), and diphthongs + /ə / /eɪə aɪə ɔɪə əʊə aʊə/ (Group 7). Next come SSBE 24 consonantal phonemes, comprising plosives /p t b d g k/ (Group 8), fricatives /f v θ ð h s z ʃ ʒ/ (Group 9), affricates /tʃ dʒ/ (Group 10), nasals /m n ŋ/ (Group 11), and approximants /l r j w/ (Group 12). Additionally, other topics addressed are aspects of connected speech (i.e., co-articulation and allophonic variation, assimilation and phonemic variation, elision, linking and gradation), as well as the prosodic features of SSBE (i.e., stress, rhythm and in-tonation), which are covered in two and three conceptual blocks, respectively. Once a group of sounds or a block of phonetic concepts are presented, summary and review activities are provided in order to assess the player's progress.

The choice of target words is framed within the *High Variability Phonetic Training* (HVPT) model (Thomson, 2018). HVPT proposes the inclusion of a variety of different speakers, phonetic contexts and/or stimuli in training tasks in order to provide the learner with the phonetic variability of real language. Ac-cordingly, only actual words rather than non-words are used. They are monosyl-labic, disyllabic and polysyllabic items, which contain CVC (*fish*), CV (*bee*) and VC (*eal*) syllabic patterns, as well as consonant clusters up to 3 C either or both in onset or/and coda position, CCCVCCCC (*strangled*), where one C belongs to one of the three following groups: /f v s z tʃ dʒ ʒ/, /p b t d k g/), (/m n/), /j w r l/ (Gómez González & Sánchez Roura, 2016). The aim is to expose SSLE to a large amount of native input while at the same time facilitating focus on those aspects of English which are most difficult for SSLE as identified in the EPSS method. This is achieved by means of the different types of minigames combined with feedback (information about the correct answer), articulatory demonstrations and/or model imitations over a self-paced period of time while walking the Way of St. James supported by the EPSS materials.

e-SoundWay (0.0) articulates these phonetic contents into 12 types of tests or challenges conceived as *multimedia* and *multi-sensorial minigames* to practice the sounds and prosody of English in individual words and longer sequences, mapping audiovisual stimuli and texts to gains in perceptual, productive and transcription phonetic capacities. Our aim is to engage students across a broad spectrum of learning capabilities in digital environments while also fostering *blended learning* or *flipped* methodologies, which are gaining ground in educa-tional settings (Baepler et al., 2014; Missildine et al., 2013). Written scripts were devised following the guidelines already described adapted to *microlearning* so that information is presented in small chunks or phonetic and pronunciation training "pills," which are objective-driven and better suited for online learning environments (Cabero & Gisbert, 2005). For most visual stimuli, we used *pictograms* from ARASAAC (*Centro Aragonés para la Comunicación Aumenta-tiva y Alternativa* "Aragon's Centre for Augmentative and Alternative Commu-nication"). The audio recordings were recorded in the premises of University College of London Speech, Hearing & Phonetic Sciences division by means of a remunerated contract, while the soundtrack was altruistically provided by two Galician groups: *Luar na Lubre* and *Resonet*.

As can be seen in Table 1, the 12 minigames train *three basic phonetic skills* (Flege, 2021; Logan et al., 1991):

a. 4 minigames target *perception*, in which players identify specific English sounds in contrast with other sounds in different phonetic settings, including allophonic variation of sounds.
b. 3 minigames focus on *production*, to assess the users' pronunciation accuracy and intelligibility on the basis of "listen and repeat" drills.
c. 3 minigames practice direct and reverse *phonetic transcription*, in which, faced with visual and/or sound stimuli, players must provide direct (from sound to phonetic symbol) and indirect (from symbol to spelling) scripts.
d. The remaining 2 minigames are pastimes that combine these three skills in the form of word search and crossword puzzles.

Table 1. e-SoundWay (0.0) Minigames

Skill	Minigame
Perception	Identification
	Odd-One-Out
	Variation
	Connected Speech
Production	Listen & Repeat
	Minimal Pairs
	Connected Speech
Transcription	Missing Symbols
	Direct
	Reverse

Skill	Minigame
Pastimes	Word Search Puzzles
	Crossword Puzzles

Turning to accent variation, although e-SoundWay (0.0) takes SSBE as the accent of reference, other English accents are also illustrated in keeping with the HVPT model. This responds to the premise that EFL learners should not be restricted to a single variety but should be exposed to different accents—at least in terms of listening/speech perception—in order to raise awareness of different pronunciation models (Mompeán, 2004; Carrie, 2016). More specifically, e-SoundWay (0.0) samples a total (T) of eight accents across 16 voices, of which 9 correspond to male (M) and 7 to female (F) native speakers recruited for this project, as specified in Table 2. Although the number of minigames per stage varies, most stages (27) target SSBE and contain 12 challenges, whereas those sampling other accents (7) generally present 6 minigames, namely those involving perception and pastimes. With the exception of pastimes, which do not appear in 6 stages (28–33), all the other minigames include a second round of testing, which in total add up 618.

Table 2. e-SoundWay (0.0) Accents and Voices

Accent		M	F	T
Within the British Isles	Southern Standard British English (SSBE)	5	3	8
	Standard Scottish English (SSE)	1		1
	West Country (West)		1	1
	Yorkshire (Yoks)	1		1
	Irish English (IrE)	1		1
Outside the British Isles	General American (GenA)		2	2
	Australian English (AuE)	1		1
	Canadian English (CaE)		1	1
T		9	7	16

Additionally, since phonetic competence involves not only cognitive (Fraser, 2001) but also perceptual (Kuhl & Iverson, 1995) and psychomotor abilities (Leather & James, 1991), which vary from one individual to another and require explicit instruction, another aim of e-SoundWay (0.0) is that each player can be aware of his/her progress in these three phonetic skills as s/he walks along the stages of the Way. For this purpose, the application has three groups of modules that manage the calculation and processing of images, data and partial as well as final results for the three targeted phonetic skills already mentioned that constitute the pillars of a *three-dimensional pyramid* represented in Figure 1.

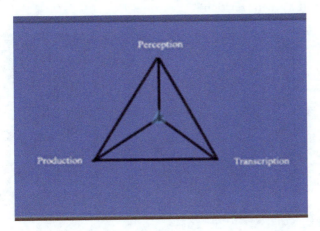

Figure 1. e-SoundWay player's phonetic skills three-dimensional pyramid.

Section III provides further details to explain how the player's phonetic skills performance is measured in the e-SoundWay three-dimensional pyramid. But first let us turn to the geographic and socio-cultural setting of this serious game.

2.2. Geographic and socio-cultural context

e-SoundWay (0.0) is set on the French Way of St. James beginning in Saint Jean Pied de Port (France) and ending at the Holy Door of the Cathedral of Santiago de Compostela (Spain) as displayed in Figure 2, which also includes a command bar with six buttons at the top. The journey starts by pressing the yellow arrow in the bottom right corner of the screen, one of the symbols of the Way to guide pilgrims to Santiago de Compostela. The player needs to "walk" 34 stages including the contents listed below, with which the route is complete.

a. 27 stages are devoted to practice SSBE, and 7 to sample the other accents already mentioned.
b. 16 stages cover 49 SSBE phonemes (Stages 1–7 on vowels; Stages 11–13 on glides; Stages 19–24 on consonants).
c. 2 stages focus on the description of connected speech phenomena (Stages 28–29).
d. 3 stages target SSBE prosody (Stages 30–32).
e. 13 stages offer summary and review activities (Stages 8–10 on vowels; Stages 14–18 on glides; Stages 25–27 on consonants; Stage 33 on prosody; Stage 34 presenting a general revision).

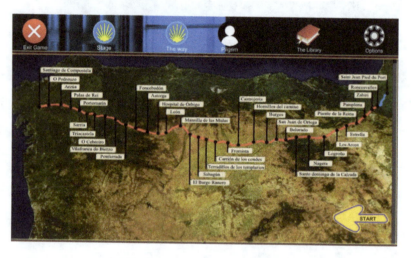

Figure 2. The stages of e-SoundWay and the French Way of St. James.

By clicking on "The Way" the player can access at any time during the game the route s/he has taken according to her/his progress, that is to say, the stage s/he is in (in blue), the stages s/he has passed (in green), and those s/he still has to go through (in red). A more detailed information about the three targeted phonetic skills is provided in the "Pilgrim" tab. It includes numerical information explaining the scores obtained that are graphically represented in the three-dimensional pyramid already introduced in the previous section. If the player selects "Stage," s/he will see a dashboard illustrated in Figure 3 containing all the stops and corresponding minigames that are included in it superimposed on a map of that section of the Way, as well as five tabs with the headings: "Who are we?," "Where are we?," "Did you know?," "Help," and "Start the Challenge." With

Figure 3. e-SoundWay stage dashboard.

a total of 300, the number of stops at each stage ranges from 12 to 4 depending on the number of minigames players need to complete, which in turn is determined by the nature of target topics already described. Within each stage, players can move forwards to the next stops or backwards to the previous ones using the corresponding directional yellow arrows.

By selecting the tab "Who are we?," the player discovers the identity of the "people" that will accompany him/her in that stage, as well as their story in relation to the Way of St. James. As portrayed in Table 3, e-SoundWay (0.0) features a total of 16 characters exemplifying the accents detailed in Table 2. The characters displayed in Table 3 were specially created for this serious game as avatars of 1 fictional character (Patience), who acts as narrator and teaching guide, and 15 pilgrims representing historical figures and current individuals that have walked the French way and are relevant figures for different reasons.[13]

The "Where are we?" and "Did you know?" tabs, on the other hand, provide geographical details and historical facts or legends related to that particular stage of the Way, respectively. Lastly, the "Help" button presents the phonetic and pronunciation training "pills" already alluded to that are necessary to successfully complete the challenge, which is accessed by clicking on "Start the Challenge." These five tabs appear at the initial stop of each stage only. The other stops just include the "Help" and "Start the Challenge" tabs.

Players can also consult the "Library" section, which gathers all the information unlocked along the Way once minigames are completed, including trilingual

---

13 All the current pilgrims represented have given their disinterested permission for their image to be used, and some of them have kindly offered to write part of the scripts in which they participate.

Accent		Avatar	
Inside the British Isles	SSBE	Patience	
		Margery Kempe	
		Kate Long	
		Andrew Boorde	
		James Francis Edward Stewart The Old Pretender	
		John Rutherford	
		St Godric of Finchale	
		George Borrow	
	SSE	Anonymous of Purchas	
	West	Annette Meakin	
	Yoks	Robert Langton	
	IrE	Walter Starkie	
Outside the British Isles	GenA	Edith Wharton	
		Rebekah Scott	
	AuE	Noel Braun	
	CaE	Laurie Dennet	

Table 3. e-SoundWay (0.0) Avatars

(English-Spanish-Galician) versions of the "Where are We?" and "Who are We?" tabs. Lastly, "Exit Game" shuts down the game while the "Options" tab corresponds to the app settings controlling three types of volume adjustments (e.g., master, music and voices) alongside the data reset. Now let us move on to the technical architecture of e-SoundWay.

2.3. Technical architecture

The game architecture has been implemented in the *Unity environment* (Unity User Manual, 2020; IBM Watson SDK for Unity, GitHub web). Unity is a multi-platform videogame engine that has everything necessary to create an interactive graphic environment compatible with multiple platforms. Among its graphics engines, e-SoundWay has been designed with OpenGL, which is compatible with Windows, Mac, and Linux. With minimal changes, it can also be adapted to OpenGL ES for Android and iOS. The language used for the most part has been C#.

The 3-module conceptual architecture of the system is represented in Figure 4. The *Game Module* manages the game interface, as well as the information contained in the minigames (e.g., stage map, road map, replayability sets), and the system dynamics underlying them. It includes corresponding submodules for the four types of minigames already described:

a. *Game submodule perception* is in charge of the game physics, sound management, answers and report of results.
b. *Game submodule production* contains mechanisms to play the target sounds and utterances, and to evaluate the player's pronunciation based on results obtained from the Third-Party Watson speech recognition module.
c. *Game submodule transcription*, which, in addition to controlling the physics involved in positioning phonetic symbols or graphemes in the right place and presenting the batteries of words for transcription and the evaluation of the answers, manages the correct implementation of a phonetic keyboard created for transcription minigames.
d. *Game submodule alphabet soup* presents a board, previously created as an object, that is devised according to the parameters required by the minigame, considering the total number of correct words to appear on the screen, their location and size, the mechanics of dragging them over the board, alongside a mechanism to monitor the results obtained.

The Game module interacts with the *Control Module* to extract the necessary information to control the graphic environment and the player's progress data

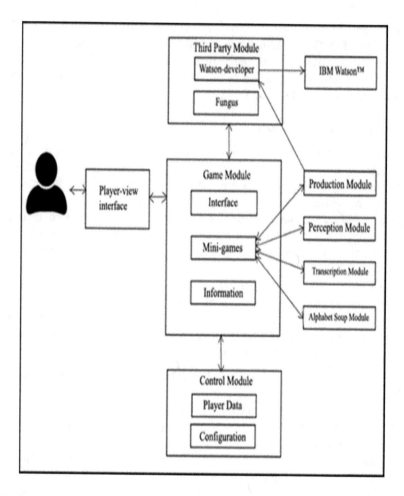

Figure 4. e-SoundWay 3-module conceptual architecture.

file to be displayed on the screen. Finally, the *Third-Party Module* facilitates the information provided by two OpenSource APIs:

a. *Watson-developer* consists of a set of subroutines used to manage audio materials and send them to the IBM Watson™ Natural Language Understanding Service speech recognition and analysis system on the IBM Cloud, currently the best STT for training in SSB-accented English-speaking speech recognition (IBM Cloud, Text to Speech [online]).

b. *Fungus* comprises a set of subroutines for managing dialogues and adding audio to them in an interactive environment, manipulating graphical elements and tracking scene interaction.

Each minigame has its own interface, but they share some common features. Upon completing each challenge, players can earn three different types of awards in the shape of *scallop shells* (i.e., bronze, silver and gold) to identify at least three different "degrees" of performance depending on the score obtained. The following section explains how the player's performance is measured after sampling three e-SoundWay (0.0) minigames.

III. e-SoundWay (0.0): Examples of use

Figure 5 shows two snapshots of Stage 1-Stop 2 (Honto)-Minigame 2 Perception: Odd-One-Out corresponding to the presentation and the game itself screens, respectively.

Figure 5. e-SoundWay perception minigame: Odd-one-out.

In other words, after having passed the first perception challenge (Identification) in Saint-Jean-Pied-du-Port, the player has arrived to the tiny hamlet of Honto (or Hunto), where there has been a refuge since ancient times for pilgrims to come and go as they please depicted in the background photo of the site. In this stop, the player will be accompanied by two SSBE speakers that will be interacting with him/her: Patience and St. Godric of Finchale. In the "Help" tab Patience offers the necessary phonetic and pronunciation training "pills" before starting the challenge or minigame, which are complemented by the game instructions

María de los Ángeles Gómez González et al.

specified in "How to Play" inside the Perception: Odd-One-Out minigame. The player will first hear audio-stimuli for 3 series of 4 target pronunciations selected with HVPT criteria with their corresponding pictograms pronounced by either St. Godric of Finchale or Patience. In this case, the SSBE target phonemes are Group 1 vowels /iː/ /ɪ/ and the challenge is to identify the one pronunciation involving such vowels that differs from the other three. As with the option in the top right-hand margin of the screen (i.e., *peke-peak-peek-pique* /ˈpiːk/), pronunciations may include *homophones*, that is, two or more words having the same pronunciation but different meanings, origins, or spelling. Once the Odd-One-Out pronunciation has been selected in each series, the right answer appears on the screen by clicking "Check" so that the target words are provided both in spelling and phonetic transcription, as well as the score obtained. In this particular example, the target words are *pick* /ˈpɪk/, *peke-peak-peek-pique* /ˈpiːk/, *peach* /ˈpiːtʃ/ and *peat* /ˈpiːt/, all monosyllabic words with the CVC syllabic pattern in which the vowel is surrounded by voiceless plosive or affricate consonants, and the right answer is *pick* /ˈpɪk/. Once the first round is completed, the player can play this minigame again, in which case s/he will hear a new set of pronunciations following the same criteria and game principles already described.

Turning to Figure 6, we can see Stage 1-Stop 12 (Roncesvalles)-Minigame 12 Pastimes: Word Search Puzzle, the images corresponding to the presentation and the game itself screens respectively. Here the player has managed to pass the preceding 11 minigames in this stage relating to perception, production, and transcription, plus a crossword puzzle. After being provided with the relevant pills and game instructions in the "Help" and "How to play" tabs, the task is now to identify the six words whose phonetic transcription appears on the screen. As noted before, they were selected according to the criteria of the HVPT model to contrast the two target vowels of Stage 1, namely Group 1 /iː/ /ɪ/. Hovering the cursor over the correct spelling of the target words in the grid highlights them in green and activates their pronunciation by either Patience or St. Godric. Wrong selections appear in solid red and are not pronounced. The secret or hidden words in Figure 6 are *lit, ship, these, scream lettuce*, and *perceived*, illustrating monosyllabic and disyllabic keywords with the CVC, CCVC, CV.CVC and CV.CVCC syllabic patterns, respectively. In this case only three of the six words have been identified. Every two stages this word search puzzle format alternates with another one in which the objective is to search the puzzle for the phonemic transcriptions of the six words offered in spelling at the start of the minigame.

To close the series of sample minigames, Figure 7 represents three snapshots of Stage 9-Stop 1 (Nájera)-Minigame1: Accent Variation Perception: SSE vs. SSBE. "Menu" (top left corner) leads to the stage dashboard (as in Figure 3)

Figure 6. e-SoundWay pastimes minigame: Word search.

where the player is equipped with the necessary contextual and phonetic information to face this challenge.

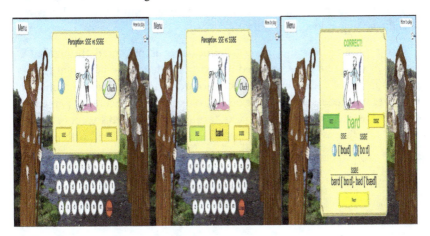

Figure 7. e-SoundWay accent perception minigame: SSE vs. SSBE.

The aim of this minigame is to reinforce knowledge and raise perception awareness of the most important characteristics of accents other than SSBE, as well as the most remarkable differences. In this particular case, the target feature is *rhoticity*, that is, when an /r/ sound is retained in RC clusters, that is when <r> is followed by a consonant. This occurs in SSE, but not in SSBE. Thus, the player will first hear the audio-stimulus corresponding to a word that contains such a cluster and which is represented in the pictogram as a clue. Then, s/he will need to write down the spelling of the word and decide whether it was pronounced in an SSE (with rhoticity) or an SSBE (without rhoticity) accent. In this case, the word is *bard* and it was pronounced by Anonymous of Purchas with an SSE accent, which is rightly answered by the player. The "Check" tab shows the first "accent variation pill" administered in this stop:

a. The correct word in spelling.
b. Two different pronunciations of the target word by native speakers of the accents in contrast by Anonymous of Purchas (SSE) and by St. Godric (SSBE).
c. Two different phonetic annotations corresponding to the two different pronunciations of the target word in SSE (with rhoticity) vs. SSBE (without rhoticity).
d. A minimal pair in SSBE with a C(+voice)VC(+voice) pattern to emphasize that the spelling <ar> in the target word corresponds to a long vowel sound / ɑː/ (*bard*) to be contrasted with the <a> spelling that is pronounced /æ/ (*bad*).
e. To obtain full credit in this minigame, the player must have both answers right: accent and word spelling.

Now regarding how the player's performance is measured throughout e-SoundWay (0.0), the score obtained in each stage depends on different factors, as the difficulty of each minigame varies according to its nature, the number of challenges it includes, and the time taken to solve them. To score the percentage of success (%success) in each minigame, formula (1) is applied, except in the case of word searches. Word soups are speed tests that are calculated with equation (2) to measure the time employed in solving them.

$$\%success = \begin{cases} if\ (success \geq mistakes) \rightarrow \frac{success - mistakes}{number\ of\ questions} \\ if\ (success < mistakes) \rightarrow 0 \end{cases}$$

$$\%\ success = \frac{Time\ at\ the\ end\ of\ the\ mini-game}{Time\ at\ the\ start\ of\ the\ mini-game}$$

The % success is used to quantify the achievement of medals and overall score in each minigame. Table 4 shows the correlations between % success, points obtained and the scallop shell medals awarded. For the quantification of global scores, the same methodology is used, adding the points obtained to those already acquired by the player. e-SoundWay (0.0) three-dimensional pyramid displayed in Figure 1 shows the player's progress in each of its three pillars corresponding to the targeted skills, that is, perception, production and transcription. It is designed as a visual system that represents the player's experience and acquisition levels, encouraging him/her to engage in the completion of minigames by obtaining medals and getting unlockable achievements. Specifically, the players' evolution is quantified with the arithmetic mean score obtained in the Stages played together with the % success reported in each of them, as indicated in equation (3).

Table 4. e-SoundWay (0.0) % Success–Points–Scallop Shell Medals Correlations

% success	Points	Scallop shell medals
0 %–50 %	3	None
50 < X < 75 %	5	Bronze
75 % < X < 90 %	7	Silver
90 % < X < 100 %	10	Gold

$$\% \text{ skill} = \frac{\sum \%success \ at \ that \ mini-game \ of \ that \ skill}{n^{\circ} \ mini-games \ of \ that \ skill \ played}$$

In addition to the achievements along the Way, there is a minimum requirement for progression from one stage to the next in order to guarantee a minimum level of competence acquisition specific to the target skill or concept. To achieve this minimum threshold, a bronze scallop shell medal must be obtained, which is equivalent to the achievement of 50 % success in each of the minigames included in one stage.

IV. Conclusion

e-SoundWay (0.0) is currently in the testing stage because it is necessary to assess the difficulty involved in the minigames as well as their playability. It will be available in the 2023/2024 academic year to EFL/English Phonetics and Phonology secondary/university students. Subsequently, once the feedback provided by these target groups is incorporated into the serious game, e-SoundWay (0.0) will be made accessible to the general public.

Ultimately, the goal of e-SoundWay (0.0) is to improve or enhance the English phonetic competence (combining specific learned and inherent skills/abilities) of SSLE, and more generally, of any learner, raising their awareness and understanding of English speech, its sounds and prosody across different accents, and the correspondence, or lack of it, between sound, spelling and phonetic symbols. Simultaneously, e-SoundWay (0.0) gives players the opportunity to become pilgrims that gain historic-cultural knowledge and get rewards as they walk the French Way of St. James, making the learning process a fun personal and multisensorial experience.

Acknowledgments

This work has been funded by the Ministry of Science, Innovation and Universities in the modality of R&D&I Projects Research Challenges in the field of Social Sciences and Humanities and Sciences with and for Society and in the field of Digital Economy, Society and Culture with reference PID2019-105678RB-C21, and subsequently by the grant and subsequently by the grant TED2021-130283B- C21 (Strategic Projects oriented to the Ecological Transition and the Digital Transition), as well as by the USC grant 2022-RC031-2.

References

Alonso, R. (2014). Teaching speaking: An exploratory study in two academic contexts. *Porta Linguarum*, *22*, 145–160.

Baepler, P., Walker, J. D., & Driessen, M. (2014). It's not about seat time: Blending, flipping, and efficiency in active learning classrooms. *Computers & Education*, 78, 227-236. https://doi.org/10.1016/j.compedu.2014.06.006

Baker, A. & Burri, M. (2016). Feedback on Second Language Pronunciation: A Case Study of EAP Teachers' Beliefs and Practices. *Australian Journal of Teacher Education*, *41*(6). Retrieved from http://ro.ecu.edu.au/ajte/vol41/iss6/1

Bakla, A. (2018). Learner-generated materials in a flipped pronunciation class: A sequential explanatory mixed-methods study. *Computers & Education*, *125*, 14–38.

Bartolí Rigol, M. (2005). La pronunciación en las clases de lenguas extranjeras. *Phonica*, *1*, 1–27.

Cabero, J., & Gisbert, M. (2005). *Materiales formativos multimedia en la red. Guía práctica para su diseño*. Eduforma/Trillas.

Calvo Benzies, Y. (2016). *The teaching and learning of English pronunciation in Spain. An analysis and appraisal of students' and teachers' views and teaching materials* [Unpublished PhD dissertation]. University of Santiago de Compostela.

Carrie, E. (2016). "British is professional, American is urban": Attitudes towards English reference accents in Spain. *International Journal of Applied Linguistics, 27*(2), 427–444.

Cenoz, J., & Garcia-Lecumberri, M.L. (1999). The acquisition of English pronunciation: Learners' views. *International Journal of Applied Linguistics, 9*, 3–15.

Chela, B. (2008). Hacia la optimización de la enseñanza de la pronunciación de un segundo idioma. In R. Monroy & A. Sánchez-Pérez (Eds.), *25 años de Lingüística en España: Hitos y retos* (pp. 285–293). Editum, Servicio de Publicaciones de la Universidad de Murcia.

CEFR. (2020). Common European framework of references. Companion volume. Retrieved July 17, 2021 from https://rm.coe.int/common-european-framework-of-reference-for-languages-learningteaching/ 16809ea0d4.

Cruttenden, A. (2014). *Gimson's pronunciation of English*. Routledge.

Crystal, D. (2003). *English as a global language*. Cambridge University Press.

Derwing, T., & Munro, M. (2005). Second language accent and pronunciation teaching: A research-based approach. *TESOL Quarterly, 39*(3), 379–397.

Estebas Vilaplana, E. (2009). *Teach yourself English pronunciation*. Netbiblo.

Filella, G., Pérez-Escoda, N., & Ros-Morente, A. (2017). Evaluación del programa de Educación Emocional "Happy 8–12" para la resolución asertiva de los conflictos entre iguales. *Electronic Journal of Research in Educational Psychology, 14*(3), 582–601. http://dx.doi.org/10.14204/ejrep.40.15164

Finch, D.F., & Lira, H.O. (1982). *A course in English phonetics for Spanish speakers*. Heinemann Educational Books.

Flege, J.E. (2021). New methods for second language speech research. In R. Wayland (Ed.), *Second language speech learning* (pp. 119–156). Cambridge University Press.

Foote, J.A., Trofimovich, P., Collins, L., & Soler Urzua, F. (2016). Pronunciation teaching practices in communicative second language classes. *The Language Learning Journal, 44*(2), 181–196.

Fraga-Varela, F., Vila-Couñago, E., & Martínez-Piñeiro, E. (2021). The impact of serious games in mathematics fluency: A study in Primary Education [Impacto de los juegos serios en la fluidez matemática: Un estudio en Educación Primaria]. *Comunicar, 69*, 125–135. https://doi.org/10.3916/C69-2021-10

Fraser, H. (2001). *Teaching pronunciation: A handbook for teachers and trainers department*. Department of Education Training and Youth Affairs (DETYA).

Gallardo del Puerto, F., García Lecumberri, M.L., & Cenoz Iragui, J. (2009). *Degree of foreign accent and age of onset in formal school instruction*. Proceedings of the Phonetics Teaching and Learning Conference, London, pp. 1–4.

Gómez González, M.A., & Lago Ferreiro, A. (Forthcoming). *Computer-assisted pronunciation training (CAPT): An empirical evaluation of EPSS Multimedia Lab*. Language Learning & Technology.

Gómez González, M.A., & Sánchez Roura, T. (2016). English pronunciation for speakers of Spanish. In *From theory to practice*. Mouton de Gruyter. https://doi.org/10.1515/9781501510977

Gómez González, M.A., Sánchez Roura, T., Torrado Cespón, M., Rollings, A., & Gómez Penas, M.D. (2019). *EPSS (English Pronunciation for Speakers of Spanish) Multimedia Lab*. https://www.usc.gal/multimlab/

Gurova, T., Riabukha, T., Zinenko, N., & Gostishcheva, N. (2020). Mobile learning in developing phonetic competence of future interpreters. *Advanced Education, 14*, 66–74. https://doi.org/10.20535/2410-8286.155398

Henderson, A., Curnick, L., Frost, D., Kautzsch, A., Kirkova-Naskova, A., Levey, D., Tergujeff, E., & Waniek-Klimczak, E. (2015). The English pronunciation teaching in Europe survey: Factors inside and outside the classroom. In J.A. Mompeán & J. Fouz-González (Eds.), *Investigating English pronunciation* (pp. 260–292). Palgrave Macmillan.

Huensch, A., & Thompson, A. (2017). Contextualizing attitudes towards pronunciation: Foreign language learners in the United States. *Foreign Language Annals, 50*(2), 410–432. https://doi.org/10.1111/flan.12259

IBM Cloud. *Text to speech* [Online]. https://cloud.ibm.com/docs/text-to-speech?topic=text-to-speech-gettingStarted#gettingStarted

IBM Watson SDK for Unity. *GitHub web* [Online]. https://github.com/watson-developer-cloud/unity-sdk

Kim, A.Y. (2012). Investigating the effectiveness of computer-assisted language learning (CALL) in improving pronunciation: A case study. *Multimedia Assisted Language Learning, 15*(3), 11–33.

Kuhl, P., & Iverson, P. (1995). Linguistic experience and the "perceptual magnet effect." In W. Strange (Ed.), *Speech perception and linguistic experience* (pp. 121–154). York Press.

Lago Ferreiro, A., Gómez González, M.Á., Fragueiro Agrelo, A., & Llamas Nistal, M. (2022). *Multi-platform application for learning English phonetics: Serious Game*. XV Technologies Applied to Electronics Teaching Conference. https://

ieeexplore.ieee.org/document/9840541.   https://doi.org/10.1109/TAEE54
169.2022.9840541

Lara, D., & Lara, L. (2009). Podcasting: An effective tool for honing language
students' pronunciation? *Language Learning & Technology*, *13*(3), 66–86.

Leather, J., & James, A. (1991). The acquisition of second language speech.
Studies in Second Language Acquisition, *13*(3), 305–341.

Levis, J.M. (2018). *Intelligibility, oral communication, and the teaching of pronunciation*. Cambridge University Press.

Levy, Y. (2007). Comparing dropouts and persistence in e-learning courses.
Computers & Education, *48*(2), 185–204.

Logan, J., Lively, S., & Pisoni, D. (1991). Training Japanese listeners to identify
English /r/ and /l/: A first report. *JASA*, *89*(2), 874–886.

Luo, B. (2016). Evaluating a computer-assisted pronunciation training (CAPT)
technique for efficient classroom instruction. *Computer Assisted Language
Learning*, *29*(3), 451–476.

Macdonald, S. (2002). Pronunciation—views and practices of reluctant teachers.
Prospect, *17*(3), 3–18.

Martínez-Adrián, M., & Gallardo, F. (2011). Hacia la mejora de la exposición
oral en inglés en ámbito universitario. *GRETA Journal*, *19*, 45–55.

Martínez-Flor, A., Usó, E., & Alcón, E. (2006). Towards acquiring communicative competence through speaking. In E. Usó & A. Martínez-Flor (Eds.),
Current trends in the development and teaching of the four language skills (pp.
139–157). Mouton de Gruyter.

Missildine, K., Fountain, R., Summers, L., & Gosselin, K. (2013). Flipping
the classroom to improve student performance and satisfaction. *Journal of
Nursing Education*, *52*(10), 597–599.

Mompean, J.A., (2004). Options and criteria for the choice of an English pronunciation model in Spain. In J. Anderson, J. M. Oro, and J. Varela Zapata (eds),
Linguistic perspectives from the classroom: language teaching in a multicul-
tural Europe. Universidade de Santiago de Compostela. 243– 259.

Mompeán, J.A., & Fouz-González, J. (2016). Twitter-based EFL pronunciation
instruction. *Language Learning & Technology*, *20*(1), 166–190.

Munro, M.J., & Derwing, T.M. (2007). The functional load principle in ESL pronunciation instruction: An exploratory study. *System*, *34*(4), 520–531.

Rossiter, M.A., Derwing, T.M., Manimtim, L.G., & Thomson, R.I. (2010). Oral
fluency: The neglected component in the communicative language classroom.
*The Canadian Modern Language Review/La Revue canadienne des langues
vivantes*, *66*(4), 583–606. http://dx.doi.org/10.3138/cmlr.66.4.583

Setter, J. (2008). Theories and approaches in English pronunciation. In R. Monroy & A. Sánchez (Eds.), *25 años de Lingüística aplicada en España: hitos y retos* (pp. 447–457). Editum.

Szpyra, J. (2015). *Pronunciation in EFL instruction. A research-based approach.* Multilingual Matters.

Thomson, R.I. (2018). High variability [pronunciation] training (HVPT): A proven technique about which every language teacher and learner ought to know. *Journal of Second Language Pronunciation, 4*(2), 208–231.

Unity user Manual 2020. 3 LTS [Online]. https://docs.unity3d.com/Manual/UnityManual.html

Walker, R. (1999). Proclaimed and perceived wants and needs among Spanish teachers of English. *Speak Out!, 24,* 25–32.

Milagros Torrado Cespón (Universidad Internacional de
La Rioja, Spain), Inmaculada Santos Díaz (Universidad de
Málaga, Spain)

Chapter VII Evaluation of the *CleverCookie* tool for learning and teaching English as a foreign language

I. Introduction

CleverCookie. English Language Resources for Speakers of Spanish (Torrado Cespón, 2021) (*CleverCookie* henceforth) is a tool specially designed considering the needs of online users of English whose first or second language is Spanish. The novelty within this tool is an audiovisual section where *CleverCookie*, a speaker of Spanish who sometimes struggles with some English grammar issues, explains in a short video how to deal with them. The topics included in these videos are not random. However, they have been carefully chosen from a learner corpus compiled from the online forums of English as a Medium of Instruction (EMI) subjects written by students at the Universidad Internacional de La Rioja (UNIR). Through a process of error analysis, the most common errors were identified and chosen to integrate this tool. During 2020–2022, the researchers working on the *CleverCookie* project included seven videos with some of the most frequent errors. This tool has been described by Torrado Cespón and Santos Díaz (2022), pointing out the clarity of its videos and usefulness in solving little doubts appearing in writing. This chapter explains the perception of voluntary students who have tested the tool based on an online questionnaire offered by the teacher. This questionnaire aimed to assess the clarity of the videos provided by *CleverCookie* so they could identify the grammatical issue that worked in each of them. In addition, the questionnaire also provided *CleverCookie*'s coordinator feedback about other functionality and applicability aspects to improve the tool during the next biennium.

II. Error analysis solutions for online environments

The use of error analysis (EA) in foreign language teaching has proved to be an interesting mechanism to improve the design of materials and resources for students bearing in mind their real linguistic needs (among many others, see: Burt,

1975; Jobeen et al., 2015; Karim et al., 2018; Serrano de Santiago et al., 2022; Xie & Jiang, 2007). In the case of non-linguistic subjects, the quality of linguistic expression should also be considered an essential part of the learning process (Bárcena Toyos, 2021, 2022). If we add an online environment to this situation, error analysis results can be conditioned by factors that are not applicable in face-to-face instruction. Torrado Cespón and Díaz Lage (2022) mentioned the difficulties in reaching adult online students due to the alienation provoked by the online setting. Therefore, designing tools which can be attractive for this target group is essential to maintain their motivation; at the same time, they do not imply spending too much time on them. Undeniably, post-pandemic teachers must work with online teaching and a more technological-like view of the teaching system (Konkin et al., 2021). Thus, understanding the factors affecting students' written performance is essential to offer them the correct tools. Considering that students read a lot online, but their attention focuses less (Delgado & Salmerón, 2021), offering them shorter formats is a solution worth considering.

2.1. *CleverCookie* as a result of error analysis

CleverCookie was designed considering the needs of online students under-taking an EMI subject. It is based on the most frequent errors made by uni-versity students in online written environments. A forum compilation process began in 2014 to create a learner corpus (Castillo Rodríguez & Díaz Lage, 2015) to analyze the most frequent errors. Once analyzed, some of those errors were represented using short videos (maximum two and a half minutes) to optimize user attention (Cilliers, 2017; Firth et al., 2019; Rothman, 2016). Together with this, *CleverCookie*'s web page (www.clevercookie.es) also includes explanations about the error or revised topic, from historical reasons to curiosities and other information that the learner may find interesting. Therefore, the result is a tool explicitly directed at online students willing to advance as fast as possible. More-over, the web page also included grammatical explanations, English and Spanish version, to facilitate understanding for users whose level is not higher than B1. Including the Spanish version of the grammatical explanations is based on the need for explicit grammatical references in the case of adult learners (Kavari, 2014; Turnbull, 2018).

2.2. Linguistic competence in online teaching

Online writing or Internet-Mediated Communication (IMC) tends to be rapid and careless due to a lack of revision and/or lack of proficiency (Torrado Cespón,

2018; Torrado Cespón & Díaz Lage, 2017). It is difficult to state clearly what proves to be more influential. Due to this, it is frequent finding software primarily addresses to facilitate this situation, from autocorrection (see Microsoft Word, for example) to online tools (*Grammarly.com* as one of the most representative nowadays). However, auto-corrective software and predictive text can result in a double edge sword, as the user stops thinking about correctness and lets the program do the job. In the case of word processors, users tend to revise less and trust autocorrections. However, this type of software is not available in all instances, and, as a result, spelling mistakes are frequent in sites where the text is not self-corrected.

Student's command of the language in this type of space contrasts with their performance in the EFL classroom. The setting provides a stress-free environment where the student gets involved in topics which are truly interesting for them, and they are not under correctness pressure. The question of if we should correct our students' misuse of the language arises. The fact is that even if we want to bring reality into the classroom as much as possible, the classroom is not an authentic environment regarding language use. As EFL teachers, we want our students to use the language accurately, so we must guide them to correctness. This does not mean that, in a suitable situation, we can allow them to use the language less precisely, especially if we are dealing with intercultural contacts or telecollaboration. This type of activity can be used later for metalinguistic reflection and feedback about error analysis with your students. Thus, you can check whether they are committing mistakes because of unawareness, because they are coping with the patterns used in IMC, or because IMC plays a role. If the case is the latter, proofreading seems to be the solution (Torrado Cespón, 2020).

Providing students with tools mainly addressed to deal with the most common mistakes can be a good idea for online teaching. *CleverCookie* englobes all this. Following Nguyen (2021), the English used in the classroom aims at being a production model. Therefore, teachers shape their discourse according to the communicative needs of their students but also consider the most problematic areas. Thus, everything done in the classroom is done for a reason turning the discourse of the English teacher into a kind of metadiscourse (Scollon & Scollon, 2001). The EFL teacher also uses reality in this sense: when seeing an interesting linguistic or cultural element, an EFL teacher thinks about its use in the classroom and takes advantage of it as authentic material for teaching. The same happens in error analysis: if teachers perceive a pattern presents problems, that pattern would be revised in class directly or indirectly.

III. Methodology

3.1. Research model and procedure

This research was carried out considering a quantitative and qualitative model. A questionnaire was offered during an online session to a group of undergraduate students during the first weeks of the semester. To accomplish it, they had to watch all the videos included in the *CleverCookie* tool.

3.2. Research context and sample

This research involved a group of students from UNIR. All of them attended the subject Advanced Didactics of the English Language from the Primary School Teacher Degree during the academic year 2021/2022, which is entirely taught in English. A total of 69 students participated in the research. The age mean was 28.43 years. No previous linguistic acknowledgment or teaching experience is required to access this degree. Thus, the group is heterogenous regarding their linguistic skills in the foreign language. Table 1 presents the sample of participants according to whether they have sex, teaching experience in teaching English as a foreign language and accredited level in English. Most students are women, precisely 75.36 % (n = 52) compared to 24.64 % of men (n = 17). Only 14.49 % (n = 10) say they do not have any certificate. The highest certified level corresponds to B2, with 63.77 % (n = 44), followed by B1 with 14.49 % (n = 10) and, finally, C1 with only 7.25 % (n = 5). Regarding the mother tongue, English is that of a small minority (2.9 %; n = 2) compared to the rest that has Spanish as its mother tongue or one of the other co-official languages spoken in Spain: monolingual (75.365, n = 52), Basque (11.59 %, n = 8), Catalan (8.70 %, n = 6) and Galician (1.45 %, n = 1).

Regarding teaching experience, 57.97 % (n = 40) stated that they did not have any experience, 23.19 % (n = 10) had experience in formal education, 23.19 % (n = 16) in non-formal education and 4.35 % (n = 3) had experience in both formal and non-formal education. In the case of respondents who have experience as a teacher, they have an average of 2.93 years, with a minimum of one year and 15 years being the maximum.

Table 1. Distribution of the Sample of Participants according to Accredited Level and Sex

Experience				Accredited English level according to the Common European Framework of Reference for Languages				Total
				None	B1	B2	C1	
No	Sex	Male	n	3	2	7		12
			%	7.50 %	5.00 %	17.50 %		30.00 %
		Female	n	6	4	18		28
			%	15.00 %	10.00 %	45.00 %		70.00 %
Yes	Sex	Male	n	0	1	4	0	5
			%	0.00 %	3.45 %	13.79 %	0.00 %	17.24 %
		Female	n	1	3	15	5	24
			%	3.45 %	10.34 %	51.72 %	17.24 %	82.76 %
	Total		n	10	10	44	5	69
			%	14.49 %	14.49 %	63.77 %	7.25 %	100.00 %

3.3. Instruments used and their validation.

To collect the data, a questionnaire was prepared in Spanish to evaluate the tool, which consists of 34 questions divided into four dimensions: (1) Sociodemographic data; (2) Questions to understand the content of the videos; (3) Quantitative assessment of pedagogical, technical and aesthetic criteria and (4) Qualitative assessment and suggestions. The questionnaire was subjected to a content validation carried out by eight experts in Foreign Language Didactics (English) and English Philology from different universities: International University of La Rioja, University of Cádiz, University of Malaga, and University of Valladolid.

In this chapter, we will primarily analyze dimension two, which shows us the degree of assimilation of linguistic contents and their norms. Here a question about the targeted error in the video was made, and students needed to provide their answers (Table 2). To avoid conditioning, all answers were open.

Table 2. Questions about Each Video

Video	Question
1 Capitalization	When can we use capitalization more flexibly?
2 Verb *to be*	What error do the hazelnuts make?
3 Collocations	Which two English verbs are usually mistaken because they share the same meaning in Spanish?
4 Adverbs	Which adverb position needs further explanation?
5 -ing and to + infinitive	What does CleverCookie recommend observing verbs in context?
6 Uses of "the"	Which rule gives SmartScone to CleverCookie?
7 Inversion in non-direct question	Why did the cookie cross the road?

The questionnaire also included a multiple-choice question about the level which the participants found CleverCookie suitable. This considered the levels established by the Common European Framework of Reference (CEFR): A1, A2, B1, B2, C1, and C2.

Finally, following the Likert scale structure, they had to assess the usefulness of the tool according to five statements: *I would recommend this app to those who want to learn English, I would use this tool in the future as a teacher, the tool could be helpful to for the flipped classroom methodology, the videos have helped me improve my English language skills,* and *the explanations in Spanish have made it easier for understanding the content addressed.*

3.4. Data analysis

Students had to express their informed consent to answer the questions through an online questionnaire made with Google Forms. For data processing, the matrix generated by the platform was used, encoded, and exported to the SPSS statistical package (version 23) to perform descriptive analysis.

IV. Results and discussion

This section contains the distribution of responses to the content of videos viewed in English. However, six questions were formulated in Spanish, and one in English and the answer box was free format text. The answers have been coded according to the following criteria: (1) *Degree of adequacy*: correct, partially correct, or incorrect and (2) *Language*: English or Spanish. Table 3 presents the frequency and percentage of responses in each variant. In addition, through a grayscale, the sections with the highest response record have been highlighted in a darker color.

Five videos exceed 90 % of correct answers. In the first place, number 3 is placed on *collocation* and (6) *Uses of "the"* with 98.55 % of responses (n = 68) in each case. It is followed by (7) *Inversion* with 97.10 % (n = 67), (4) *Adverbs* with 95.65 % (n = 66), and (1) *Capitalization* with 92.75 % (n = 6). The two videos that are below the 90 % threshold are (2) *Verb "to be"* with 88.41 % (n = 61) and (4) *-in/to + infinitive* with 84.06 % (n = 58).

Concerning the selected language, in most cases, it is Spanish, except in three questions. The first corresponds to the only question asked in English, (7) *Inversion in non-direct* questions since the question is formulated in English and answered with the specific information of the video "To get to the other side." However, there are 23.19 % (n = 16) who translate what the video says. The next question with the highest percentage of answers in English is (3) *Collocations*, since they have to provide specific verbs in English (verbs *make* and *do*), so the use of English reaches 57.97 % (n = 40). The third question is (4) *Adverbs*, in which 50.72 % (m = 35) answered correctly in English with the exact words of the video "in front position."

It should be noted that the answers were considered partially correct since the students, instead of directly answering the questions, tried to give grammatical explanations. For example, student number 50 indicated the following in question 2, without mentioning the two specific failures of the *CleverCookie*: "making translations literally from Spanish to English, which makes the use of grammar, in many cases, incorrect."

Table 3. Answers

Question	Answers	n	%	Language	N	%
Video 1	Correct	64	92.75	English	24	34.78
				Spanish	40	57.97
	Partially incorrect	4	5.8	English	1	1.45
				Spanish	3	4.35
	Incorrect	1	1.45	Spanish	1	1.45

Question	Answers	n	%	Language	N	%
Video 2	Correct	61	88.41	English	19	27.54
				Spanish	42	60.87
	Partially incorrect	8	11.59	English	4	5.8
				Spanish	4	5.8
Video 3	Correct	68	98.55	English	39	56.52
				Spanish	29	42.03
	Partially correct	1	1.45	English	1	1.45
Video 4	Correct	66	95.65	English	35	50.72
				Spanish	31	44.93
	Partially correct	2	2.9	English	1	1.45
				Spanish	1	1.45
	Incorrect	1	1.45	Spanish	1	1.45
Video 5	Correct	58	84.06	English	23	33.33
				Spanish	35	50.72
	Partially incorrect	5	7.25	English	1	1.45
				Spanish	4	5.8
	Incorrect	6	8.7	English	1	1.45
				Spanish	5	7.25
Video 6	Correct	68	98.55	English	30	43.48
				Spanish	38	55.07
	Incorrect	1	1.45	English	1	1.45

Question	Answers	n	%	Language	N	%
Video 7	Correct	67	97.1	English	51	73.91
				Spanish	16	23.19
	Partially incorrect	2	2.9	English	1	1.45
				Spanish	1	1.45

The number of correct answers reflected in Table 3 shows that the videos are easy to understand and straightforward. Thus, *CleverCookie* functions as a valuable resource considering the demands of online students (Delgado & Salmerón, 2021; Konkin et al., 2021).

The participants were also invited to check all the resources available on the web page to judge the level where it could be applied (Table 4).

Table 4. Suitable Level

N	%	A1	A2	B1	B2	C1	C2
1	1.45	X	X				
2	2.90	X	X	X			
5	7.25	X	X	X	X		
2	2.90	X	X	X	X	X	
3	4.35	X	X	X	X	X	X
5	7.25		X				
8	11.59		X	X			
8	11.59		X	X	X		
1	1.45		X	X	X	X	
18	26.09			X			
11	15.94			X	X		
1	1.45			X	X	X	
1	1.45			X	X	X	X

N	%	A1	A2	B1	B2	C1	C2
2	2.90				X		
1	1.45				X	X	

Even though a higher percentage of participants considered *CleverCookie* a valuable resource for a B level (42.03 %), many others also signaled it as a helpful tool even for a higher level. Consequently, this can be a tool not only for learning but also for clear doubts that may emerge no matter the user's proficiency.

Participants also stated the usefulness of the tool for different aspects (Figure 1)

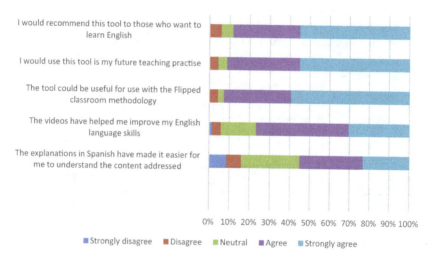

Figure 1. Usefulness.

Most participants corroborate the usefulness of *CleverCookie* as a tool for learning. Over 55 % strongly agree, and 33.33 % agree with the first statement. Statement 2 received almost the same perception, so although this tool was created bearing in mind the needs of secondary students and adults, most participants find it also valuable for their future target groups (primary). Statement 3 presents a higher level of agreement, with 59.42 % of participants strongly agreeing and 33.33 % agreeing that it is a useful tool for the flipped classroom. This can be directly related to the need for online tools that suit post-pandemic teaching needs (Konkin et al., 2021). The inclusion of *CleverCookie* as flipped classroom tool is part of the new project their creators are involved in, being offered now to the students in the master's degree on TEFL at UNIR for their application. It is also part of the ESOL TEFL Wonderland courses (ElHayawi et al., 2022).

Regarding the usefulness of videos at a personal level, opinions vary. However, over 76 % agree or strongly agree with their validity. The part that presents more differences relates to the use of Spanish as a clarifying resource for adults, where 29 % of participants do not consider this a relevant part. Still, those agreeing or strongly agreeing surpass the percentage of those who do not (55 % vs. 16 %).

Finally, although not a primary objective within this research, it was also interesting to know the mode participants chose to access *CleverCookie*'s web page (Table 5). This helps the creators design future resources considering the preferred mode of access. Despite the universal use of the smartphone among the target group, it was not a popular device in this case. We may assume this is due to the use of a computer for their assignments and attending lectures: as the information about *CleverCookie* was provided during a live session, using a computer would be easy as they were already doing so. However, the research teams plan to transform *CleverCookie* into an app so it can be adapted to the current needs of students nowadays.

Table 5. Access

How did you access www.clevercookie.es?					
		Fre-quency	Per-centage	Valid per-centage	Cumula-tive per-centage
Valid	Smart-phone	1	1.45	1.4	1.4
	Com-puter	64	92.75	92.8	94.2
	Tablet	4	5.80	5.8	100.0
	Total	69	100.0	100.0	

V. Conclusions

CleverCookie's videos proved to be clarifying and easy to understand. Moreover, participants also pointed at it as a useful tool for their future teaching practice and even as a resource for themselves. All this information is considered for the design of new videos. Once these videos have been created with their corresponding sections, the research group has planned to offer them to secondary school students to improve their qualifications in the EBAU exams. Introducing *CleverCookie* in secondary will be the definitive proof to check its validity in teaching English as a foreign language to speakers of Spanish.

Acknowledgments

This work is part of VILEO Project: *Implementación de vídeos instructivos para la mejora de las producciones escritas en inglés como lengua extranjera de estudiantes universitarios en entornos online* (RETOS de investigación UNIR, 2020–2022) and VIEALI-Rioja project: *videos formativos y material complementario para la mejora de enseñanza/aprendizaje de la lengua inglesa como lengua extranjera entre los alumnos de bachillerato de la comunidad autónoma de La Rioja* (proyectos propios UNIR 2022–2024), coordinated by Dr. Milagros Torrado Cespón.

References

Bárcena-Toyos, P. (2021). Teachers' classroom practices to achieve integration of content and language in CLIL. *NABE Journal of Research and Practice.* https://doi.org/10.1080/26390043.2021.1890989

Bárcena-Toyos, P. (2022). CLIL and SIOP: An effective partnership? *International Multilingual Research Journal.* https://doi.org/10.1080/19313152.2022.2075191

Burt, M.K. (1975). Error analysis in the adult EFL classroom. *TESOL Quarterly, 9,* 53–63. https://doi.org/10.2307/3586012

Castillo Rodríguez, C., & Díaz Lage, J.M. (2015). Exploitation of a learner corpus: Analysing openings and endings in academic forums. *Opción, extra, 6,* 192–201. https://www.redalyc.org/pdf/310/31045571012.pdf

Cilliers, E.J. (2017). The challenge of teaching Generation Z. *People: International Journal of Social Sciences, 3*(1). https://grdspublishing.org/index.php/people/article/view/322

Delgado, P., & Salmerón, L. (2021). The inattentive on-screen reading: Reading medium affects attention and reading comprehension under time pressure. *Learning and Instruction, 71,* 102396. https://doi.org/10.1016/j.learninstruc.2020.101396

ElHayawi, M., Benali Taouis, H., Bekaryan, L., Zonoubi, R., Monfared, R., Safari, P., & Leonard, S. (2022). *ESOL TESOL wonderland teaching training.* https://teflwonderland.com/guided-teaching-practice/

Firth, J., Torous, J., Stubbs, B., Firth, J.A., Steiner, G.Z., Smith, L., Alvarez-Jimenez, M., Gleeson, J., Vancampfort, D., Armitage, C.J., & Sarris, J. (2019). The "online brain": How the Internet may be changing our cognition. *World Psychiatry, 18*(2), 1129–129. https://doi.org/10.1002/wps.20617

Jobeen, A., Kazemian, B., & Shahbaz, M. (2015). The role of error analysis in teaching and learning of second and foreign language. *Education and Linguistics Research, 1*(2), 52–62. https://doi.org/10.5296/elr.v1i1.8189

Karim, A., Mohamed, A.R., Ismail, S.A.M.M., Shahid, F.H., Rahman, M.M., & Haque, H. (2018). Error analysis in EFL writing classroom. *International Journal of English Linguistics, 8*(4), 122. https://doi.org/10.5539/IJEL.V8N4P122

Kavari, K.M. (2014). To use or not to use the mother tongue in ELT classrooms, that is the question. *Spectrum: A Journal of Multidisciplinary Research, 3*(6), 206–212.

Konkin, A.A., Dronova, A.Y., Tretyakova, G.V., Bermudez-Alekina, A.E., Kotenko, V.V. (2021). *Prospects of using innovations in post-pandemic higher education.* International Linguistic Science and Practice Conference "Methods of Teaching Foreign Languages 2.0: Real vs. Virtual," SHS Web of Conferences, Vol. 127. Article 01001. https://doi.org/10.1051/shsconf/202112701001

Nguyen, V.M. (2021). English language-learning environments in COVID-19 era. *AsiaCALL Online Journal, 12*(3), 39–46. https://www.academia.edu/45430575/English_language_learning_environments_in_COVID_19_era_Nguyen_Van_My

Rothman, D. (2016). *A tsunami of learners called Generation Z.* http://www.mdle.net/Journal/A_Tsunami_of_Learners_Called_Generation_Z.pdf

Serrano de Santiago, O., Velazquez Recendez, J.M., De Avila Sifuentes, G., Acosta Cruz, L.G., & Méndez Murillo, M.A. (2022). A case study of error analysis in Mexican EFL middle school students. *English Linguistics Research, 11*(1), 20–28 https://ideas.repec.org/a/jfr/elr111/v11y2022i1p20-28.html

Scollon, R., & Scollon, S. (2001). *Intercultural communication. A discourse approach.* Blackwell.

Torrado Cespón, M. (2018). Interlanguage or technology when using English as vehicular language: What influences students productions online? *The Eurocall Review, 26*(2), 41–49. https://doi.org/10.4995/eurocall.2018.9924

Torrado Cespón, M. (2020). Proofreading, the net and foreign language anxiety in the use of apology formulae in an online forum. A learner corpus study. In M.L. Carrió Pastor (Ed.), *Corpus analysis in different genres: Academic discourse and learner corpora.* Routledge.

Torrado Cespón, M. (Coord.). (2021). *CleverCookie: English language resources for speakers of Spanish*. https://www.clevercookie.es/

Torrado Cespón, M., & Díaz Lage, J.M. (2017). Error analysis and interlanguage in the use of the term "ICT" in an online learner corpus. *Complutense Journal of English Studies, 25*, 105–123. https://doi.org/10.5209/CJES.56354

Torrado Cespón, M., & Díaz Lage, J.M. (2022). Gamification, online learning and motivation. A quantitative and qualitative analysis in higher education. *Contemporary Educational Technology, 14*(4), Article ep381. https://doi.org/10.30935/cedtech/12297

Turnbull, B. (2018). Examining pre-service ESL teacher beliefs: Perspectives on first language use in the second language classroom. *Journal of Second Language Teaching and Research, 6*(1), 50–76. https://pops.uclan.ac.uk/index.php/jsltr/article/view/482

Xie, F., & Jiang, X.M. (2007). Error analysis and the EFL classroom teaching. *US-China Education Review, 4*(9), 10–14. https://eric.ed.gov/?id=ED502653

Irene Doval (University Santiago, Spain)

Chapter VIII The English–Spanish parallel corpus PaEnS

I. Introduction: The PaCorES project

The English-Spanish Parallel Corpus PaEnS is part of a major ongoing project, PaCorES, acronym for Spanish Parallel Corpora, which aims to collect a series of bilingual parallel corpora with Spanish as the central language. Parallel corpora contain translations of texts from a source language into one or more other languages with the translated elements linked or aligned across languages in units consisting of words, phrases, or sentences (McEnery & Hardie, 2012, p. 20).

Parallel corpora have become an essential resource for a wide range of applications. Five major fields of applications of parallel corpora can be distinguished, each with its specific users: (a) basic research in contrastive linguistics and translatology, (b) lexicography, (c) translation, (d) teaching of foreign languages and of translation, and (e) natural language processing, most prominently in the field of machine translation (McEnery & Xiao, 2007, p. 2).

In general research in contrastive linguistics, parallel corpora provide an easily accessible empirical basis, producing patterns of correspondence, allowing for the analysis of similarities and differences between two linguistic systems and providing quantitative data (Johansson, 2007). In translation studies, they are very useful for discovering collocational and syntactic patterns between two languages (Bernardini, 2004, p. 28). Moreover, in the case of bidirectional corpora (in which a given language can function as both the source and target language), they can also be used to compare monolingually the original language and the translated language and to test Baker's hypothesis (1996, pp. 175 ff) on the so-called "translation universals," typical phenomena exclusive to translated texts.

Heid (2008, pp. 137 ff) provides an overview of the applications of parallel aligned corpora for bilingual lexicography, highlighting their usefulness at various levels and providing syntagmatic data on word usage in both languages. The usefulness of parallel corpora in language teaching has been frequently addressed in the specific literature (Doval, 2018, pp. 65 ff; Johansson, 2009, pp. 33 ff). On the one hand, they can serve as a basis for the elaboration of teaching materials and reference grammars. Moreover, bilingual concordance systems can be used in addition to bilingual dictionaries, or even instead of them, as they provide valuable contextual information in a multitude of translated usage examples (Doval, 2019, p. 116). Finally, parallel corpora are a fundamental resource for a wide range of natural language processing tasks (Doval, 2022, p. 187), such as multilingual terminology and information extraction and especially machine translation. As Wetzel and Bond (2012, p. 28) point out, large, high-quality parallel corpora are an indispensable resource for training statistical and neural machine translation systems.

Each of these applications has distinct user groups with very different starting premises (from specialists in linguistics and language technology to English or Spanish learners) and with specific requirements related to the corpus's design, the type of texts, their degree of annotation and the metadata to be stored. Considering that the creation of parallel corpora is a vast undertaking in terms of both time and effort—more time consuming and technically complex than that of monolingual corpora—it is intended that the corpora of the PaCorES Project can be exploited for multiple purposes. Thus, it is our intention that, in addition to linguistic and translation research, the corpora are useful to lexicographers, translators and NLP researchers. Special effort has been made to make them a useful and user-friendly tool in language and translation classrooms, so that the corpora can be used by intermediate to advanced learners of the given foreign language or Spanish to obtain a large number of translation suggestions shown in examples of usage.

Since existing parallel corpora with Spanish as the central language have major drawbacks (see section II) in order to be fully exploited by all the above-mentioned groups of users, the project PaCorES is driven by the aim of addressing these shortcomings. Within the project, high-quality, sentence-aligned parallel corpora are being compiled for different languages that are paired with Spanish. For the time being the German-Spanish corpus (www.corpuspages.eu) and the English-Spanish corpus (www.corpuspaens.eu) are already available online. It is expected that the Spanish-Chinese and Spanish-French corpora will be added to these in the near future.

The remainder of this paper is structured as follows: Section II briefly describes other similar resources and their drawbacks for many of the applications listed above. Section III is devoted to the description of the design and composition of the English-Spanish PaEnS corpus. The remaining sections then deal with text preprocessing (IV), segmentation and alignment (V). The web presentation of the corpus and the search possibilities are then described (VI) and, finally, future work is outlined and a brief recapitulation of the distinctive features of the corpus is made (VII).

II. Related work

By far, the most important parallel language resources come from different institutions of the European Union. Steinberger et al. (2014) give a comparative overview of the different multilingual resources available, which include, among others, the Europarl corpus (see below), the Digital Corpus of the European Parliament (DCEP),[14] or the JRC Acquis.[15] In addition, the European Union supports projects aimed at the exploitation and use of these resources, and in general at the enhancement of multilingualism by means of parallel corpora, like the MultiParaCrawl[16] corpus, which is made up of parallel corpora from web crawls collected in the ParaCrawl project and further processed to make it a multi-parallel corpus by pivoting via English.

Particular mention should be made of OPUS[17] a huge, constantly-growing collection of freely available multilingual text collections compiled by a crawler, which automatically searches the web for bilingual web pages, and also includes already aligned resources, such as some of those mentioned above (Tiedemann, 2012, pp. 2214 ff.). All preprocessing is done automatically. No manual corrections have been carried out. It also provides tools for data processing, as well as multiple search systems for corpus queries. This vast collection is maintained by Jörg Tiedemann and currently consists of more than 90 languages (cf. Tiedemann, 2016). Obviously, not all language pairs are equally represented. The English/Spanish language pair consists of 36 million aligned bisegments (Tiedemann, 2012, pp. 2214 ff.). The main fields covered by OPUS are legislative and administrative, as a large part of the texts come from the European Union or other international institutions. There are also, although to a lesser extent, other

---

14 The DCEP is a multilingual sentence-aligned parallel corpus in 23 official EU languages (253 language pairs) consisting of European Parliament texts produced between 2001 and 2012 and containing over 1.3 billion words. It excludes the documents already available in the Europarl corpus to avoid overlapping. https://wt-public.emm4u.eu/Resources/DCEP-2013/DCEP-Download-Page.html.

15 JRC-Acquis is a collection of legislative texts from the European Union and is currently comprised of selected texts written between the 1950s and the present day (https://ec.europa.eu/jrc/en/language-technologies/jrc-acquis).

16 The last version ParaCrawl Corpus release v9 (March 2022) includes 705 parallel corpora and 41 languages. It contains for the Spanish-English language pair 269,394,967 aligned sentences. https://paracrawl.eu/.

17 http://opus.lingfil.uu.se/.

text types such as subtitles, journalistic texts and some other smaller collections from various Internet sources, such as subtitles and technical documentation

We will now turn to the shortcomings, given that these corpora have laid the groundwork for the creation of the PaCorES corpus collection and their extension to new language pairs. In the corpora created automatically from the web by means of a web crawler, it is impossible to identify the direction of the translation. Therefore, they lack the identification of the source and the translated language (Doval, 2017). Closely related to this point is the fact that it is not known whether the translations have been made directly between the two working languages, or rather indirectly as independent translations from a third language acting as the pivot language. In many of the European Union resources, source texts are translated into English in the first step, from which they are then translated into other languages. While these issues might not pose a major problem for NLP applications, they are nevertheless key drawbacks for translation and cross-linguistic research.

On the other hand, to make the corpora a suitable tool for use in the language and translation classroom, both source and target texts must be of high quality, and the translations must be unambiguously carried out by professional human translators. This aspect cannot be verified by corpora automatically produced by gathering web pages, where it is not known if the texts have undergone any quality control.

All in all, perhaps the main drawback of these corpora is, despite their huge size, the poor variety of their texts, as they are limited to very specific domains, mainly administrative, legal and commercial language (cf. Steinberg et al., 2014, p. 4) where the general language is not well represented. Therefore, these corpora are poorly suited for different user groups, and especially for use in translation and second-language learning.

Finally, it should be noted that users without specific training have difficulties to use these resources due to their lack of a web interface. This makes it difficult for the common occasional user to access and use the system. This is the case with the resources from the European Union, which, although they can be downloaded in XML format, do not offer a web interface to be consulted online. The project PaCorES aims at making the resources easily available to researchers and students in different fields, even if they lack programming skills.

III. Design and composition of PaEnS

The PaEnS corpus consists of two major well-differentiated parts: the core corpus and the supplements. The core corpus was entirely developed within the project and will be the focus of this paper. The supplements are texts of different origins, which have been added subsequently and should be considered as mere complements to the core corpus.

3.1. The core corpus

Here we will describe the data of the PaEnS core corpus in terms of size, text types, language varieties, number and publication date of the texts.

A corpus is not just an arbitrary collection of electronic texts, but they must be "selected and ordered according to explicit linguistic criteria in order to be used as a sample of the language" (Sinclair, 1996, p. 4) in order to ensure that the corpus is suitable for the intended purpose. In the case of translation corpora, however, an important limitation regarding the available material must be kept in mind. The vast majority of texts are not translated at all and, if translated, only a tiny proportion has passed any quality control. Hence, the basic criterion for gathering texts for a parallel corpus must be an opportunistic one, that is, it is necessary to resort to what is available (Doval, 2017). For this reason, the requirements placed on monolingual corpora in terms of representativeness and balance (Biber, 1993; Egbert et al., 2022) representing a relevant range of subjects and registers are hardly applicable here (Nádvorníková, 2017).

In addition to this major constraint, another one is the requirement of the quality of the data (originals and translations). Apart from the aforementioned institutional language resources, the only way to ensure text quality is to make use of written texts from reputable publishers, where both original texts and translations are subjected to strict quality control.

Therefore, the PaEnS core corpus contains original texts in English and Spanish and their published translations. So far it comprises a collection of 75 works[18] and their translations. The corpus is bidirectional and quite balanced regarding translation direction, where English originals are only slightly more prevalent (26 %) vs. Spanish Originals (23 %). Figure 1 displays the structure of the corpus. The arrows between the boxes indicate the types of studies this structure enables, which include, among others: contrastive and translation studies based on original texts and their translations (solid horizontal arrows) or based on parallel original texts (dotted vertical arrows) and general features of translated texts (dashed diagonal arrows).

---

18 The full list of authors and works can be found here: shorturl.at/hjoy2.

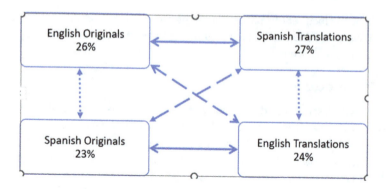

Figure 1. Structure of the PaEnS corpus.

Eighty percent of the works are fiction (fantasy, thriller, historical fiction, children's and young adult literature among others) and 20 % are non-fiction of various genres (essays, advice literature, biographical and popular science texts). This type of texts not only guarantees high quality but also a greater lexical diversity and, especially in children's and young adult literature, a fictional spoken informal language, which is a very important resource for a bilingual corpus, since it is a very scarce register in the translated language.

In regard to the geographical provenance of the works, a certain dialectal diversity has been pursued by including works from British, American, Irish, and Australian writers for English, and European and Latin-American writers for Spanish. As our aim is to build up a corpus of present-day texts, all of them were published after 1960, with special emphasis on twenty-first-century works, as shown in Figure 2.

The works were not included in their entirety but in excerpts in order to comply with the constraints for copyrighted publications. Moreover, consequently this leads to a greater variety of texts. These omissions in the text flow are indicated according to an ellipsis in square brackets [...]. Table 1 gives an overview of the current composition of PaEnS, that contains nearly 17 million tokens and over a half million bisegments, that is, pairs of aligned text chunks (sentences or smaller segments).

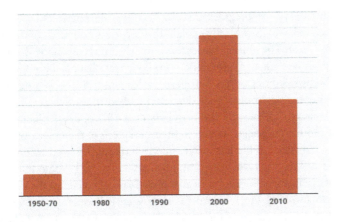

Figure 2. Texts by time period.

Table 1. Number of Works, Tokens and Bisegments by Language and Original Text in the PaEnS Core Corpus (July 2022)

Language	Works	Tokens	Bisegments
English Original	37	4.446.050	279.624
Spanish Translation		4.521.373	
Spanish Original	38	3.755.859	235.866
English Translation		3.948.366	
TOTAL	75 (x2)	16.671.648	515.490 (x2)

3.2. The supplements

As its name implies, this part of the corpus was designed only as a supplement to the core corpus in order to cover certain, such as administrative and legal language, which the corpus' core collection lacked. Unlike the core corpus, the texts had previously been automatically aligned at the sentence level without manual review. The texts have subsequently undergone different automatic control and cleaning procedures. So large segments above 350 characters (in Spanish or English, respectively) were excluded as well as unbalanced bisegments or any others considered to lack linguistic value. These omissions are not indicated. Currently, this supplementary part includes three collections: Europarl, TED Talks and Global Voices. We will now briefly explain the key features of each of them.

Europarl,[19] created by Philipp Koehn, is a parallel corpus containing the minutes of the European Parliament (Verbatim reporting). It was obtained by automatically gathering the proceedings of the European Parliament from its website (Koehn, 2005). The proceedings contain the edited and revised transcripts of all speeches delivered in plenary debates by the members of the European Parliament, usually in their mother languages, as well as the translations of the transcripts into all other official languages of the European Union (Bernardini, Ferraresi & Miličević, 2016, pp. 68–69). However, a certain number of statements have no information about the original language. The latest version (release v7) contains the transcripts between 1996 and 2011 in 21 official EU languages. PaEnS uses the cleaned and structurally enriched version of the CoStEP[20] Corpus as well as its metadata. The English-Spanish portion comes to over 40 million words per language after the aforementioned cleaning procedures (s. Table 2).

The TED Talks are a collection of transcribed and translated talks published by the TED Conference website.[21] Since 2007, the TED Conference has been posting all video recordings of its talks together with subtitles in English and their translations into more than 80 languages (Cettolo et al., 2012, p. 261). TED Talks are mostly originally held in English and their videos are available through the TED website together with subtitles. The talks have been translated by volunteers into different languages. The version used in PaEnS is that provided by the Web Inventory of Transcribed and Translated Talks.[22] It is comprised of the Spanish translations and the original English transcripts of 4,043 TED Talks from 2006 to 2020 aligned at the sentence level. The automatic alignment was manually reviewed within the project.

---

19 http://www.statmt.org/europarl.
20 http://pub.cl.uzh.ch/purl/costep/ It was made freely available as the Corrected & Structured Europarl Corpus (CoStEP) in order to further enhance the usefulness of Europarl and to compensate for some of its drawbacks (Graen et al. 2014).
21 http://www.ted.com.
22 https://wit3.fbk.eu/>. For more information, see Cettolo et al. (2012). Special thanks are due to Mr. Cettolo, who kindly made the talks from 2018 onwards available to the PaEnS corpus.

The most recent collection added to the corpus is Global Voices,[23] a corpus of texts written by an international, multilingual, primarily volunteer community of writers, translators, academics, and human rights activists. A group of volunteers translates the stories into dozens of languages. The texts, taken from release v2018q4, are sentence aligned and include data up to December 2018.

The summary statistics for all three Supplements included so far in PaEnS are presented in the Table 2.

Table 2. Number of Tokens and Bisegments in the Supplements (July 2022)

Resource	Language	Tokens	Bisegments
Europarl	English	42.178.712	1.550.421
	Spanish	44.128.158	
TED Talks	English	8.676.842	430.667
	Spanish	8.338.726	
Global Voices	English	15.285.853	680.530
	Spanish	16.361.642	
TOTAL	English	66.141.407	2.661.618
	Spanish	68.828.526	

The following sections describe the steps that have been carried out for the creation of the PaEnS core corpus.

IV. Data preprocessing

This section describes the data preprocessing steps that prepare the incoming texts for further processing: alignment (section V) and linguistic annotation. The data preprocessing involves three tasks: text normalization, annotation of textual divisions and annotation of metadata.

Each work is assigned a unique ID, the texts are converted to txt-format and the characters are encoded to UTF-8. Then both versions are tested for

---

23 https://globalvoices.org/ The parallel corpus included here was compiled and provided by Casmacat (http://casmacat.eu/corpus/global-voices.html) and it was adjusted for OPUS (Tiedemann, 2012).

discrepancies and non-corresponding text fragments are removed. Essentially the aim is to achieve as much parallelism as possible between the source and target data to obtain the best alignment results. First, all text fragments that are not part of the body of the text are removed, such as bibliographic information, dedications, tables of contents, tables, diagrams, indexes, footnotes, headers and footers, and author's or translator's notes. Similarly, any appendix with no equivalent in the other version is deleted.

Second, both sets of data (original and translation) are checked for errors associated with the digitization process. Typical errors include the insertion of a space or a hyphen within a word, the deletion of spaces between words, or the occasional confusion of certain characters.

Most works include some sort of segmentation in terms of parts or chapters that are tagged as divisions to make it easier to refer back to the source. Further subdivisions such as page breaks in the source text, paragraphs or lines are not marked, given that most of the texts were primarily digital. Typographical highlighting (italics or bold) is not marked.

The metadata is used to capture relevant information about the source texts to retrieve it from the corpus. Each of the works included in the PaEnS corpus is provided with a metadata list containing, among other things: author and translator, title, year of publication and other bibliographic information, original language and version language, genre, manual reviewer, and information on the basic statistics (number of characters, tokens, and bisegments) of the documents. These additional metadata tags are attached to the individual text files and stored locally with each text document.

V. Segmentation and alignment

Corpus alignment is a central task in the construction and exploitation of a parallel corpus. The type of alignment is determined by the previous type of segmentation of the text into different segments, such as paragraphs, sentences or words.

Tiedemann (2011) defines alignment as "the process of linking corresponding parts with each other" (p. 123). Alignment is the task of making this correspondence explicit, by linking segments of the bitext (source and target text) that are equivalent and assigning the segments of the translation to corresponding segments of the original. These aligned segment pairs, one from each half of the bitext, are called bisegments (Tiedemann, 2011, p. 24).

Based on this segmentation a parallel corpus can be aligned at different levels. For the PaEnS corpus, it was decided to focus on sentence alignment, since this level of alignment is the most established for parallel corpora (see among others Tiedemann, 2011; Volk et al., 2014).

In this alignment process, two tasks are combined: First, segmentation of the monolingual texts into sentences is performed, and then the English and Spanish sentence segments are linked to each other, as shown in Figure 3:

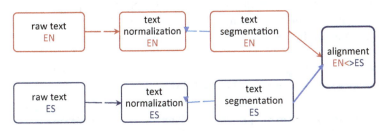

Figure 3. PaEnS Core Corpus: Workflow.

In the PaEnS corpus, the open-source program LF-Aligner[24] is used for sentence alignment because it has achieved the best results in several tests. It is based on Hunalign (Varga, 2012, pp. 92–119), a very common alignment software for multilingual corpora. Hunalign combines both a length-based and a lexical matching approach and is therefore a so-called hybrid algorithm (Tóth et al., 2008; Varga et al., 2005).

Alignment is performed in four steps:

(a) The texts are segmented based on punctuation. A sentence ends after a full-stop, question-mark or exclamation-mark (.?!)

(b) Then they are aligned using a modified version of Brown et al's (1991) sentence length-based model.

(c) The program creates an automatic dictionary based on this initial alignment, and

(d) finally, it refines the alignment in a second run using the automatic dictionary.

The accuracy of alignment depends, first on the type of texts; specifically, fictional texts, as in the case of the PaEnS corpus, present greater problems than other types of texts, such as administrative or technical texts, as pointed out by Zanettin (2012, p. 155). Moreover, within fictional texts, the degree of correspondence

---

24 http://sourceforge.net/projects/aligner/.

of the bitext varies depending on the author, the translator, the texts themselves and the direction of the translation.

Sentence alignment would be trivial if a sentence were translated into exactly one sentence, but, obviously, a one-to-one correspondence is not always possible since during the translation process, sentences in the target text can be omitted (Table 3) or inserted (Table 4), the translator can split a sentence (correspondence 1:2, Table 5), merge two sentences (correspondence 2:1, Table 6), or rearrange them to produce a natural translation in the target language (Varga, 2012, p. 94).

Table 3. Omission of a Segment in the Target Text (3101, chap. 1)

Junto a los dólares había dos pasaportes: el suyo y el del Güero.	With the dollars were two valid US passports—hers and Guero's.
Los dos tenían visas norteamericanas vigentes.	[n_t_s]
Contempló un momento la foto del Güero:	She studied his photo:

Table 4. Addition of a Segment in the Target Text (3007, part 3, chap. 7)

| "The Ministry's not too happy." | Al Ministerio no le ha hecho ninguna gracia. |
| [a_s_t] | —El trébol es el símbolo de Irlanda. |

Table 5. Misalignment due to 1:2 Correspondence (3132, part 5, chap. 9)

| —He llamado a Héctor casi todos los días, saben que estoy preocupado. | "I've been calling Héctor almost every day. |
| | They know I'm worried." |

Table 6. Misalignment due to 2:1 Correspondence (3012, chap. 4)

You decide that you want a better life, in a manner that will also make the life of your family better.	Decides que quieres una vida mejor que al mismo tiempo suponga una mejora para la vida de tu familia, *o la de tu familia y la de tus amigos, o la de todos ellos y también los desconocidos que los rodean.*
Or the life of your family, and your friends, and the strangers who surround them.	

In the project an effective procedure was developed to manually review and validate the results of the automatic alignment of the selected bitexts, and hence to improve its quality. This is done in three steps. First segments of more than 350 characters are split by inserting manually breaks at appropriate places in both segments. In a second step, the empty alignments are identified. As previously stated, they may be due to misalignments or to deletions or insertions in the translated text. If the segment is misaligned, the necessary corrections are made. If the segment has been omitted in the translation, the mark [n_t_s] (=non-translated segment) is inserted in the empty cell (Table 3). If the segment has been added in the translated text, the mark [a_s_t] (=text added in the translation) is inserted (Table 4). Finally, to reduce manual work, we find unbalanced bisegments in terms of the number of characters in English and Spanish. These unbalanced bisegments are more likely to be misaligned. We apply a ratio, comparing the number of characters in both, the English and the Spanish segment, order the bisegments by the value of this ratio and focus on the range 10:- 10 (Doval et al., 2019). This way manual checking of the automatic alignment is done more efficiently and takes less time. This procedure is a compromise to minimize the tedious work involved in review, while ensuring a high level of accuracy.

VI. Search and display

As Dörk and Knight (2015) assess, many existing corpora are "aimed mainly at people with expertise with linguistics" (p. 84). Thus, there is less reflection on the decisions involved in designing search and visualization of corpora and corpus analysis for non-expert users.

As mentioned at the beginning of this chapter, to make the corpus a real multipurpose tool, useful for very different user groups, from cross-linguistics and translation researchers to lexicographers and NLP researchers to occasional or regular users, as well as English or Spanish learners, it is essential to provide an adequate interface for displaying and retrieving data, including corpus texts, metadata and linguistic annotation. To achieve this aim, the web interface of PaEnS presents relevant functionalities.

It has a fast and user-friendly search: the search engine allows queries to be carried out very quickly through large amounts of data. The basic query language is very simple and an advanced, more complex, query language is only displayed if required. Therefore, it was designed as a three-level search. The first level is the simple or standard search. In this case, to search for a concordance (all occurrences of a given word displayed in context) the user need only enter the search term (a word or a phrase) in English or Spanish in the search field. Figure 4 provides an example of the standard search menu and some of its features.

Figure 4. Standard search in the PaEnS corpus.

In these types of queries, lemmatization is applied by default. With multiword queries, all search words within a specific distance are found. The search habits of Internet users are exploited, emulating the google search language as the basic model. So, if the term or phrase is enclosed between quotation marks (" "), the search only returns concordances that exactly match the entered word form or phrase (s. Figure 6). To expand the text search, wildcards (*?) can be used to search for characters that do not exactly match the search criteria.

The search results are displayed in an easy-to-read format. The matching segments are displayed side-by-side. We discarded the most common concordance format, KWIC (Key Word in Context)—the node word occupies a central position with all lines vertically aligned around the node—because this presentation of the results for bilingual corpora is not user-friendly (Doval et al., 2019), since it does not allow the original and the translation to be displayed side-by-side. For this reason, we decided on a two-column html table for the display of the query results, where the left column corresponds to concordances of the search term in the source texts

(English or Spanish). The corresponding segment with the translation is displayed in the same row in the right column. Occurrences of the search term in the translations are shown afterward in the right column. The search term or phrase is displayed with some context and highlighted in bold (Figure 4). With each query, information on the number of hits, the total number of pages, as well as the current page number is shown.

At the bottom of the table, a set of links are available to allow the user to navigate through the pages and to download (feature only available for registered user) the query results in two formats: ODS and CSV. In each cell, information concerning the text ID, the corresponding part or chapter are displayed in blue square brackets. By clicking on the work ID, the user can select a larger language context. Moreover, this screen shows detailed information concerning the bibliographic information, as shown in Figure 5.

Figure 5. Context with and bibliographic information in the PaEnS corpus.

The second level of search is the advanced one (Figure 6). At this level, the user can control and restrict the scope of the search by applying the following drop-down search filters: text ID, author, publication year, original or translated text, genre and dialectal variety. Moreover, here bilingual searches can be performed at the same time, returning concordances where a given word in English corresponds to a specific word in Spanish (Figure 7).

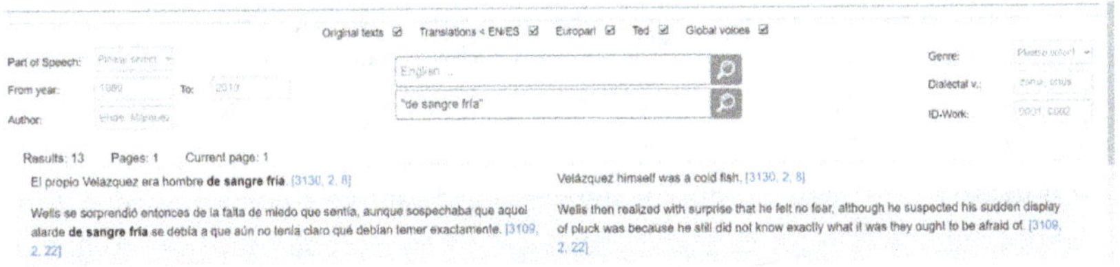

Figure 6. Advanced search in the PaEnS corpus.

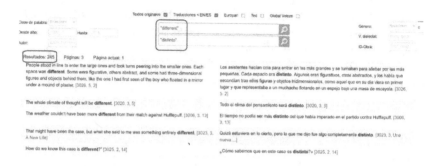

Figure 7. Advanced bilingual search in the PaEnS corpus.

The last search level is the most complex and it gives the user full command of the powerful query syntax used in the underlying query tool: Solr. (Version 7.5.0).[25] This supports searches using regular expressions (RegEx),[26] that expands considerably the power of the query language. The search term has to be preceded by [SS] (Solr Search). The search expression must be constructed word by word, and for each word, it will be possible to specify several parameters. Figure 8 shows a formal search. At this level the search system allows for complex queries across multiple layers of linguistic annotation, combining text string and PoS-tags searches.

VII. Concluding remarks and future work

The corpus PaEnS is part of a larger project, PaCorES, started at the University Santiago de Compostela in 2014, that intends to create a large collection of Spanish bilingual parallel corpora of high quality and considerable size. So far there are two corpora available online: the German-Spanish corpus, PaGeS, with nearly 40 million tokens, and the English-Spanish corpus, PaEnS, with more than 16 million tokens (core corpus), to which this paper is devoted. As has also been previously stated, the stated purpose of the project is to build qualitative multifunctional parallel corpora so that they become useful tools for a multiplicity of users.

This paper describes the different steps we have completed in the construction of PaEnS. Since this is an ongoing project, we want to continue and complete

25 http://lucene.apache.org/solr/.
26 https://www.regular-expressions.info/.

it in several dimensions. On the one hand, we plan to add new texts to the nuclear corpus to reach some 50 million words, 25 per language. We also intend to include new collections in the supplements to complement the domains of the existing ones. On the other hand, we are implementing two new features: PoS tagging and word alignment. The English texts have already been tagged with Treetagger and the Spanish texts with Freeling and both tagsets have been mapped to the universal part-of-speech tagset.[27] However, the tagged texts are not yet indexed, but they are expected to be available online soon. Regarding word alignment, several tools (Berkeley Aligner, Giza++, NaTools and Nile)[28] are being tested, but a final resolution has not yet been reached.

Despite the existence of other Spanish-English parallel corpora, PaEnS has a number of distinctive features, which make it stand out from similar resources.

The typology of texts included is very diverse: it ranges from fiction and non-fiction texts in the core corpus to the administrative and legal texts of the Europarl, journalistic texts (Global Voices) and oral texts covering a wide variety of topics (TED Talks). It includes domains like the fictional spoken language for which few resources exist.

It is bidirectional and well-balanced enabling not only comparison between the original language and the translation, but as well between originals and translations in the same language or between translations into two languages. The data is complemented with metadata that provides relevant information about the source text.

The high quality of the source texts and translations of the core corpus is assured by using only texts already published by renowned publishers. This makes it a very reliable data source. Moreover, a quality control system for each step of the corpus construction was performed. The corpus has been checked manually at different levels, including compilation, preprocessing, sentence splitting, and alignment. Finally, PaEnS is equipped with a user-friendly web interface allowing for efficient and refined searches tailored to the needs of each user.

---

27 TreeTagger: http://www.cis.uni-muenchen.de/~schmid/tools/TreeTagger/, Freeling: https://nlp.lsi.upc.edu/freeling/index.php/node/1, Universal PoS Tags: https://universaldependencies.org.

28 Berkeley Aligner: https://github.com/mhajiloo/berkeleyaligner, Giza++: http://www2.statmt.org/moses/giza/GIZA++.html, NaTools: http://linguateca.di.uminho.pt/natools/, Nile: https://jasonriesa.github.io/nile/.

All these features make PaEnS a very useful resource for multiple applications, from contrastive research, through translation studies to foreign language learning and teaching.

Acknowledgments

The research reported in this paper has been developed as part of the project *PaGeS 2.0 Optimization of a multipurpose resource* (2017–2022, FFI2017-85938-R) and the project *PaCorES: Online Spanish Parallel Corpora* (2022–2026, PID2021-125313OB-I00), funded by the State Research Agency (AEI) of Spanish Ministry of Science, Innovation and Universities.

References

Baker, M. (1996). Corpus-based translation studies: The challenges that lie ahead. In H. Somers (Ed.), *Terminology, LSP and translation* (pp. 175–186). Benjamins.

Bernardini, S. (2004). Corpora in the classroom. In J. Sincalir (Ed.), *How to use corpora in language teaching* (pp. 15–36). John Benjamins.

Bernardini, S., Ferraresi, A., & Miličević, M. (2016). From EPIC to EPTIC. Exploring simplification in interpreting and translation from an intermodal perspective. *Target: International Journal of Translation Studies, 28*(1), 61–86.

Biber, D. (1993). Representativeness in corpus design. *Literary and Linguistic Computing, 8*(4), 243–257. https://doi.org/10.1093/llc/8.4.243

Brown, P.F., Lai, J.C., & Mercer, R.L. (1991). Aligning sentences in parallel corpora. In Proceedings of the 29th Annual Meeting on Association for Computational Linguistics, ACL '91, *Stroudsburg, PA* (pp. 169–176). ACL.

Cettolo, M., Girardi, C., & Federico, M. (2012). *WIT3: Web inventory of transcribed and translated talks.* Proceedings of EAMT, Trento, Italy, pp. 261–268.

Dörk, M., & Knight, D. (2015). WordWanderer: A navigational approach to text visualisation. *Corpora, 10*(1), 83–94.

Doval, I. (2017). La construcción de un corpus paralelo bilingüe multifuncional. *Moenia. Revista lucense de lingüística y literatura, 27*, 125–141.

Doval, I. (2018). Corpus paralelos en la enseñanza de lenguas extranjeras: un ejemplo de aplicación basado en el corpus PaGeS. *CLINA, 4*(2), 65–82. https://doi.org/10.14201/clina2018426582

Doval, I. (2022). Parallelkorpora: Ergänzung oder Ersatz bilingualer Wörterbücher? Möglichkeiten und Grenzen der didaktischen Nutzung von Parallelkorpora vs. bilingualen Wörterbüchern für den Fremdsprachenunterricht.

In I. Leibrandt & K. Jahn (Eds.), *Arbeitswelten von gestern bis heute* (pp. 185–210). Lang.

Doval, I., Fernández Lanza, S., Jiménez Juliá, T., Liste Lamas, E., & Lübke, B. (2019). Corpus PaGeS: A multifunctional resource for language learning, translation and cross-linguistic research. In I. Doval & M.T.S. Nieto (Eds.), *Parallel corpora for contrastive and translation studies: New resources and applications* (pp. 103–121). John Benjamins.

Egbert, J., Biber, D., & Gray, B. (2022). *Designing and evaluating language corpora: A practical framework for corpus representativeness*. Cambridge University Press. https://doi.org/10.1017/9781316584880

Graën, J., Batinic, D., & Volk, M. (2014). Cleaning the Europarl corpus for linguistic applications. In *Konvens*. Stiftung Universität Hildesheim.

Heid, U. (2008). Corpus linguistics and lexicography. In A. Lüdeling & M. Kyto (Eds.), *Corpus linguistics. An international handbook* (Vol. 1, pp. 131–153). Walter de Gruyter.

Johansson, S. (2007). Using corpora: From learning to research. In E. Hidalgo, L. Quereda, & J. Santana (Eds.), *Corpora in the foreign language classroom* (pp. 17–30). Rodopi.

Johansson, S. (2009). Some thoughts on corpora and second-language acquisition. In K. Aijmer (Ed.), *Corpora and language teaching* (pp. 33–44). John Benjamins.

Koehn, P. (2005). *EuroParl: A parallel corpus for statistical machine translation*. Proceedings of the Machine Translation Summit, Phuket, Thailand, pp. 79–86. http://www.statmt.org/europarl/

McEnery, T., & Hardie, A. (2012). *Corpus linguistics*. Cambridge University Press.

McEnery, T., & Xiao, R. (2007). Parallel and comparable corpora: What are they up to?. In G. James & G. Anderman (Eds.), *Incorporating corpora: Translation and the linguist*. Multilingual Matters. http://someya-net.com/104-IT_Kansai_Initiative/corpora_and_translation.pdf

Nádvorníková, O. (2017). Pièges méthodologiques des corpus parallèles et comment les éviter. *Corela HS-21*. http://corela.revues.org/4810

Sinclair, J. (1996, mayo). Preliminary recommendations on corpus typology (EAGLES Document EAG-TCWG- CTYP/P). Expert Advisory Group on Language Engineering Standards. http://www.ilc.cnr.it/EAGLES96/corpus typ/corpustyp.html

Steinberger, R., Ebrahim, M., Poulis, A., Carrasco-Benitez, M., Schlüter, P., Przybyszewski, M., & Gilbro, S. (2014). An overview of the European Union's highly multilingual parallel corpora. *Language Resources and Evaluation Journal (LRE)*. https://doi.org/10.1007/s10579-014-9277-0

Tiedemann, J. (2011). *Bitext alignment*. Morgan & Claypool.

Tiedemann, J. (2012). *Parallel data, tools and interfaces in OPUS*. Proceedings of the 8th International Conference on Language Resources and Evaluation (LREC 2012). http://www.lrec-conf.org/proceedings/lrec2012/pdf/463_Paper.pdf

Tiedemann, J. (2016). OPUS—parallel corpora for everyone [Special issue]. *Baltic Journal of Modern Computing (BJMC)*, 4(2). Proceedings of the 19th Annual Conference of the European Association of Machine Translation (EAMT). https://www.bjmc.lu.lv/fileadmin/user_upload/lu_portal/projekti/bjmc/Contents/4_2_28_Products.pdf

Tóth, K., Farkas, R., & Kocsor, A. (2008). Sentence alignment of Hungarian–English parallel corpora using a hybrid algorithm. *Acta Cybern, 18*, 463–478.

Varga, D. (2012). *Natural language processing of large parallel corpora* [PhD dissertation, Eötvös Loránd University].

Varga, D., Halácsy, P., Kornai, A., Nagy, V., Németh, L., & Trón, V. (2005). *Parallel corpora for medium density languages*. Proceedings of the RANLP, pp. 590–596.

Volk, M., Graën, J., & Callegaro, E. (2014). *Innovations in parallel corpus search tools*. Proceedings LREC 2014 (Language Resources and Evaluation Conference), pp. 3172–3178.

Wetzel, D., & Bond, F. (2012). *Enriching parallel corpora for statistical machine translation with semantic negation rephrasing*. Proceedings of the Sixth Workshop on Syntax, Semantics and Structure in Statistical Translation, pp. 20–29.

Primary sources

[3007] Rowling, J.K. (2000). *Harry Potter and the Globet of Fire*. Bloomsbury Publishing. *Harry Potter y el cáliz de fuego*. Salamandra.

[3012] Peterson, J.B. (2018). *12 Rules for Life*. Allen Lane. *12 Reglas para Vivir*. Planeta.

[3101] Pérez Reverte, A. (2002). *La reina del sur*. Alfaguara. *The Queen of the South*. Picador.

[3132] Pen, P. (2011). *El aviso*. RBA Libros. *The Warning*. Amazon Crossing.

Carina Soledad González González (Universidad de La
Laguna, España)

Chapter IX   Gamification and immersive learning in AR/VR virtual learning environments

I. Introduction

Gamification has become a popular educational innovation strategy among thousands of teachers worldwide in recent years, with the goal of enhancing students' learning motivation (González, 2019; Kapp, 2012; Llorens et al., 2016). The game as a didactic strategy is one of the most used resources in teaching-learning processes since it constitutes the natural way of learning as a universal activity of human beings (Huizinga, 1955). In this sense, The primary goal of gamification is to enhance motivation by incorporating game characteristics into non-game environments, the best-known definition being "the use of game design elements in non-game contexts" (Deterding et al., 2011).

Gamification can be designed and implemented in a variety of teaching and learning environments, including digital or analog formats, virtual, face-to-face, or hybrid settings (González, 2019, 2022). We can then speak of plugged or unplugged gamification (González, 2019, 2022). Moreover, Gamification can be applied within the classroom, as well as outside of school through gamified reinforcement activities. Additionally, it can be combined with other innovative methodologies, such as the flipped classroom or blended learning (Akçayır & Akçayır, 2018).

The chapter outlines an educational experience that gamifies virtual environments using diverse tools and techniques, such as virtual reality and augmented reality, in higher education. Research has demonstrated that gamification is an effective strategy for motivating students, encouraging their active engagement within the various virtual environments utilized (Majuri et al., 2018). The conducted experience indicates that introducing gamification techniques into virtual environments is achievable (Tenório et al., 2017; Villagrasa et al., 2014). We have also used the narrative of video games of great success among students, such as Among Us, as the basis for one of the gamification activities, which was also developed in a virtual and augmented reality environment (González, 2020). In addition, this study showcases various gamification techniques that combine distinct virtual environments, along with the highly satisfactory outcomes in student motivation and academic performance.

II. Pedagogical design of the innovation experience

2.1. Objectives, competencies, and contents

The learning objectives of the innovation experience in the subject are the following, in addition to the objectives and competencies defined by the teaching guide of the subject:

- Apply ethical values in the design and creation of technology.
- To understand diversity and human limitations in the use of technology.
- Identify "dark" design patterns that generate addiction to technology.
- To know the professional opportunities of the "user experience" (UX) specialty from the hand of companies.

On the other hand, Table 1 describes the competencies described in the teaching guide of the subject "Human-Computer Interaction Systems" of the 3rd year of the Computer Engineering Degree at the University of La Laguna.

Table 1. Competencies of the Subject

Competencies	Description
Specific	C23—Ability to design and evaluate human-computer interfaces to ensure accessibility and usability of computer systems, services, and applications.
General	CG3—Ability to design, develop, evaluate and ensure the accessibility, ergonomics, usability, and security of computer systems, services, and applications and the information they manage.
Transversal	T1—Ability to act autonomously.
	T2—Have initiative and be decisive.
	T3—Have the initiative to contribute and evaluate alternative or novel solutions to problems, demonstrating flexibility and professionalism when considering different evaluation criteria.
	T4—Act in professional development with responsibility and professional ethics following current legislation.

Competencies	Description
	T5—Consider the economic and social context when engineering solutions, recognizing and valuing diversity and multiculturalism, and prioritizing sustainability and respect for human rights.
	T7—Ability to communicate orally and in writing effectively (in expression and comprehension), with particular emphasis on drafting technical documentation.
	T8—Ability to communicate effectively with users in non-technical language and to understand their needs.
	T9—Ability to argue and logically justify decisions and opinions.
	T10—Ability to integrate quickly, work efficiently in unidisciplinary teams, and collaborate in a multidisciplinary environment.
	T13—Ability to find, relate and structure information from diverse sources and to integrate ideas and knowledge.
	T15—Ability to make decisions based on objective criteria (available experimental, scientific, or simulation data).
	T19—Ability to adapt to organizational or technological changes.
	T20—Ability to work in situations lacking information and/or with time and/or resource constraints.
	T23—Ability to abstract: ability to create and use models that reflect real situations.
	T24—Ability to design and perform simple experiments and analyze and interpret their results.
	T25—Ability to analyze, synthesize and evaluate.

Source: Own elaboration.

The contents of the course in the first block have been organized weekly. They have been developed online: Introduction to Human-Computer Interaction, Human Factors, User-Centered Design, UX Methodologies, Information Architecture, Interaction Design, Design of Interactive Interfaces, and Methods and techniques for evaluation. All the topics developed in the didactic experience have used different technological tools, which are mentioned below:

- Interactive digital content (Genial.ly, H5P) (Figures 1 and 2).
- Virtual Classroom (Moodle)

- – Gamified quizzes (Quizizz) (Figure. 3)
- – Videoconference rooms (Google Meet)
- – Online questionnaires (Google Form)
- – Virtual reality and augmented reality rooms (Mozilla Hubs) (Figure 4)
- – Voice interaction devices (Alexa) (Figure 5)

Figure 1. Organization of the interactive content in Genial.ly.
Note: Source: Own elaboration.

Figure 2. Interactive videos in H5P.
Note: Source: Own elaboration.

Figure 3. Gamified quizzes in Quizizz.

Figure 4. Gamified rooms in RV and RA in Mozilla Hubs.

Note: Source: Own elaboration.

Figure 5. Questionnaire in Google Form about the game developed with Alexa.
Note: Source: Own elaboration.

2.1. Didactic methodology

The central teaching methodology used was the inverted classroom and gamification as an active learning strategy. Different learning activities have been carried out as follows: interactive video lectures, discussion groups (synchronous and asynchronous), problem-based learning, guided practical activities, self-assessment, and peer evaluation activities and lessons given by professionals in the sector.

For the development of the experience, the following gamification procedure was followed in the teaching-learning process (González & Mora, 2015; Moreira & González, 2015), as indicated below:

- *Step 1.* Analysis of users and context: To analyze our students, we conducted the first survey to get to know them, see the starting point, and understand their learning expectations about the subject.
- *Step 2.* Definition of learning objectives: We have defined the competencies and objectives for each activity to be performed in the subject and an evaluation section that allows students to know if they passed or failed the activity in question.
- *Step 3.* Design of the experience: The experience has been structured in a progressive and weekly sequence. The contents, in audiovisual format, have been progressively unlocked according to the time constraints of the activity

restrictions designed in the virtual classroom. The weekly problems and challenges could be carried out synchronously or asynchronously. In the online classes via videoconference, the main contents were reinforced, and active work dynamics were carried out, such as the division of the large class group into small discussion groups, with gamified quizzes and contests for peer evaluation of the solutions created by the students themselves.

- *Step 4.* Resource identification: The different activities and milestones that are gamified in the learning experience were identified, including a tracking mechanism, unit of measurement, rules, and feedback given by the teacher every week about the progress of the students in each activity.

The tracking mechanism included measuring student progress in learning through "karma" points that were updated and displayed in the virtual classroom through a leaderboard with different colors by score obtained through partial deliveries made by students in the periods established for each one and attendance to online classes via videoconference. A progress bar was also enabled in the virtual classroom where students could see their current progress in the subject. Different badges were given for the activities performed, which could be considered in the virtual classroom.

The unit of measurement to determine achievement was points (for activity performed and fulfillment of the continuous evaluation), the level for the amount of the unit of measure (points) needed to reach the karma level, and the rules about what students could do or not do to move up the level and get the points. The feedback given by the teacher every week about the progress of the students in each activity was also part of the resource identification.

Progreso Bloque 1

Figura 6. Progress bar in Moodle.
Note: Source: Own elaboration.

To elaborate on the leaderboard, it was considered:

a. Attendance to video classes: 40 % of the total (according to connection time, the first two classes are not considered because there is no connection data for the meet) and

b. Delivery of weekly problems, 60 % of the total.

The results will give four colors of karma: (1) Blue (you are doing very well, and your actions will be rewarded generously in the evaluation of Block 1); (2) Green (you are doing well, your actions will be awarded for the assessment of Block 1); (3) Yellow (you have not given your full potential, but you can improve, and your actions will be rewarded in the evaluation of Block 1) and (4). Red (you have not demonstrated your potential so far, you will not be rewarded in the evaluation of block 1)

- *Step 5* of the gamification procedure involved applying the gamification elements. The gamification mechanics were divided into individual elements, such as points, badges, and levels, and social elements, such as competition and collaboration. For example, a leaderboard was established based on the Karma level, individual scores were given for a Mockup contest, and a game based on Among Us was used where students competed in groups, and the rewards were given to the group.

2.3. Educational resources, tools materials

Different devices were used in the experience: computers, cell phones, tablets, virtual reality glasses, and voice assistants (Alexa). Also, video lessons were used (recorded in OBS, edited in Shotcut, and/or Camtasia). The video lessons were organized in Genial.ly. Interactive videos were created in H5P. Gamification of the Moodle virtual classroom was performed using badge management, a progress bar, and a weekly scoreboard (Karma). For the video classes, Google Meet was used as videoconferencing software. Discussion group dynamics were conducted, with room division in Google Meet for collaboration, as well as gamified dynamics of discussion groups and competition based on the Among US game in Virtual and Augmented Reality rooms in Mozilla Hubs, where there were randomly chosen "impostors" and "crew members" in each group. Games were played in videoconference classes introducing Alexa as a voice device (related to one of the practices of the subject). Gamified quizzes were used using Quizizz. Contests were held with voting by the students themselves, according to criteria previously established by the teacher, to evaluate the best designs (related to another of the practices of the subject).

SISTEMAS DE INTERACCIÓN PERSONA-COMPUTADOR: Insignias

Número de insignias disponibles: 10

Imagen	Nombre ^	Descripción
	WINNER MOCKUP	Ganadora Concurso MOCKUPS
	WINNER AMONG UX	WINNER AMONG UX
	UX Research	Insignia otorgada por cumplimentar el cuestionario final obligatorio
	UX Engineer	Insignia que se obtiene al realizar el ejercicio sobre Metodologías UX
	UX Designer	Insignia otorgada al completar el ejercicio sobre DCU
	UX_Beginner	Insignia que se obtiene por realizar el ejercicio de modelos mentales (buenos y malos diseños en el foro)
	UI Designer	Insignia que se obtiene al realizar el ejercicio de Diseño de Interfaces Interactivas
	Interaction Designer	Insignia que se obtiene al realizar el ejercicio sobre Diseño de la Interacción
	Information Architect	Insignia que se obtiene al realizar el ejercicio sobre Arquitectura de la Información
	Human Factors Designer	Insignia que se obtiene al completar el ejercicio (foro) sobre Factores Humanos

Figure 7. Badges in Moodle.

Note: Source: Own elaboration.

On the other hand, different Digital Didactic materials of own creation have been made, such as video lessons, games, and virtual and augmented reality rooms in Mozilla Hubs, Gamified quizzes in Quizz, interactive videos in H5P, presentations in Google Presentations (36 in total). There has also been a Mock-ups contest, in 3 different categories, with more than 200 interfaces, organized in Google Photos for viewing and voting. A video playlist has been created on YouTube (36 videos).

In addition, the gamified instructional design of the virtual classroom stands out, with the management of badges, progress bars, weekly Karma score rankings, online attendance tracking, questionnaires developed for contests, and the design of educational games, among other different resources developed during this semester.

2.4. Evaluation of the experience

In order to assess the success of the educational experience, an initial survey was conducted to gather information about the students' knowledge of the subject matter, their career prospects, and their expectations. The survey yielded 106 responses, and the sample was composed of students of various ages, with 49.5 % of respondents being 20 years old, 23.3 % being 21 years old, 8.7 % being 23 years old, 6.8 % being 19 years old, and the remaining 6.8 % being over 24 years old. As for sex, 80 % were male, 18.1 % were female, and 1.9 % preferred not to answer this question. Only two persons were repeaters. 61.3 % thought they had very little or little knowledge of the subject, 29.2 % thought they had some prior knowledge, and 9.4 % felt they had a high understanding of the subject. 56.6 % were completely unaware of the professional opportunities of the subject's specialty, while 40.4 % thought they knew about the professional opportunities. A total of 85.8 % of the students recognize that they have changed their study habits due to COVID-19. Regarding learning expectations, asked in a non-binding open question, the students mainly commented that they expected to learn to design better interfaces, new forms of interaction, new forms of communication, and learning technologies. However, some students limited themselves to saying that they wanted to learn what they needed to "pass" the subject.

As an evaluation procedure, there was continuous monitoring of the student's learning progress and performance; rubrics were developed for each activity performed, weekly feedback was given on each problem/challenge posed, selecting the best practices and providing recommendations for improvement. In addition to the teacher's evaluation, self-evaluation and peer evaluation activities were developed. Based on the progress made by the students, it appears that they were highly engaged with the subject. Their weekly activity scores were very positive and their attendance to online classes remained high throughout the eight-week course, with 80 to 95 students connecting per session and 106 active students submitting to the forums each week. Of these 106 active students, 83 (78.3 %) have achieved blue karma, indicating that they are performing very well on the subject with daily assignments. Additionally, 10 students (9.4 %) are doing well, 8 are regular (7.5 %), and only 5 (4.7 %) have not been following the topic daily.

Furthermore, a partial evaluation of the subject was conducted, which included a questionnaire completed by 104 students. In the first attempt, the average success rate was 75 %, which demonstrates that the students learned the subject contents. Moreover, professionals from companies in the sector have interacted with our students outside the institution and have seen how they apply and work the skills that companies need.

At the end of Block 1, the degree of motivation with the topics of Block 1 was also evaluated, which is 83.4 % was high (36.7 %) or very high (46.7 %) and average (16.7 %). Ninety percent of the students rated their learning of the topics as high (26.7 %) or very high (70 %). 96.7 % rated the quality of the resources and content as high or very high. And 99 % rated their degree of satisfaction with the teacher as very high (90 %) or high (6.7 %). They were also asked what they liked most in an open-ended question and responded that they mainly wanted the dynamics and interactivity of the classes, the proximity of the teacher, the availability of the materials, the gamification and fun, the adequate amount of content and weekly tasks, the talks by external professionals and the video lessons. Regarding what they liked the least, they mainly felt that some activities or topics were more complicated than others or that some tools were too demanding for their connectivity and ordering capacity (Genial.ly or Mozilla Hubs). And as suggestions for improvement, they reinforced the idea that the course was well-designed for blended learning.

III. Conclusions

This work has presented a gamified didactic experience in virtual learning environments using different innovative technological tools, such as H5P, Genially. ly, Google Meet, Google Photos, gamified quizzes in Quizz, gamified rooms in virtual and augmented reality in Mozilla Hubs. In addition, the gamification of the Moodle virtual classroom has been carried out using the elements available in the platform, such as the progress bar, badges (automatic and manual), leaderboards, karma levels, surprise unlockable features, conditional activities, automatic feedback planned in forums depending on the activity performed and delivery dates, etc.

Taking into account the learning results obtained by the students in the evaluation as well as the motivation and the logs analyzed in the platform, which show a high engagement in the planned activities, we can confirm that gamification is a very effective educational strategy for the dynamization of virtual learning environments and combined with the inverted classroom allows increasing interactivity and student learning.

References

Akçayır, G., & AkAkçayçayır, M. (2018). The flipped classroom: A review of its advantages and challenges. *Computers & Education, 126*, 334–345.

Deterding, S., Dixon, D., Khaled, R., & Nacke, L. (2011, September). *From game design elements to gamefulness: Defining "gamification."* Proceedings of the 15th International Academic MindTrek Conference: Envisioning Future Media Environments, pp. 9–15.

González, C. (2019). Gamificación en el aula: ludificando espacios de enseñanza-aprendizaje presenciales y espacios virtuales. *Researchgate.net*, pp. 1–22.

González, C., & Mora, A. (2015). Técnicas de gamificación aplicadas en la docencia de Ingeniería Informática. *ReVisión, 8*(1), 25–40.

González González, C.S. (2020, December). A case of gamification in virtual environments with RV/RA. In *2020 X International Conference on Virtual Campus (JICV)* (pp. 1–3). IEEE.

González González, C.S. (2022). *Unplugged gamification: Towards a definition.* Proceedings of the 10th Technological Ecosystems for Enhancing Multiculturality (TEEM), Salamanca, Spain.

Huizinga, J. (1955). *Homo Ludens: A study of the play-element in culture.* Beacon Press.

Kapp, K. (2012) *The gamification of learning and instruction: Game-based methods and strategies for training and education.* Pfeiffer.

Llorens-Largo, F., Gallego-Durán, F.J., Villagrá-Arnedo, C.J., Compañ-Rosique, P., Satorre-Cuerda, R., & Molina-Carmona, R. (2016). Gamification of the learning process: Lessons learned. *IEEE Revista Iberoamericana de tecnologías del aprendizaje, 11*(4), 227–234.

Majuri, J., Koivisto, J., & Hamari, J. (2018). Gamification of education and learning: A review of empirical literature. In *Proceedings of the 2nd international GamiFIN conference, GamiFIN 2018.* CEUR-WS.

Moreira, M.A., & González, C.S.G. (2015). De la enseñanza con libros de texto al aprendizaje en espacios online gamificados. *Educatio Siglo XXI, 33*(3 Noviembr), 15–38.

Tenório, M.M., Reinaldo, F.A.F., Góis, L.A., Lopes, R.P., & Santos Junior, G.D. (2017, September). Elements of gamification in virtual learning environments. In *International conference on interactive collaborative learning* (pp. 86–96). Springer.

Villagrasa, S., Fonseca, D., Redondo, E., & Duran, J. (2014). Teaching case of gamification and visual technologies for education. *Journal of Cases on Information Technology (JCIT), 16*(4), 38–57.

Flávio Costa and Carlos Vaz de Carvalho (GILT R&D,
Instituto Superior de Engenharia do Porto, Porto, Portugal)

Chapter X   Promoting higher education through games

I. Introduction

Digital games, defined by Dörner et al. (2016) as "games that use some kind of computing equipment," have contributed to the exponential growth of the entertainment industry. Beyond entertainment, they have been shown to develop a variety of personal and social skills and competencies (Wiemeyer & Hardy, 2013). So, serious games, according to Corti (2006), "leverage the power of computer games to captivate and engage end-users for a specific purpose, such as to develop new knowledge and skills." Zyda (2005) describes serious games as "a mental contest, played with a computer in accordance with specific rules that uses entertainment to further government or corporate training, education, health, public policy, and strategic communication objectives." Dörner et al. (2016) also refer to serious games as "digital games created with the intention to entertain and to achieve at least one additional goal (e.g., learning or health)." While serious games are most commonly used in education and training (also known as educational games or game-based learning/training), they can also serve other purposes, as detailed by Sawyer and Smith's (2008) taxonomy.

This study focuses on advergames, the application of games for marketing, advertising, and communication purposes. As digital games have evolved into a media channel, companies have recognized their potential to promote their brands and products. Consequently, game developers have begun to incorporate product and brand references into game contexts and even design games entirely around specific products or brands.

II. Advergames

The classification of advertising in games is based on its dynamic nature and impact on gameplay. Static advertising refers to the elements in the game that cannot be edited later and can be used for single-player games or to ensure long-term brand advertising deals (Terlutter & Capella, 2013). Dynamic advertising, on the other hand, offers flexibility in changing the brands and products displayed in the games and is beneficial for games like Fortnite (2017) that require an Internet connection (Skinner, 2020).

In-game advertising involves the insertion of brands, products, or ideas into a game, and product and brand placements create a more realistic game environment (Skinner, 2020). The placement of items that contain brand images to boost the player's character or progress through a game's story has a more significant influence on the player's perception of the product and brand (Terlutter & Capella, 2013). This type of placement makes the player aware of the purpose of the product and can associate feelings of usefulness and practicality with the brand, leading to a more favorable perception outside of the game.

Mobile games, in particular, use advertising videos to allow players to earn in-game benefits, with advertising in mobile apps becoming increasingly popular (Leontiadis et al., 2012; Gui, 2017). Small developers can use mobile ad networks such as Google Mobile Ads and Apple iAD instead of making financial deals with advertising companies.

Fully branded games, also known as standalone advergames, are developed entirely around the brand or product being advertised. They are intended to promote services or ideas and are usually short and easy to play, downloadable for free, and made available by the brand itself (Terlutter & Capella, 2013). The majority of standalone advergames are related to food and drinks, and they tend to gravitate toward genres that make their brands seem more exciting and thrilling (plinq, 2019).

2.1. Exemplary cases

This section provides exemplary cases of fully branded games, with details about their features, gameplay, and relevance to the project. The first example is Tapper, an arcade game from 1983 developed by Marvin Glass and Associates and sponsored by Anheuser-Busch. Players act as a bartender serving Budweiser tap beer to customers. Tapper received good reviews, with over 3,300 arcade machines sold, and Compute!'s Gazette describing it as a "well-designed strategy game." The game includes the Budweiser logo in the background, on the taps, and the mugs, creating an association between the brand and the concept of beer (Keizer, 1985; plinq, 2019).

Another example is Cool Spot, a 1993 game developed by Virgin Games and sponsored by 7up for the Sega Mega Drive and the Super Nintendo Entertainment System. Players control Cool Spot, the 7up mascot, through 11 platforming levels to find a caged ally and release them. The game focuses on coolness, with the playable character being portrayed as cool by surfing on top of a 7up bottle.

The game aims to associate the concept of coolness with the 7Up brand, as cool brands are often associated with being extraordinary, energetic, rebellious, and popular (Jenkin et al., 2014; Warren, et al., 2019).

America's Army is a 2002 tactical first-person shooter game developed and published by the United States Army and released for free. The game features accurate depictions of the United States military training grounds, practices, and values, providing players with an immersive experience. Players take part in training courses and military missions, with the game serving as a recruitment tool for the US Army. The game was well received, and players appreciated the realism and features such as being able to lean around corners and automatically switching out of the weapon's zoom mode when changing stances (Osborne, 2002) (Kennedy, 2002) (GamePolitics, 2009).

Lastly, Magnum Pleasure Hunt is a 2011 web-based game developed by the Lowe Brindfors Stockholm marketing agency and sponsored by Unilever. In the game, players control a "pleasure hunter" who seeks the ultimate Magnum pleasure, collecting Magnum bonbons to increase their score while navigating depictions of popular brand websites. Magnum Pleasure Hunt was successfully spread across social media, with over 725,000 unique visits in just five days, making it the most tweeted website in the world on April 14, 2011 (MindJumpers, 2011; MullenLowe Group, 2013).

III. ISEP game concept

This project proposes the development of an advergame for ISEP—Instituto Superior de Engenharia do Porto, a higher education institution. An advergame was chosen as the promotional method because it offered several advantages over traditional methods like open days, printed material or even websites. It was a more effective way to target the intended audience, could be used repeatedly, and could reach students through the Internet.

The primary goals of this project were to recruit more and better students at a lower cost by showcasing the higher education experience at ISEP and to create a distinct image for the institution that emphasizes its scientific and technological capabilities. The advergame also addresses a list of obstacles that are preventing the organization from achieving its objectives, such as the high cost of recruiting new students, the lack of student motivation to join ISEP due to the reputation of other similar institutions, and the difficulty of reaching students in person.

3.1. Game genre definition

Game genres are used to categorize games and provide players with a general idea of what type of game they are playing based on the available mechanics (Apperley, 2006; Drachen, et al., 2013). Existing advergames have shown that taking a more literal approach to advertising a product is not always the best strategy, and that detaching the product presentation from its real-world environment can be more effective in motivating players during gameplay. Therefore, it is important to select a game genre that is suitable for the product, client, or concept being advertised. Although some studies have investigated the correlation between game genres and serious objectives (Baptista et al., 2015), this process is highly individualized and depends on the specific brand or product and target audience. As a result, a significant portion of the study was focused on identifying the optimal game genre and how to align the key brand concepts with the game mechanics and elements.

The Analytic Hierarchy Process (AHP) was employed in this project to select the game genre, as it provides "an organised way to make decisions and collect information relevant to them" (Saaty, 2008). AHP was selected for its ability to compare the importance of criteria being analyzed, as well as the importance of each alternative when associated with each criterion. To ensure the consistency of the judgments made during the evaluation process, a consistency ratio is calculated. The consistency ratio is obtained by comparing the consistency index with a random index, which is expressed in the following equation:

$$CR = \frac{CI}{RI}$$

CR is the consistency ratio,
CI is the consistency index,
RI is a random index.
The consistency index is calculated as follows:

$$CI = \frac{\lambda max - n}{n - 1}$$

λ_{max} is the highest eigenvalue of the matrix, and n corresponds to the size of the matrix. The random index is extracted from studies of large populations of matrixes (see Table 1).

Table 1. Relation between Size of a Matrix (n) and RI (Saaty, 1987)

n	1	2	3	4	5	6	7	8	9	10
RI	0.00	0.00	0.58	0.90	1.12	1.24	1.32	1.41	1.45	1.49

If the resulting consistency ratio is over 0.1, it can be considered that the comparisons were paired randomly, thus making the results inconsistent. Once all pairing matrixes have been tested for consistency, the weight of every alternative for each criterion is inserted into a matrix, and then multiplied by the weight of criteria, resulting in a value that represents how ideal the alternative is. The alternative with the highest value becomes the solution.

For our study, we selected five criteria for analysis, namely realism, challenge, narrative, interaction, and management:

- Realism was considered crucial as ISEP desires the game to be an authentic portrayal of what it's like to be a part of the institution, implying that there must be a direct correlation between the elements in the game and their real-life counterparts.
- Challenge was included to depict the obstacles a student experiences in a higher education degree, such as exams, projects, presentations, etc.
- Narrative reflects the story-driven nature of a game, which should have a storyline that players can follow from beginning to end, similar to a student's journey in ISEP that has a start and end.
- Interaction in games has diverse implications, but in this context, it refers to the amount of feedback and engagement the game provides to the player. Some games present challenges to the player, while others allow them to explore their surroundings without any hindrance. Although this criterion is essential, it is not as representative of ISEP as realism and challenge, which share the same level of importance as narrative.
- Lastly, management pertains to the way players assess their options and make decisions accordingly. In the context of ISEP, students must manage their time, energy, and classes in a way that benefits them, leading to positive academic results but also causing stress.

Given the importance of each criterion, a pairwise comparison matrix was created and it was possible to estimate the weight of each of the criteria by normalizing the matrix (Table 2 where R stands for realism, C for challenge, N for narrative, I for interaction, and M stands for management). Realism and

challenge were the most important criteria, with a weight of 34.24 %, while management featured the lowest importance, at 5.57 %.

Table 2. Normalized Criteria Matrix

	R	C	N	I	M	Weight
R	0.3488	0.3488	0.3600	0.3600	0.2941	0.3424
C	0.3488	0.3488	0.3600	0.3600	0.2941	0.3424
N	0.1163	0.1163	0.1200	0.1200	0.1765	0.1298
I	0.1163	0.1163	0.1200	0.1200	0.1765	0.1298
M	0.0698	0.0698	0.0400	0.0400	0.0588	0.0557

The game genres used in this process are simulation, strategy, role-playing,
platformer, and arcade, based on the most frequent advergame cases (Drachen
et al., 2013; Apperley, 2006). While there may be creative approaches to developing the ISEP advergame through other genres like beat'em up, fitness, or music
games, these are likely to be inferior to the chosen alternatives. It should be noted
that these genres are not mutually exclusive, and combining them may be an
option if the results obtained from applying the AHP returned high values for
multiple genres.

Simulation games accurately depict an aspect of life or fiction, such as driving
or managing a business, and are considered the most realistic genre. Strategy and
role-playing games can be played in fantasy worlds, but their mechanics work
in realistic environments as well, making them equally realistic but less so than
simulation games. Platformers and arcade games can be detached from real-life
concepts and rules, making them the least realistic, although they are not entirely unrealistic.

The challenge can vary between games of the same genre, with certain genres
intrinsically more difficult than others. Platformers contain several hazards
around their environment, making them more challenging than arcade games,
which feature simple controls. Strategy games require players to create plans and
execute them, offering a level of challenge that rivals that of arcade games. Role-
playing and simulation games do not focus on challenge but rather on story and
intuitive mechanics, respectively.

Lastly, simulation and strategy games possess the most potential in terms of
management. Simulation games include management games that show how to

run businesses, while strategy games motivate players to make the best use of their resources to solve puzzles and fight battles. Platformers and role-playing games also require management but in different ways, such as managing space and upgrading skills, respectively. Arcade games possess fewer resources, but management is still essential.

To compare the relative impact of the criteria for a specific game genre, a table was created for each criterion. For instance, Table 3 compares the alternatives in terms of management (SIM for simulation, STR for strategy, RPG for role-playing games, ACT for action, ARC for arcade, and PLT for platformers).

Table 3. Management Pairwise Comparison

	SIM	STR	RPG	ARC	PLT
SIM	1	1	3	5	3
STR	1	1	3	5	3
RPG	1/3	1/3	1	3	1
ARC	1/5	1/5	1/3	1	1/3
PLT	1/3	1/3	1	3	1

After constructing the matrix for pairwise comparison among all the options, the significance of each genre with respect to every criterion was determined. The resulting table, Table 4, displays an overall matrix of these weights. It demonstrates that simulation, platforming, and role-playing games hold considerable importance in terms of realism, challenge, narrative, and management.

Table 4. Global Weight Matrix

	R	C	N	I	M
SIM	0.4624	0.0737	0.0436	0.1075	0.3424
STR	0.1952	0.1952	0.2017	0.2805	0.3424
RPG	0.1952	0.0737	0.4641	0.0509	0.1298
ARC	0.0737	0.1952	0.0888	0.2805	0.0557
PLT	0.0737	0.4624	0.2017	0.2805	0.1298

The importance of these values is weighted by associating with each criteria (Table 5).

The final significance of each option was determined by adding the products of their weights in relation to a particular criterion and the weight of that criterion itself. For example, the importance of simulation games to the project was determined by multiplying its weight of 0.4624 on the realism criterion with the weight of realism, which is 0.3424 in comparison to other criteria. This calculation was carried out for each criterion and then summed up, resulting in a value of 0.2222 for simulation games. The same approach was used for other alternatives, as depicted in Table 6, which shows the weight of each game genre for the project.

Table 5. Weight of Each Criterion

	R	C	N	I	M
Weight	0.3424	0.3424	0.1298	0.1298	0.0557

Table 6. Resulting Weight of Each Game Genre

	SIM	STR	RPG	ARC	PLT
Weight	0.2222	0.2153	0.1661	0.1431	0.2533

Based on the results, it can be inferred that the platformer game genre is the most significant for this project since it received the highest score. Nonetheless, it is worth noting that simulation and strategy games also obtained high values, 0.2222 and 0.2153 respectively. This suggests that the game should still incorporate elements that are characteristic of simulation and strategy games, such as realism, problem-solving, and management. Furthermore, while the narrative of role-playing games and the simplicity of arcade games may still be valuable features, they should not be prioritized over the aforementioned game elements. One way to implement these concepts would be to introduce resources that the player must manage, in place of the typical health bar or hit points found in platformers. For example, the player might need to keep track of time, stamina, knowledge, and stress to progress through a level. Table 6 provides the weights for each game genre in this project.

3.2. Level design

The game is structured as a series of levels, each of which represents a project that the player must complete. These projects can take the form of class assignments, exams, or research projects. During each level, the player must fight enemies that represent tasks they must perform and interact with various facilities, such as teachers and research groups, to gain benefits at the cost of time. For example, facilities and teachers in the first level increase the player's speed, while those in the second and third levels increase the number of platforms and decrease enemy speed, respectively.

To progress through the levels, the player must manage their resources, such as stress, stamina, and knowledge. Each of these elements is associated with one or more of ISEP's values, such as course diversity, resource availability, connection to industry, and teaching quality. For instance, each level is themed around a different engineering field, showcasing ISEP's course diversity. The buildings and facilities present in the levels, such as research groups and the library, increase the player's knowledge, while facilities like ISEP|GO and aeISEP decrease the player's stress. Labs present in the levels showcase ISEP's connection to the industry.

To cater to the game's target audience of high school graduates with varying levels of gaming experience, the difficulty of the game gradually increases as the player progresses through the levels. Design decisions were made to ensure that the game is enjoyable and engaging for this audience.

3.2.1. Level example

The initial level serves as a benchmark for the game's difficulty. If a player struggles with the first level, they may lose interest in the game since it will likely become progressively more challenging. Figure 1 illustrates the start of the level, where the player is introduced to basic movement mechanics.

The level layout incorporates instructions, allowing players to read them at their own pace without any additional inputs or interruptions from menus or dialog boxes. Through these instructions, players are introduced to the stress mechanic and its purpose, as well as the timer and stamina concepts. Players must perform a series of small jumps to cross a pit, providing further opportunities to demonstrate the effects of stress. The game also progressively introduces concepts such as risk and reward and resource management in a similar manner. It is crucial to establish the game's mechanics and difficulty level early on in the first level, as it sets the tone for the rest of the game and can impact player motivation to continue playing. Figure 1 illustrates the start of the level.

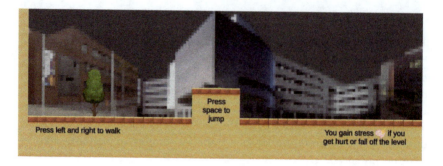

Figure 1. Start of the first level.

IV. Results

Conducting pilot testing and gathering feedback from players through question-naires can provide valuable insights to developers regarding the game's features and areas that require improvement (Thabane et al., 2010; van Teijlingen & Hun-dley, 2001). To evaluate the feasibility of the created methods and procedures, a pilot testing session was conducted near the end of the project, using online sessions due to the pandemic. In each session, participants were asked to com-plete the first three levels of the game and then respond to three questionnaires, namely the System Usability Scale survey, the Game Experience Questionnaire, and a set of questions on the game's impact as an advergame. The aim was to first obtain a report of the participants' experience, followed by their personal evaluation of the game's impact. The testing sessions were conducted between September 24 and October 2, 2021, with a total of 19 participants from the target demographic group.

The majority of participants (68.4 %) reported having five or more years of experience playing digital games, while only four participants reported having no experience with digital games. In the next question, participants were asked about their typical level of involvement in gaming (see Figure 3) and shows a quite balanced distribution between all the levels.

The results displayed in Figure 4 depict the number of participants who had prior knowledge of serious games (left side of the figure) and advergames (right side of the figure) before their involvement in this project.

Upon reviewing the charts, it becomes apparent that the responses vary by only one participant, indicating that there may be a correlation between knowledge of serious games and advergames. It appears that the majority of participants had

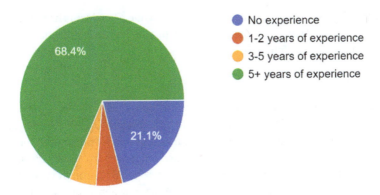

Figure 2. Participant previous gaming experience.

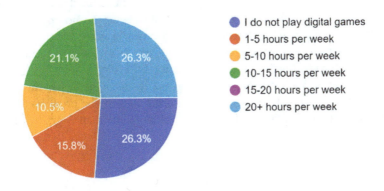

Figure 3. Participant usual gaming practice.

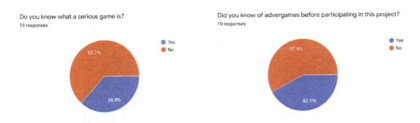

Figure 4. Participant knowledge of serious games and advergames.

no familiarity with either concept. In summary, while participants had extensive experience playing games, they seemed to be unaware of their potential benefits for non-entertainment purposes.

4.1. Usability

Essentially, digital games are software applications, which is why it's important to evaluate their usability. To assess usability, the System Usability Scale (SUS) was created by John Brooke in 1986. This questionnaire is widely used for subjective end-of-test assessments of usability and comprises ten survey questions. The answer scale ranges from 1 ("Strongly disagree") to 5 ("Strongly agree"). The list of questions was designed so that odd-numbered items represent positive effects, while even-numbered items represent negative experiences. To calculate the score, 1 must be subtracted from user responses for odd-numbered items, and user responses to even-numbered questions must be subtracted from 5. The final score of each question ranges from 0 to 4, with 4 being the most positive answer. To obtain the overall SUS score, the results must be added and then multiplied by 2.5, which yields a scale from 0 to 100. This result must then be adjusted according to the identified commonly obtained results (Fig 5).

The average SUS score is 68, which suggests that scoring higher than this in a SUS test means that the system outperforms 50 % of the products tested. Additionally, a score of 80.3 or higher is required to attain an A grade, which

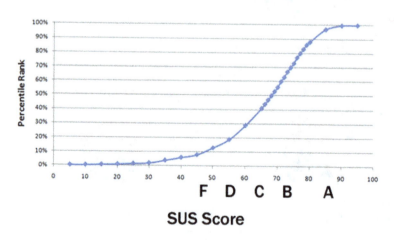

Figure 5. SUS scores associated with percentile ranks and letter grades (Sauro, 2011).

represents the top 10 % of scores. Conversely, an F indicates that a product ranks in the bottom 15 % of scores, with a SUS score below 51.

The overall SUS score for the ISEP advergame was 86.18, with a standard deviation of 10.22, placing this project in the top 10 % of scores. This clearly reflects the positive experience of the users with the game.

4.2. Game experience

The Game Experience Questionnaire (GEQ), developed by IJsselsteijn, Kort, and Poels, is a collection of surveys that can be employed at various stages of a game testing session. Despite some studies that have questioned the GEQ's validity (Law et al., 2018) and others that have highlighted the need for modifications when evaluating games designed to evoke negative emotions, such as survival horror games (Norman, 2013), the questionnaire was employed in this study because it had been previously assessed in a variety of research settings (Johnson et al., 2018) and was the International Communications Union's standardized recommendation for evaluating gaming quality (Schmidt et al., 2018).

Each survey has scoring guidelines that evaluate different aspects of the game, such as competence, sensory and imaginative immersion, flow, tension/annoyance, challenge, negative affect, and positive affect (IJsselsteijn et al., 2013). The response values range from 0 ("Not at all") to 4 ("Extremely"), which are then used to calculate the score for each component.

In this study, the Core and Post-game Module surveys of GEQ were used. Table 7 displays the outcomes of the Core Module survey, revealing that competence and positive affect scored the highest among the positive components, while immersion and flow rated the lowest. Although these values are above average, they indicate that the game could be more immersive. Immersion is a crucial characteristic for advergames since it allows users to feel as if they are the character using the product or brand in question.

Table 7. Results of the GEQ Core Module

Variable	Mean	Standard deviation
Competence	3	0.9
Sensory and imaginative immersion	2.7	0.7
Flow	2.7	0.7
Tension/annoyance	0.9	1

Variable	Mean	Standard deviation
Challenge	1.7	0.5
Negative affect	0.7	0.7
Positive affect	3.3	0.7

The player's experience was enjoyable, as indicated by the low ratings for negative components such as tension/annoyance and negative affect. However, the challenge component received a slightly below-average rating, suggesting that the game was less challenging than expected.

Table 8 presents the results of the Post-game Module, which show an average result for the positive experience component. This indicates that although the game was enjoyable during gameplay, it did not leave a lasting impact on the players. While this aligns with the goal of the advergame to have a subconscious effect, it is important to consider. The other results are consistent with those of the Core Module, with low ratings for tiredness and negative experience, and a low value for the reality variable indicating a lack of immersion.

Table 8. Results of the GEQ Post-game Module

Variable	Mean	Standard deviation
Positive experience	2.3	0.9
Negative experience	0.4	0.5
Tiredness	0.2	0.4
Returning to reality	1	0.6

The results of the GEQ were highly positive, reflecting the enjoyable experience of the users but still revealing some improvements to be made in the immersion, challenge and lasting effects.

4.3. Game impact

To assess the marketing impact of the proposed advergame, a brief questionnaire was developed following established guidelines (Williams, 2003). The questionnaire used a 1–5 scale for responses and gathered information on the players' perspectives toward digital games, serious games, and advergames. The

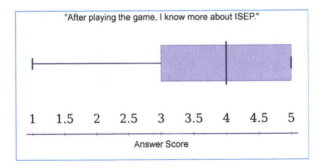

Figure 6. Answers to the "I know more about ISEP question."

19 responses collected from the questionnaire were plotted and analyzed as can be seen in the following figures.

The plot reveals a wide range of answers with a higher prevalence toward the higher values, with 75 % of responses having a score of 3 or above, 50 % scoring 4 or above, and 25 % achieving the highest score. The mean value of approximately 3.94 and standard deviation of approximately 1.10 suggest that most participants learned more about ISEP through the game and feel confident in this assertion. These results are highly encouraging as they indicate that the advergame was successful in promoting ISEP's image to the participants. The second question was also plotted using the same technique, as depicted in Figure 7.

The box plot depicted in this figure displays the range of scores for the third question, which spans from 3 to 5. The majority of responses (75 %) received a score of 4 or higher, with half of the participants giving the maximum score.

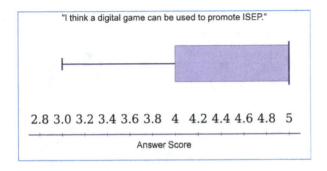

Figure 7. Answers to "A digital game can be used to promote ISEP" question.

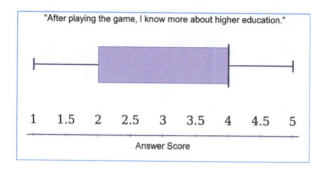

Figure 8. Answers to the "I know more about higher education" Question.

The mean value of the data is around 4.47, while the standard deviation is approximately 0.68. These results demonstrate a high level of agreement among the participants regarding the potential of digital games in promoting ISEP, or any other higher education institution for that matter. This indicates that there is ample room for digital games to play a role in the promotion of ISEP.

The plotted data in Figure 9 displays a range of responses, with 75 % of answers scoring 3 or higher, and 50 % scoring at least 4. The mean value of approximately 3.63 and standard deviation of approximately 1.16 indicate that participants generally agreed that the advergame helped them better understand ISEP's facilities, courses, and resources. However, there were some lower scores, possibly due to the limited scope of the game's content outside of ISEP. This further emphasizes the importance of designing an advergame that is tailored to the specific brand or institution being promoted.

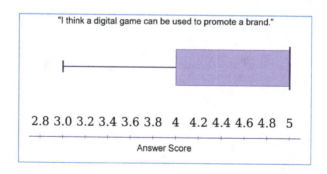

Figure 9. Answers to "A Digital game can be used to promote a brand" question.

The box plot for the fourth question is similar to the one for the second question, with answers ranging from 3 to 5. The plot indicates that 75 % of the answers scored at least 4, and 50 % achieved a score of 5. However, the mean and standard deviation for this question are slightly different, with a mean of approximately 4.53 and a standard deviation of approximately 0.68. Like the results for question 2, these results suggest that all participants agreed with the statement, indicating that advergames have the potential to be successful and that there is room for such projects in the gaming industry.

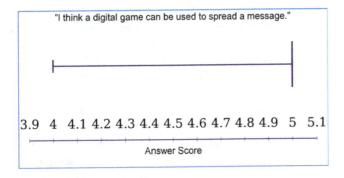

Figure 10. Answers to "A digital game can be used to deliver a message" question.

The chart presented in Figure 10 appears unique due to the significant concentration of answers with a score of 5. The majority of the defining features of the box plot, such as the first quartile, median, and third quartile, are situated at the highest value on the scale, indicating that 75 % of users gave their answer the maximum score. These results demonstrate the overwhelmingly positive response that participants have toward the effectiveness of digital games in conveying messages. Out of all the participants, only 25 % answered with a score of 4, while the remainder gave a score of 5. The mean for this data is approximately 4.84, with a standard deviation of around 0.36, further supporting the consensus among participants that digital games can be a potent tool for promoting brands and spreading messages. Overall, the questionnaire responses indicate that this game was successful in promoting ISEP, and that digital games have significant potential as a medium for spreading messages.

194 Costa and Vaz de Carvalho

4.4. Game analytics

The user experience can be analyzed through game analytics, which involves discovering and communicating patterns in data to solve business problems or make predictions (Drachen et al., 2013). This project utilized game telemetry, which involves collecting data remotely without direct player contact. Attributes associated with objects in the game, such as characters, enemies, and items, are measured and analyzed. These attributes can include distance traveled, number of deaths, damage dealt, items obtained and used, and more. Game developers can use this data to understand how players interact with the game, which parts they struggle with, and which elements of the game enhance or worsen the user experience.

For platformer games like the one analyzed in this project, gameplay metrics such as progression speed, areas interacted with, damage taken, and sources of damage are important. These metrics can provide insight into the player's playstyle, which sections of the game are problematic, and which resources the player manages effectively.

The Damage Taken event tracked all sources of damage and the amount of damage taken, providing information on which parts of the game were the most challenging for players. Over 50 sources of damage were analyzed, with a focus on the most significant ones for improving the player experience (Drachen et al., 2013).

Table 9. Most Common Sources of Damage

Damage Source	Enemy1.1	Enemy 3.2	Enemy 3.1	Death-Zone1.3	Enemy3.3
Amount of Damage Inflicted	36	24	19	18	18

This table reveals that the primary source of damage for players was enemy1.1, the initial enemy that players encounter upon starting the game. While this is to be expected, as all players are required to face this enemy and fail the level at least once, it also suggests that players may not have fully grasped the game's movement mechanics by the time they encountered this enemy. To address this issue, the game should feature a larger initial area without enemies, complete with stairs and platforms that allow players to practice moving and jumping without the threat of falling into a death zone or taking damage from enemies.

The third level begins with a sequence of jumps that feature enemies 3.1 and 3.2 on the players' landing platform. While this was intended to encourage players to learn the charging enemies' patterns, it may have created an environment that was too hostile for the beginning of a level. Finally, it is worth noting that players took damage a total of 373 times. With 50 hazards present in the game, this means that players averaged 7.46 damage per hazard. This figure is much higher than the optimal value of 2, indicating that enemies should have been placed in more controlled environments and separated from each other.

The Interacted Building events track which buildings and teachers players interacted with during the game. This section will focus on the buildings that were least interacted with, as understanding why players avoided them can provide valuable insights into design flaws. Table 10 displays this list.

Table 10. Facilities that Were Least Interacted with

Facility	Level 3 Office	Level 2 Office	Level 1 Office	Level 3 aeISEP	Level 2 ISEP|GO
Number of times interacted	3	9	11	12	13

This table illustrates that the teacher's offices situated at the end of each level were rarely used by players. When players possess enough knowledge to complete the level, they may choose to skip the facility to save time. The other two buildings, aeISEP and ISEP|GO, also had low interaction rates as they serve as stress-reducing facilities that players may not need if they have already managed their stress levels well. These findings indicate that players have a good understanding of the resources available and their benefits. However, since these facilities are located at the end of each level, players may not interact with them as frequently. Nonetheless, the disparity in usage between these facilities and the others supports the previous theories.

The Player Data and Game Over events function similarly by recording data on the player's resource management. The Player Data event is triggered when a player completes a level, whereas the Game Over event is triggered when a player fails a level. Despite their different triggers, both events capture similar attributes. By analyzing these events, it is possible to observe the values of each resource that the player managed at the time of the event. Figure 11 provides an example of this analysis.

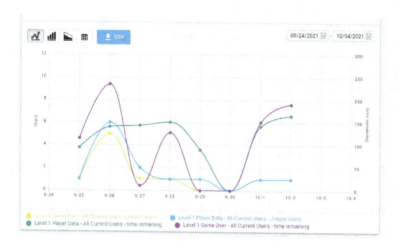

Figure 11. Analytics spline chart displaying time remaining when users finished level 1.

The presented chart illustrates the average time remaining on each day of testing, with the finishing of level 1 and level failure events depicted in green and purple, respectively. Additionally, it displays the number of occurrences of both events, with level completions in blue and level fails in yellow. The testing dates are indicated on the horizontal axis. This graph effectively demonstrates that the number of level fails is roughly equivalent to the number of level clears. By examining the values for all levels, it is evident that on average, players required approximately 1.77 tries to complete the first level, 1.46 attempts to finish the second, and 2.43 attempts to pass the third level. These values satisfy the objective of creating levels that could be completed in three or fewer attempts, with the exception of a few participants who gave up on level 3. Further analysis of the Player Data and Game Over events revealed that players managed their resources well, with an average of 2 minutes to spare when finishing a level and failing with an average of 3 minutes remaining. Stamina management was also not an issue, with averages ranging from 40 to 55 on level clears and between 58 and 75 when failing. The knowledge resource ranged from 70 to 80 on level clears and between 25 and 56 when failing, but this did not cause level failure. Finally, players kept their stress under control, with an average of 50 to 59 across all levels. Stress was the most common cause of level failure, as anticipated, due to design flaws in the Damage Taken event that led to additional stress in the player's character.

In conclusion, game analytics were critical in identifying design flaws in hazard placement across levels and suggesting potential solutions. Furthermore, the intuitive game mechanics, such as the facilities and resources presented to the player, were demonstrated, as well as the strategies used by players to manage these resources.

V. Conclusions

The project's objectives as an advergame were assessed using pilot testing surveys. The System Usability Scale determined that the system's usability ranked in the top 10 % with a final score of 86.18, indicating the advergame's success as a system. The Game Experience Questionnaire showed the importance of user experience and demonstrated that while the game was generally enjoyable, it could benefit from features that enhance immersion and consistency. Adjustments to the challenging aspects of the game could also improve the user's experience. The Game Message Impact Questionnaire produced highly positive results, indicating that digital games can be used to promote brands and spread messages. Specifically, participants agreed that the advergame was effective in promoting ISEP, and many learned more about ISEP through playing the game. Game analytics during testing highlighted areas where the game was too difficult and suggested solutions to improve interaction with hazards and enemies, as well as demonstrating the intuitiveness of game features such as facilities and resource management.

Overall, the project accomplished most of its development objectives. However, some implementation issues were encountered, particularly in the gameplay dimension, including difficulty and progression factors. The game lacked persistence of progression upon application closure and mid-level checkpoints in its levels, though these omissions were intentional to prioritize other areas of the game's development during the allotted time.

Conflict of interest

The authors declare that the research was conducted in the absence of any commercial or financial relationships that could be construed as a potential conflict of interest.

Author contributions

FC conducted the study, designed and developed the game and wrote the document. VC designed the study, monitored the study and revised all the documents.

References

Apperley, T. (2006). Genre and game studies: Toward a critical approach to video game genres. *Simulation & Gaming—Simulat Gaming, 37*, 6–23.

Baptista, R., Coelho, A., & Vaz de Carvalho, C. (2015). Relationship between game categories and skills development: Contributions for serious game design. *Proceedings of the European Conference on Game Based Learning, 1*, 34–42.

Corti, K. (2006). Games¬based Learning; a serious business application. *Informe de PixelLearning, 34*(6), 1–20.

Cruz-Lara, S., Manjón, B.F., & Vaz de Carvalho, C. (2013). Enfoques innovadores en juegos serios. *IEEE VAEP RITA, 1*(1), 19–21.

Dörner, R., Göbel, S., Effelsberg, W., & Wiemeyer, J. (2016). *Serious game: Foundations, concepts and practice.* Springer.

Drachen, A., Seif El-Nasr, M., & Canossa, A. (2013). Game analytics—the basics. In M. Seif El-Nasr, A. Drachen, & A. Canossa (Eds.), *Game analytics: Maximizing the value of player data* (pp. 13–40). Springer.

GamePolitics. (2009). Army's video game-equipped recruitment center fuels controversy (archived) [Online]. Accessed January 15, 2021, from https://web.archive.org/web/20111217162928/http://gamepolitics.com/category/topics/americas-army?page=1

Gui, J., Nagappan, M., & Halfond, W.G. (2017). What aspects of mobile ads do users care about? An empirical study of mobile in-app ad reviews. *arXiv preprint* arXiv:1702.07681.

IJsselsteijn, W.A., de Kort, Y.A.W., & Poels, K. (2013). *The game experience questionnaire.* s.n.

Jenkin, G., Madhvani, N., Signal, L., & Bowers, S. (2014). A systematic review of persuasive marketing techniques to promote food to children on television. *Obesity Reviews, 15*(4), 281–293.

Johnson, D., Gardner, M.J., & Perry, R. (2018). (GEQ), Validation of two game experience scales: The player experience of need satisfaction (PENS) and game experience questionnaire. *International Journal of Human-Computer Studies, 118*, 38–46.

Keizer, G. (1985). Seven cities of gold. *Compute!'s Gazette, 3*(19), 114–115.

Kennedy, B. (2002). Uncle Sam wants you (to play this game) [Online]. Accessed January 14, 2021, from https://www.nytimes.com/2002/07/11/technology/uncle-sam-wants-you-to-play-this-game.html?sq=wardynski&scp=1&st=cse

Law, E.L.-C., Brühlmann, F., & Mekler, E.D. (2018). *Systematic review and validation of the game experience questionnaire (GEQ)—implications for citation and reporting practice* (pp. 257–270). s.n.

Leontiadis, I., Efstratiou, C., Picone, M., & Mascolo, C. (2012). *Don't kill my ads! balancing privacy in an ad-supported mobile application market.* s.n.

MindJumpers. (2011). Impressive digital campaign: Magnum Pleasure Hunt [Online]. Accessed January 18, 2021, from https://www.mindjumpers.com/magnum-pleasure-hunt/

MullenLowe Group. (2013). Pleasure Hunt on Youtube [Online]. Accessed 2015 January 2021, from https://www.youtube.com/watch?v=gEDSAnU5rM4. Accessed 15 January 2021

Norman, K.L. (2013). Geq (game engagement/experience questionnaire): A review of two papers. *Interacting with Computers, 25*(4), 278–283.

Osborne, S. (2002). America's army: Operations review [Online]. Accessed January 14, 2021, from https://www.gamespot.com/reviews/americas-army-operations-review/1900-2895424/

plinq. (2019). List of Advergames [Online]. Accessed December 5, 2020, from https://www.plinq.co/advergames-by-year

Saaty, R. (1987). The analytic hierarchy process—what it is and how it is used. *Mathematical Modelling, 9*(3), 161–176.

Saaty, T.L. (2008). Decision making with the analytic hierarchy process. *International Journal of Services Sciences, 1*(1), 83–98.

Sauro, J. (2011). Measuring usability with the System Usability Scale (SUS) [Online]. Accessed February 1, 2021, from https://measuringu.com/sus/

Sawyer, B., & Smith, P. (2008). *Serious games taxonomy.* s.n.

Schmidt, S., Zadtootaghaj, S., Möller, S., Metzger, F., Hirth, M., & Suznjevic, M. (2018). *Subjective evaluation methods for gaming quality* (P. GAME). ITU Publications.

Skinner, O. (2020). Product placement in video games [Online]. Accessed December 4, 2020, from https://www.voices.com/blog/product-placement-in-video-games/

Terlutter, R., & Capella, M.L. (2013). The gamification of advertising: Analysis and research directions of in-game advertising, advergames, and advertising in social network games. *Journal of Advertising, 42*(2–3), 95–112.

Thabane, L., Ma, J., Chu, R., Cheng, J., Ismaila, A., Rios, L., Robson, R., Thabane, M., Giangregorio, L., & Goldsmith, C. (2010). A tutorial on pilot studies: The what, why and how. *BMC Medical Research Methodology, 10*, Article 1.

van Teijlingen, E., & Hundley, V. (2001). The importance of pilot studies. *Social Research Update, 35.*

Warren, C., Batra, R., Loureiro, S.M.C., & Bagozzi, R.P. (2019). Brand coolness. *Journal of Marketing, 83*(5), 36–56.

Wiemeyer, J., & Hardy, S. (2013). Serious games and motor learning: Concepts, evidence, technology. In *Serious games and virtual worlds in education, professional development, and healthcare.* IGI Global.

Williams, A. (2003). How to… write and analyse a questionnaire. *Journal of Orthodontics, 30*(3), 245–252.

Zyda, M. (2005). From visual simulation to virtual reality to games. *Computer, 38*(9), 25–32.

José Carlos López Ardao (Universidade de Vigo, Spain)

Chapter XI   Gamification in learning English as a second language (LESL)

I. Introduction

Gamification is the use of game mechanics and dynamics together with the game thinking of players in non-game contexts and applications, such as education.

A common problem in education, perhaps always, has always been to get students to achieve an adequate level of motivation and greater engagement in studying a subject. Gamification aims precisely to boost students' motivation, effort, dedication and satisfaction. It should be clarified that the educational use of gamification should not be confused with the use of educational games (there are thousands on the web and in toy stores), serious games (video games with specific learning objectives in some discipline), simulators (games to imitate real-life situations and scenarios for learning and training purposes) or game-based learning, which consists of using games such as SimCity, Civilization, World of Warcraft, Minecraft, etc. in educational contexts.

There are numerous research papers that report good practices and success cases in introducing gamification into the classroom. Yukai Chou (2021) shows a list of successful use cases of gamification in education including many of the most successful online education platforms, such as TEDed, Khan Academy, Coursera, Udemy, Microsoft Virtual Academy, SoloLearn or CodeAcademy.

A recent meta-analysis of the literature (Bai et al., 2020) analyses the results of 32 papers comparing academic performance between groups that use gamification (experimental) and groups that do not (control). This paper concludes that academic performance was significantly better for students in the experimental groups, in which gamification techniques were used, than in the control groups.

If we focus on the specific field of second-language learning, Garland (2015) carries out a systematic review of research papers published in this field between 2013 and 2015 in his doctoral thesis. In the end, 14 studies were selected, most of them using experimental and control groups, showing that it is feasible to achieve, in many cases, a higher level of motivation, dedication and satisfaction on the part of the learner with the help of gamification.

Another more comprehensive systematic review has recently been published (Dehghanzadeh et al., 2021), which presents an overview of the state of the art on the use of gamification for Learning English as a Second Language (LESL) in digital environments. For this systematic review, 22 publications were selected between 2008 and 2019. Most of the studies reviewed indicated that the use of gamification for LESL was beneficial in terms of learners' experiences. In terms of language content learning, most studies reported positive results. In addition to the learning of language content, 17 studies additionally pointed the increase of relevant indicators such as engagement, motivation or satisfaction.

When we talk about motivation, we can distinguish between intrinsic motivation, which is innate to the individual and comes from within, and extrinsic motivation, which corresponds to stimulation coming from outside in the form of rewards and incentives.

Intrinsic motivation is that which leads us to do things for the simple pleasure of doing them, for personal satisfaction, and without the need for extrinsic reinforcement. There are several theories related to intrinsic motivation that have been commonly applied in the gamification literature.

According to Goal-setting theory (Locke et al., 1981), goals that are immediate, specific and moderately stringent are more motivating than those that are long term, vaguely defined, or those that are too easy or too difficult. To this end, it is essential to provide immediate feedback so that learners can measure their progress in relation to the goals, and also to let them know if they need to make adjustments in their strategy or dedication.

Self-efficacy theory (Bandura, 1977) refers with this concept to confidence in one's own ability to achieve desired goals and outcomes. Self-efficacy usually increases when the learner successfully completes a sequence of tasks that are progressively increasing in difficulty. In this sense, it is useful to use a system that allows the student to measure his or her progress and to have direct feedback on his or her performance.

The social comparison theory (Festinger, 1954) states that people evaluate their abilities and opinions in relation to those of others. There are quite a few studies that point out that upward comparison positively influences students to be more engaged in their learning.

The operant conditioning theory (Skinner, 1950) argues that a behavior can be reinforced by the consequences it carries. In this sense, Skinner points to the reinforcement of intrinsic motivation using extrinsic rewards or incentives.

The self-determination theory (SDT) (Ryan & Deci, 2000), that is considered the most important theory of human motivation, is based on the assumption that all humans have three innate (unlearned) psychological needs, which we seek to satisfy for excellent functioning and well-being: *Competence*, or the need to acquire skill or mastery in those areas of knowledge in which we are interested; *Relatedness*, or the need to relate to other people; and *Autonomy*, or the need to be free to be able to make the decisions one considers appropriate at any given moment.

Dan Pink (2009) considers that intrinsic motivation is driven by competence, autonomy and purpose (relatedness is not mentioned). Marczewski (2013) proposes his model of intrinsic motivation for gamification by including purpose in the SDT model. Purpose refers to as the human need to want to give meaning to what we do, and which is closely linked to altruism, help, charity or social compromise. In this way, Marczewski refers to his model as *RAMP: Relationship, Autonomy, Mastery and Purpose*. An important added value of Marczewski's work was to relate these motivators to the types of users (or behaviors) that can be found in a gamified system:

- *Philanthropists*, especially motivated by purpose.
- *Achievers*, mainly motivated by mastery.
- *Socializers*, especially motivated by relatedness.
- *Free Spirits*, mainly motivated by autonomy.

It is worth mentioning that, in practice, all students have a little of each type of user, although usually one type of behavior clearly stands out from the others. The RAMP model is now considered a very useful model in the design of gamified systems. In Bai et al. (2020), the authors argue that the better academic performance of groups in which gamification techniques were used can be explained by the theories of intrinsic motivation mentioned above. Gamification promotes goal setting and, as a result, students tend to achieve better results. On the other hand, gamification can satisfy the need for recognition cited in social comparison theory and SDT (need for relatedness). Even operant conditioning theory points to social recognition as a positive external reinforcement. In addition, gamification provides the learner with feedback on their performance, which helps to satisfy the SDT need for mastery.

The fact that Skinner's operant conditioning studies argue that extrinsic rewards can reinforce intrinsic motivation means that special attention should be paid to extrinsic motivation. Zichermann and Cunningham (2011) identify four types of extrinsic rewards or incentives, ranked according to the priority given by humans. This is the well-known SAPS model of extrinsic motivation:

- *Status*: People place the higher value on being able to achieve a position of privilege and recognition above all others.

- *Access*: On a second level, we value having restricted or exclusive access to advantages, spaces, information, resources, elements, etc. to which others do not have access.
- *Power*: Next, we value the ability to exercise some kind of power, rank, command, etc. over others.
- *Stuff*: Finally, it is curious to note that "things," that is, tangible or material rewards, occupy the last position in terms of preference.

This ranking is also due to the fact that it is common for each element of the pyramid to imply the availability of the elements below it. Status usually implies access, but not the other way around. Access usually implies power, and power is usually accompanied by the possibility of having things.

Zichermann and Cunningham (2011) also consider the relationship between the two types of motivation, indicating that intrinsic motivation is necessary in the medium/long term, but is not always sufficient or explicit. As examples, intrinsic motivation may exist and the person may be aware of it, but it may not be sufficient, and in that case extrinsic motivation may help to enhance it and serve as a trigger (e.g., losing weight or quitting smoking). On the other hand, intrinsic motivation may be hidden, or the person may not be aware of it, and extrinsic motivation may help to uncover it and make it explicit (e.g., reading or playing chess).

A key issue when bringing gamification into the classroom is choosing the most appropriate application or digital environment for our objectives. In this respect, although in other fields we can find implementations of gamification using learning management system (LMS) platforms, especially Moodle (Ekici, 2021), in the field of LESL, as far as we know, there are hardly any cases of use of this type of platform. The work of Homer et al. (2018) uses ClassDojo, a gamification-oriented LMS, but it is more common to use tools focused on language learning that incorporate gamification, such as Duolingo (James & Mayer, 2019), or to use quiz-based tools such as Kahoot, Quizziz or Jeopardy (Dehghanzadeh et al., 2021).

To fill this gap, in this paper we propose a gamification architecture to be implemented in any general LMS, focusing on the teaching of English as a second language. More specifically, we will use Moodle given the great possibilities it offers for gamification.

II. A gamification architecture for LESL

The main idea of this work is to propose a gamification architecture general enough to be implemented in any LMS, focusing on the teaching of English as a second language. When we talk about proposing an architecture, we are referring to defining the necessary gamification elements and the interrelationships between them. Let's start by defining the different elements.

2.1. Points and leaderboards

We start from the usual scenario of a virtual classroom to support teaching based on an LMS, typically Moodle. In this virtual classroom, teachers share resources with students and propose activities through workshops, assignments, quizzes, forums, etc. The idea is to convert this virtual space into a gamified virtual classroom, where students become players and the different types of activities become challenges, battles, missions, etc. As a result of performing these activities, students get points. In a normal course, these points are used as grades which, with the appropriate weighting, and combined with other grades from exams and written tests, are used to obtain a final grade for the course. In our gamified classroom, the points will be accumulated in a leaderboard, which can be displayed in an orderly way.

In a simple gamification architecture design, we can choose to use a single type of points and all activities would contribute to points of this type. In the case of Moodle, the leaderboard would be a grading category to which we would assign all activities. However, in a more complex design, the architecture could consider using several types of points. The reason for this is that if users can exhibit a combination of different types of behaviors (Achievers, Philanthropists, Socializers and Free spirits), we could use different types of points to motivate different types of behaviors. We propose to use the following types of points:

- *Merit points* would be used to assess the performance level in the activities. That is, it would be the actual grade of an activity. These points will be especially interesting for "achiever" behavior. As we said, these points would be collected in Moodle using a grading category to which the desired activities would be assigned.
- *Activity points* will be used to reward the completion of the tasks, regardless of the grade obtained, as well as to encourage activity on the platform (using the forum, regularly accessing the virtual classroom, etc.). In other words, work and effort are rewarded, not merit or level of performance. These points are attractive for "free spirit" behavior. In the case of using Moodle, there is a

plugin called "Level-Up" (available at https://moodle.org/plugins/block_xp), which allows us to configure which events receive points automatically on the platform (submitting an assignment, starting a discussion, answering a quiz, doing a peer assessment, etc.), which automates and greatly simplifies the management of this type of points (referred to as eXperience Points).

- *Karma* (or reputation) *points* will be used to reward altruism, outstanding collaboration in group work, reputation among peers, help in the forums, etc. These points are very attractive for philanthropic and socializer behavior. The appropriate way to account for these points in Moodle is to use an additional category for grades in forums or for group works.

When several types of points are used, the best way to simplify gamification management is to use a generic main category of points, which could be called *Game Points* (GP) or *eXperience Points* (XP) that accounts for all types of points. In this way, the main ranking in the course would be established based on these game points, which would consider all behaviors, and not only merit, for example. The Moodle plugin "Level-Up," in its paid version, allows points earned in a Moodle grading category or element to be added up as XP points, which makes this module an ideal mechanism for counting the main game points and visually displaying the overall ranking with different possibilities.

Regardless of whether merit points are used to contribute to the course game points, we consider them to be the most important points from an academic point of view and therefore recommend that these points are converted to a grade that can also be used in the calculation of the Final Grade for the course. As an example, if we want the activities completed throughout the course to have a weight of 20 % in the final grade, we can distribute 200 merit points among the different activities of the course, so that the student sees a direct relationship between the accumulated merit points and their contribution to the final grade (by simply dividing the points by 100).

2.2. Course progress and access restrictions

In gamification it is essential to give feedback to the student on their progress and performance level in the course. To this end, Moodle offers the possibility of using *activity completion tracking*, which allows the teacher to establish the completion conditions for each activity, such as having received a passing or failing grade on an assignment or quiz or having created a certain number of discussions or forum replies. As activities are completed, a completion mark is displayed next to them.

To show the learner their progress more clearly, it is highly recommended to use the *progress bar*, a block that visually displays the completion status of selected activities.

Another feature of Moodle that is extremely useful in gamification is *access restrictions*. Moodle allows the teacher to configure the conditions that must be met in an activity, section or resource for students to be able to access that element. These access conditions can be to obtain a minimum grade in a category or activity, to complete a certain activity, to belong to a certain group, or to reach a certain XP level.

Although we will talk about other uses of access restrictions later, a very interesting use is to offer students a specific learning sequence, which can also be different according to the conditions of each student. For example, we could define several groups of learners, who would see different sets of activities, and even have these unlocked in sequence as they are completed. Another example of use would be to offer learners different reinforcement tasks based on their grade on a pronunciation test. Access restrictions offer many possibilities for defining multiple personalized learning sequences.

2.3. Achievements and levels. Virtual objects

To increase student motivation, we must set short-term goals or objectives. These objectives can be of two types:

- On the one hand, the goal can be to reach a *point level*, that is, a certain number of points of some kind. If different types of points are used, it is best to use one main point category and define levels for it. The "Level-Up" plugin allows us to define levels for XP points, so it is an ideal ally for gamification in Moodle once again.
- On the other hand, the objective can be to obtain an *achievement*, which is an intermediate milestone defined by the teacher, to provide feedback on the student's progress and serve as an extra motivation to study and perseverance. Examples of achievements would be:
  - Achieving a minimum grade for all the activities for a period.
  - Being among the top performers in an activity or set of activities.
  - Doing all the activities for a period.
  - Attending all class sessions during a certain period, etc.

When a student reaches a new level or obtain an achievement, a *reward* or recognition by means of a *badge* (or both) should be given to the student. For continuous feedback and a greater sense of progress, it is advisable to reward on a regular basis. Therefore, one type of reward that it is very interesting for gamification are virtual objects, which are *intermediate rewards* to be collected by the learner little by little and finally exchanged for final rewards. In Moodle there is a specific plugin called "Stash" (available at https://moodle.org/plugins/block_st ash), which allows to create, award and exchange virtual objects.

To implement achievements in Moodle we will also use *access restrictions*, since the achievement is nothing more than a set of conditions. For this purpose, there is an extremely useful resource in Moodle, which is the *label*, a text box that is displayed on the main page of the course, but only if the conditions configured as access restrictions allow it. Since the virtual objects in the Stash plugin are displayed by means of a special code (snippet) to be inserted into a text box, an achievement and its reward (the virtual object) can be easily created by pasting the code of a virtual object into a label and configure the conditions of the achievement.

A very interesting possibility offered by the "Stash" plugin is the use of a *virtual economy* within the course, which is very useful for gamification. For example, we can define a virtual currency that we will use to reward achievements or levelling up with one or more coins. At the end of the course, we can open the "market" for students to exchange their coins for final rewards. Another possibility is to define two or three different virtual objects that are obtained in different types of achievements or levels. In this case, it is interesting to have to collect objects of different types to get a reward. Since the "Stash" plugin allows us to define exchange rules between different virtual objects, we will also create a virtual object to represent each finalist reward, so that, at the end of the course, each student will have in his/her inventory the set of finalist rewards obtained.

2.4. Finalist rewards and badges

When defining finalist rewards, we must consider the SAPS model of Zichermann and Cunningham (2011). In this sense, we can consider that badges are really rewards that grant *status* and, therefore, must be publicly visible. Similarly, another "status" reward is the use of public rankings, as students will, as far as possible, wish to occupy top positions.

We should mention that Moodle badges are used to certificate acquired competences and skills and, therefore, they are not suitable for recognizing achievement in gamification. Instead of using Moodle badges, we propose to create a group for each badge to be awarded. If the group is set up with an illustrative icon image, this will be displayed in the forum posts next to the learner's name and avatar, giving the Moodle forums a visual aspect related to status and recognition. To automate the process of joining a group ion Moodle, and thus avoid the teacher having to do it, it is advisable to use a *group choice activity* in which we have configured the access restrictions necessary to reach the achievement related to the badge represented by the group.

Within the type of rewards that grant *access*, one possibility is to restrict access to certain sections of the course or to a certain set of resources and activities. For this we can again use *access restrictions*. The conditions can be to have passed a certain quiz, to have reached a certain XP level, to belong to a certain group or to have certain virtual object, such as a VIP pass, a ticket or a certain number of coins. Other finalist "access" rewards that are highly valued by students are being able to enjoy advantages in assignments, exams, written tests, etc. that other students do not have, such as cheats, extra time, extra attempts at quizzes or homework submissions, etc.

Finally, if we wanted to reward our learners with "power," we could do so by giving them roles such as "forum moderator," "group leader," "assessment reviewer," etc. This is feasible in Moodle by defining roles and managing permissions associated with activities.

III. Activities for LESL

Once we have designed our gamified virtual classroom, the next step is to configure it in Moodle and this involves creating and configuring the Moodle activities that we consider most suitable for our students, in this case, focused on the learning of a second language such as English.

- *Quizzes* are excellent activities for LESL, since the evaluation and feedback is automatic and immediate and they allow us to ask many kinds of questions to work on phonetics, vocabulary, reading comprehension or grammar. We can use multiple choice, gap-fill, short answer or matching questions, and we can use embedded audio directly in the statements to work on listening. Multiple-choice questions can be used to create a "Do you want to be a millionaire?" activity and short answer (one word) questions can be used to create a crossword-type activity. In both cases the availability of the "Game" plugin (available at https://moodle.org/plugins/mod_game) is required.
- *Glossary* is an interesting activity to work on vocabulary belonging to different semantic fields. Besides, the glossaries created can be used later as the definitions of thematic crosswords (requires the availability of the "Games" plugin).
- *H5P interactive video* is an activity that allows us to take a YouTube video and enrich it with questions of different types that appear throughout the video.

This makes it possible to create activities with a similar utility to the quizzes, i.e., to work on phonetics, vocabulary or grammar, but the video allows the questions to be contextualized and to work mainly on listening activities.

- Within the different *H5P interactive activities* there are additional activities which are very interesting for language learning:
  - You can create *dictation* activities with immediate feedback to work on listening.
  - *Find the Words* activities are useful for vocabulary learning.
  - In *Mark the words* activities, the student must mark words that meet certain criteria (a certain phoneme, grammatical category, a verb tense, etc.).
  - *Sort the paragraphs* activities allow us to work on reading comprehension and grammar.
  - *Speak the words* is a basic pronunciation activity. The student must read a word or text, which is recorded by the system to perform an audio-to-text conversion, to check if there is a match with the original text, and so the pronunciation is acceptable.
  - *Essay* activity allows the creation of a writing activity where the teacher can configure which words or regular expressions should appear in the text to provide immediate feedback to the learner.
- *Assignments, workshops* and *forums* are the suitable activities for writing and speaking work. Assignments should be used when the assessment and feedback is to be done by the teacher, while workshops are suitable when the number of assignments is very large or when self- and/or peer assessment is preferred. Forums are useful when we want the work to be public for the whole class and we want students to rate and/or make critical comments on the work of their peers. Moodle assignments are also the suitable activity for group work.

IV. Practical guide to gamification

In short, in our gamified virtual classroom the *players* are the students. The different types of activities that we usually propose to the students in the classroom or as homework will be converted into challenges, battles, missions, etc. As a result of make these activities, students get *points*, which are accumulated on a board which can be displayed in an orderly way as a *leaderboard* or ranking. An essential task in gamification design is to define a set of objectives that learners can achieve. These objectives can be of two types: obtaining a new score *level* or reaching an intermediate *achievement*. Levels and achievements will be rewarded with *virtual objects* and/or recognized by means of *badges*. Virtual objects can be exchanged for *finalist rewards* and merit points will usually contribute to the final grade of the course. Figure 1 shows the different elements of the gamification architecture and their interrelationships.

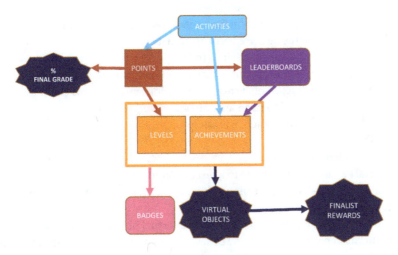

Figure 1. Gamification proposal.

Finally, we are going to give the basic instructions and steps to follow to set up a gamified virtual classroom in Moodle using all the gamification elements and Moodle plugins mentioned in this paper.

1. We create two grading categories referred to as "merit points" and "karma points." The maximum number of merit points should be related to their weighting in the final grade of the course (100 points per each 10 %).
2. We create the activities we consider most suitable and assign them to the category "merit points." If we create workshop activities, we assign the assessment grade to the category "karma points."
3. We create "forum" activities to share work with peers and to discuss doubts and problems. We assign forum activities to the category "karma points." Teachers will grade the shared material, comments relevant to this material and forum posts that are helpful to classmates.
4. Using the Stash plugin, we create the virtual objects to represent the finalist rewards and the virtual objects to reward levels and achievements.
5. We define the achievements and point levels (karma and XP are enough) to be rewarded with virtual objects. Then, we use a Moodle label with access

restrictions (an instance of the virtual object must be created in the Stash plugin for each label). Possible achievements could be:

   a. Reaching a new score level

   b. Completing one or more activities

   c. "Passing" one or more activities (obtaining a minimum grade)

   d. Obtain one of the best grades in an activity.

   e. Complete/pass a set of activities (of a type, in a period, etc.).

6. We set up the rules for obtaining activity XP points in the Level-Up plugin. Some examples of relevant events for obtaining activity points could be:

   a. Submit a submission in an assignment or workshop activity.

   b. Do a peer assessment in a workshop activity.

   c. Finish a quiz.

   d. Complete an activity.

   e. Start a discussion or reply to a discussion in a forum activity.

7. We set in Level-Up (paid version only) that "merit points" and "karma points" contribute to XP points.

8. We create rules for the exchange between virtual objects and finalist rewards in the Stash plugin. We place the codes of these rules in labels within a hidden section (which we can call "Marketplace"). This section will be shown at the end of the course.

References

Bai, Shurui, Hew, Khe Foon, & Huang, Biyun. (2020, June 30). Does gamification improve student learning outcome? Evidence from a meta-analysis and synthesis of qualitative data in educational contexts. *Educational Research Review*. Article 100322. https://doi.org/10.1016/j.edurev.2020.100322

Bandura, A. (1977). Self-efficacy: Toward a unifying theory of behavioral change. *Psychological Review*, 84(2), 191–215. https://doi.org/10.1016/0146-6402(78)90002-4

Chou, Yukai. (2021). The 10 best educational apps that use gamification for adults in 2021. https://yukaichou.com/gamification-examples/top-10-education-gamification-examples

Dehghanzadeh, H., Fardanesh, H., Hatami, J., Talaee, E., & Noroozi, O. (2021). Using gamification to support learning English as a second language: A systematic review. *Computer Assisted Language Learning*, 34(7), 934–957. https://doi.org/10.1080/09588221.2019.1648298

Ekici, M. (2021). A systematic review of the use of gamification in flipped learning. *Education and Information Technologies*, *26*, 3327–3346. https://doi.org/10.1007/s10639-020-10394-y

Festinger, L. (1954). A theory of social comparison processes. *Human Relations*, *7*(2), 117–140. https://doi.org/10.1177/001872675400700202

Garland, C.M. (2015). *Gamification and implications for second language education: A meta analysis* [Tesis doctoral, St. Cloud State University]. https://repository.stcloudstate.edu/engl_etds/40/

Homer, R., Hew, K.F., & Tan, C.Y. (2018). Comparing digital badges-and-points with classroom token systems: Effects on elementary school ESL students' classroom behavior and English learning. *Journal of Educational Technology & Society*, *21*(1), 137–151.

James, K.K., & Mayer, R.E. (2019). Learning a second language by playing a game. *Applied Cognitive Psychology*, *33*(4), 669–674. https://doi.org/10.1002/acp.3492

Locke, E.A., Shaw, K.N., Saari, L.M., & Latham, G.P. (1981). Goal setting and task performance: 1969–1980. *Psychological Bulletin*, *90*(1), 125–152. https://psycnet.apa.org/doi/10.1037/0033-2909.90.1.125

Marczewski, A. (2013). *The intrinsic motivation RAMP.* https://www.gamified.uk/gamification-framework/the-intrinsic-motivation-ramp/

Pink, D.H. (2009). *Drive: The surprising truth about what motivates us.* Riverhead Books.

Ryan, R.M., & Deci, E.L. (2000). Self-determination theory and the facilitation of intrinsic motivation, social development, and well-being. *American Psychologist*, *55*(1), 68–78. https://doi.org/10.1037/0003-066X.55.1.68

Skinner, B.F. (1950). Are theories of learning necessary? Psychological Review, 57(4), 193-216. https://doi.org/10.1037/h0054367

Zichermann, G., & Cunningham, C. (2011). *Gamification by design: Implementing game mechanics in web and mobile apps.* O'Reilly Media.

Jonathon Reinhardt (University of Arizona, USA)

Chapter XII   Researching gameful L2 teaching and learning: Challenges and potentials

I. Introduction

As the field of gameful L2 (second/foreign/additional language) teaching and learning (GL2TL) grows, it needs to focus on both research and teaching practice. The digital game industry has grown massive and global over the past few decades with technological advances, surpassing in profit the film and music industries combined. Within the industry, educational gaming is growing at a record pace—valued at US$ 9.2 billion in 2019, it is projected to reach US$ 88.1 billion by 2027, a faster pace than even electric vehicles. (Verified Market Research, 2022). This means that whether or not applied linguists and L2 educators are involved in the development process, increasing numbers of educational games for L2TL will be created and sold to individual learners and schools around the world. If there is a healthy body of research on L2 learning and teaching with games, the industry will recognize the value of working with practitioners of both research and teaching when developing these games. If not, they may develop them without our involvement, leading to more failures than successes.

Formal GL2TL has promise for several reasons. Millions or maybe even billions of people already play digital games all over the world, and many do so in an L2, as most games are available only in the major global languages. In addition, because of international online game communities and international, multilingual servers for MMO games, it is easier than ever to play intentionally in an L2 or in a translingual context—in other words, as a casual way to pick up an L2. Gameful L2 learning experiences can motivate hard-to-reach learners, especially younger ones, and make L2 learning relatable and relevant to them. They can be surprised to find that something they enjoy but that is rarely acknowledged in school can actually be an enjoyable and effective way to learn. In addition, as generations of gamers grow older, more and more students will be familiar with gaming, will respond to it well, and may even come to expect it. Finally, formal gameful L2 learning can develop important skills that are important to successful language learning but that are also sometimes overlooked in traditional communicative language teaching materials, like goal setting or achieving, exploring, risk-taking, collaborating, and competing.

Research on GL2TL has shown great potential. Importantly, successful GL2 learning is contingent on the alignment of many variables, for example, learner variables like gaming literacy and L2 proficiency levels, design variables that focus on mechanics and game features, and gameplay variables like context of play, that is, where and why the game was played. When these variables align positively, research has found that a well-designed game, or well-designed gameful pedagogy, can effectively:

- teach association of L2 form, meaning, and function (Purushotma, 2005);
- contextualize L2 learning through narrativization, or turning experiences into stories (Neville, 2010);
- support practice to mastery through repetition and targeted feedback in sheltered, scaffolded spaces—in other words, giving learners a place to make mistakes and to learn from them (e.g., Reinders & Wattana, 2012);
- promote goal setting and achieving behavior similar to task-based approaches (e.g., Purushotma et al., 2008);
- promote languaging or collaborative negotiation of meaning (e.g., Zheng et al., 2009);
- support identity work and play (e.g., Warner et al., 2019);
- leverage situated, place-based learning, as a game can be played on a portable smart device (e.g., Holden & Sykes, 2011); and
- promote learner autonomy, as a game can be played at non-traditional times and places (e.g., Chik, 2014).

While there is still much to be explored, and there can be failure when variables do not align, the promise of GL2TL is difficult to deny.

II. Reasons for researching gameful L2TL

Considering the number of individuals who give up on L2 learning before gaining much proficiency, a key purpose of L2TL research more broadly is to understand better how L2 learning happens and thus inform how it might be supported in formal and informal learning contexts. As an applied endeavor, research on L2 learning has implications for the design of L2 learning experiences and environments, including materials, curricula, teaching methods, and assessments. L2TL research is also important because it helps educate new and practicing teachers, especially if the goal is to imbue an understanding of teaching as praxis, where teaching and research practice mutually inform one another, and teaching is understood as both an art and a science.

The same can be said about the purpose of gameful L2TL, that we want to better understand what it is, how it happens effectively, and how we might design environments that afford or facilitate it. Individuals learning to become L2 teachers and practicing teachers should learn how game designs can afford learning and how materials, curricula, methods, and assessments can complement them. Games and gameful pedagogy are not magical or mysterious boxes that work without us being able to know why, and if we figure out why and how through careful research design, we can reproduce it and apply what we have learned to new contexts. Ideally, teaching can inform game design and development and integrate it into the research-teaching dialectic.

There are additional pragmatic reasons for studying gameful L2TL that don't have exact parallels in other L2TL fields. For one, the field is quite young and we need to legitimize it to the rest of academia by nurturing it and doing rigorous, high quality research in it. In order for people to get credit for doing work in the field, and to continue doing it, the field has to be recognized as a legitimate area of scholarship. Research credentials can also give us authority to speak about the growing popularity of gaming and to respond to those who think educational gaming is just the latest buzzword or bandwagon. We also need to position ourselves as contributors of useful, applied knowledge in the educational design and development industry, because educational game developers need us and our knowledge if they want to build effective products. When we are invited to be involved in game development because of our credentials, we should be able to explain research findings and implications to people like game developers who may not be familiar with what research is, or even that the fields of L2TL, CALL, SLA, or applied linguistics exist.

III. Challenges to researching gameful L2TL

Unfortunately, there are many challenges as well that can discourage research practice, and sometimes they are hard to overcome. First, there is considerable societal skepticism toward gaming as a legitimate means of learning as well as concerns about the effects of gaming on psychological health. Although their concerns may be grounded in anecdotal evidence or hearsay, many have strong opinions about whether gaming can lead to anti-social or violent behavior and whether it is addictive and what that means for whether we should use games for educational purposes. To these concerns we need to have responses ready, for example, that these are questions that can and should be answered empirically, and that there is also considerable research showing the benefits of gaming.

Another challenge is the considerable academic skepticism toward recognition of gaming as a legitimate field of scholarship. This has resulted in research on gameful L2TL not being recognized for promotion and tenure, lab space and technological support not being available, or games and gameful innovations not being allowed into existing curricula. Compounding this skepticism is a third challenge, that there is no real single disciplinary home for gameful L2TL, since the field is dispersed among applied linguistics, education, languages, game design, game studies, and computer science. While journals and conferences for GL2TL research may be found in CALL, language education, education, or game studies and design, there are few native models for practice of research, teaching, or game development available, and it is difficult to find applicable theory and scholarship. It is challenging to do meaningful research when one feels isolated and not taken seriously.

Yet with these challenges come silver linings. We can be objective providers of facts about learning with games, both benefits and drawbacks, without necessarily taking sides. While game-based learning is something of a buzzword, administrators will normally support innovations and arguments for taking it seriously if they see that the field is expanding, that it is developing academic rigor, and that games are coming whether researchers have anything to do with it or not. Moreover, while it may be easier to do research by simply going to a single conference and relying on journals fully devoted to a field, searching in and finding theories and methods from other fields provides synergy and promotes innovation. These qualities are already evident in the research that has been done.

IV. Approaches to researching gameful L2TL

Reflecting the diversity of the field, research on gameful L2TL has involved pedagogical intervention, evaluation of L2 learning games, analysis of game design, exploration of informal L2 gaming practices, description of L2 gaming communities, building L2 learning games, and by surveying and synthesizing research. A variety of theories and research methodologies have been used, and although languages and audiences have been mostly English and mostly university age learners, findings have been relatively diverse and promising.

First, there have been many formal game-enhanced pedagogical interventions that take an existing, commercial, non-educational or vernacular game and test out how it can be used for L2 learning in a formal context. Usually the games are simulation, strategy, or puzzle games that are not difficult to learn and do not pressure players with time constraints, like *The Sims* or the browser-based strategy game *Forge of Empires*. Since these games are not designed for language learning, an intervention study might focus on the design of supplemental pedagogy or wraparound materials that draw learner attention to particular language features in the game. They usually attempt to measure what is successfully learned—usually vocabulary knowledge—with a pre-test/post-test design. For example, Shintaku (2016) asked whether game-enhanced learning of L2 Japanese could result in prolonged vocabulary retention, and whether the game functionality of vocabulary items impacted their learning. By that, she meant the differences between primary and secondary vocabulary embedded in the game—primary meaning vocabulary the player had to know in order to move through the game, and secondary meaning vocabulary that was peripheral to game play. The game was *Mysteries of the Haunted House*, a free, browser-based adventure/puzzle point-and-click game in Japanese, which was level appropriate for her intermediate-level university students. She created materials to teach all the vocabulary items before and during play and found that knowledge of the primary vocabulary was retained longer than knowledge of the secondary vocabulary. Implications were that the game design had an impact on vocabulary retention, as did the design of the wraparound materials and their implementation.

A second approach to researching GL2TL is by evaluating existing L2 learning games. Since these games are not always developed in consultation with L2TL research, their designs may leave something lacking. Often, they are evaluated through analysis of the game design and by playtesting with learners, that is, by testing learning outcomes and having learners share their opinions of the game. For example, Gonzalez-Lloret, Ortega, and Payne (2020) evaluated the game *Practice Spanish: Study Abroad* by comparing the experiences and outcomes of a group using it with a control group using equivalent Internet activities. In addition, they tested its adaptability for formal classroom use by having students play it in pairs, even though it was designed for solo play. Findings were that there was no significant difference in learning outcomes and that dyads actually outperformed individuals, who were generally bored with the game. Players used far more English than Spanish, although the English they used was focused meta-linguistically on Spanish. The study shows that educational games truly should be subjected to classroom research if their developers want them to be successful, preferably before they are released to market, so that unanticipated issues can be addressed.

Similar to evaluating games, a third approach is to analyze not the learning
outcomes of gameplay but the designs of existing games, implicating learning potential based on the analysis. For example, Dixon (2021) compiled a large corpus
of all the language used for the mechanics of dialogue trees, quest objectives,
and quest stage explanations in two games, *Skyrim* and *Fallout*. After analyzing
and comparing these mechanic-based sub-corpora, he found that the language
of a particular mechanic in one title is more similar to the language of that same
mechanic in other titles from different genres than it is to language of other mechanics found in the same title or genre. The finding counters the claim made
that certain genres should be associated with particular learning affordances,
and in fact we should be associating game mechanics and designs, not game
titles or genres, with L2 learning outcomes.

A fourth approach is to have learners independently play games and then
attempt to assess their informal L2 learning experiences, not by setting up a pedagogical intervention, conducting an experiment, or evaluating or analyzing the
game, but by explaining the game briefly to the learners, having them play on
their own for considerable amounts of time, and then surveying or conducting
interviews with them. While these studies tend to be descriptive, they may also
involve discourse analysis of gameplay sessions. The games are carefully chosen
by the researchers for their potential for independent language learning at the
learner's proficiency level. As an example, Scholz (2016) traced the L2 develop-
mental trajectories of several advanced German learners who played *World of
Warcraft* over several months. Although they had an initial orientation session,
the learners were free to play as much as they desired. Scholz then conducted
an analysis of their L2 learning using complex adaptive systems theory, showing
how dynamic, non-linear, and dissimilar from others each learner's trajectory
was. While all the players improved and found the experience motivating, they
did so in very different and unpredictable ways. The point of the research was
in some ways to show the explanatory capacity of the learning theory, with the
results implying that some games might function as effective informal learning
environments for some learners, but not for others.

Another kind of research practice describes L2 gaming practices in the wild,
usually taking descriptive, ethnographic, or sociolinguistic approaches and focusing on the attendant discourses around and about games, rather than (or in
addition to) the interactions in or through games. These studies consider gaming
a social practice rather than an individual psycho-cognitive phenomenon and
ask how users engage in these socio-literacy practices and what we can learn
from them. An example of this sort of research is Vazquez-Calvo's (2021) analysis of the literacy practices of a multilingual gamer community that decided

to produce crowd translations of popular games into Catalan. Vazquez-Calvo takes an ethnographic, discourse analytic approach, focusing on detailed analyses of specific actions to illustrate his main thesis, that language learning occurs not only through individual translation but also, and maybe even more importantly, by means of social interaction around and about translation and translation skills. This approach clearly reflects the L2 learning theory espoused by the researcher, that language learning entails literacy development in social contexts and through affinity practices, that is, doing what one enjoys for social and personal identity reasons. While this sort of research is not generalizable, it is highly ecologically valid and serves, like Dixon (2021) and Scholz (2016), as a model for, and illustration of, how the research methodology a study uses is interwoven with the learning theory it espouses.

Research involving the building of games for L2 learning from the ground up are usually quite complex projects, and so the reports we see on them are usually redacted and not reflective of all the processes involved. The appeal of building our own games is that we can target learners and what we want them to learn more precisely, instead of relying on vernacular games or on educational games that may not be exactly what we need and that may present other issues. We can also take this approach to build minigames or just sections of games in order to test out how particular designs and mechanics potentially correlate with learning dynamics and outcomes (e.g., Cornillie et al., 2015), without committing to an entire game. As an example of a multi-phase project involving design, playtesting, and analysis of learning outcomes, Perry (2021) reports on an extensive project where she built augmented reality place-based games and had learners of French play them in order to see whether and how the different designs support high-level co-regulation, which is associated with co-construction of meaning as opposed to simple knowledge acquisition. The development of the game was done through design-based research, which meant that at various stages of creation the game was play-tested to gauge attitudes and record behaviors and to inform the next design stage. Once Perry had built the games she had 58 players play them in teams and recorded player interactions, finding different levels of co-regulation and surmising that certain quest designs led to more high level, group co-regulation than other quest designs.

Finally, research can be surveys of games or surveys of research on games, sometimes involving meta- or synthetic analysis. This research is important to the growth of a field because it builds the ontological and epistemological grounding that supports the field over time, ultimately guiding practice. There have been a number of game surveys and research syntheses that have helped conceptualize the GL2TL field by taking certain angles or perspectives on research, or by categorizing games for their usefulness as learning tools. A survey of games tries to make sense for practitioners by selecting specific games and organizing them according to heuristic categories, and a synthesis attempts to find patterns in studies that are dispersed and may not necessarily reference one another. For example, Filsecker and Bündgens-Kosten (2012) categorize games according to the SLA theory their designs match, while Reinhardt and Sykes (2012) categorize research according to whether they looked at vernacular or educational games, and Reinhardt and Thorne (2020) categorize research findings according to L2 learning affordances. Peterson (2016) as well as Jabbari and Eslami (2019) examined MMORPGs in particular, and Peterson (2021) looks specifically at simulation games. As a recent example, Blume (2021) provides a survey of games that can be used for teaching inclusivity and developing transcultural communicative competence. By presenting a selection of LGBTQIA+ inclusive games like *Coming Out Simulator, Dream Daddy, Spring,* and *Butterfly Soup* and outlining wraparound language-learning activities for use with them, Blume makes the argument that language educators can use GL2TL to counter the heteronormativity found in traditional language-learning materials. Blume presents the work as a rhetorical argument to promote this practice, as well as to make key pedagogical points and advice.

V. Discussion

To date, research on GL2TL has shown eclectic diversity of research purposes, approaches, and outcomes. While most research uses a wide variety of theories and methodologies from different fields in social sciences, education, and humanities, most all highlight, claim, or imply a theory of L2 learning, and most have implications for future research and/or gameful pedagogy. They have used experimental, interventionist, descriptive, ethnographic, analytic, qualitative, and quantitative techniques, and often particular theories implicate particular methodologies and vice-versa. Some examine vernacular and some educational games, while others examine gaming practices and communities, and still others build their own games. While some focus on learners or players, others do not and instead focus on game design, and still others focus on both learners and design. As difficult as it may be to apprehend this diversity, it should not be thought of as a liability, but rather an asset that reflects the potential of GL2TL to disrupt and refresh current practices in language-learning research and teaching more broadly. While it may seem divergent and disunified, research is laying the broad ontological and epistemological foundations—what it is we are looking for and how we should do it—that our field needs in order to grow into the future.

Research has tended to focus on one or the other end of several parameters. First, it can focus either on GL2TL in the wild or in autonomous contexts, or in formal/controlled environments, usually a classroom or in a course. The former is especially important because it implicates the design of the other; in other words, how people L2 game outside of classrooms informs what we do with games in them. Second, research seems to either take the perspective of gaming as a social practice or a game as a learning object. In the first, games and gaming are part of an ecology, while in the second, the game is an ecology itself; the latter can benefit from perspectives on the former because it recognizes that games are not truly realized as learning objects until they are played, and that the context of play can make a difference. Third, research seems to either look at vernacular, commercial off the shelf games, or at educational games, which would include games that the researcher themselves design. Clearly there are benefits and drawbacks of each, but the distinction is important because the locus of the pedagogy and who designs it—an educational gaming company, the teacher, or someone else—can make a difference in how the game is experienced.

There are also several gaps or lacunae that should be pointed out because these point to research opportunities. First, there is a need for more research on educating teachers how to incorporate gameful L2TL in their teaching. It's not clear if we should have them play games, read and analyze gameful lesson plans, design gameful lesson plans, or design games, etc., or in which courses, workshops, or curricula gameful L2TL should be incorporated. Although research is important to share with teachers because it teaches an evidence-based mindset toward practice we don't really know which research to discuss, or how research might inspire or perhaps even alienate teachers. Second, to continue with a focus on teachers, we also need to analyze current formal practices and examine who incorporates games into L2T, and how they do so, exploring their successes, failures, and frustrations. Third, we also need to study L2 gamers who have informally learned languages using games, asking who they are, which games have they used, and how they did it. Thousands of people around the world have L2 gamed, especially in English, but there are very few case studies on them, which would be helpful for their implications on formal GL2TL. Finally, we also need more focus on non-digital gameful approaches like using minigames, analog (board/card) games, and gamification, asking how they have been used and what effective practices are, not just what has been done or what could be done. Just because a game is not digital does not mean it is not gameful, and the fact that GL2TL has its origins in CALL has meant that work on the use of non-digital games has not been welcome there.

VI. Conclusion

The purpose of this paper has been to argue for researching gameful L2TL, by exploring reasons for doing it and the challenges it faces, and by presenting examples of different approaches to research. It is undeniable that GL2TL holds considerable promise and potential, but because of the many challenges that teaching and research practitioners face, it may sometimes seem that the field is not living up to its promise. Maybe change will come slowly, and as generations of learners who L2 gamed mature into L2 teachers, they will not be discouraged by barriers to researching and teaching with games. Whether or not they do, however, it is inevitable that educational games for L2 learning will appear and will begin entering formal and informal usage, regardless of whether they are quality products or not. We can hope that practitioners of GL2TL are able to respond in ways that are recognized as authoritative and legitimate, since their practice is grounded in not only teaching but also a diverse base of research.

References

Blume, C. (2021). Inclusive digital games in the transcultural communicative classroom. *ELT Journal, 75*(2), 181–192.

Chik, A. (2014). Digital gaming and language learning: Autonomy and community. *Language Learning & Technology, 18*(2), 85–100.

Cornillie, F., Van den Branden, K., & Desmet, P. (2015, July 6–8). From language play to linguistic form and back again. Lessons from an experimental study for the design of task-based language practice supported by games. In J. Colpaert, A. Aerts, M. Oberhofer, & M. Gutiérez-Colón Plana (Eds.), *Proceedings of XVIIth International CALL Conference. Task design and CALL, Tarragona, Spain* (pp. 214–222). Universiteit Antwerpen.

Dixon, D. (2021). The linguistic environments of digital games: A discriminant analysis of language use in game mechanics. *CALICO Journal.* http://dx.doi.org/10.1558/cj.20860

Filsecker, M., & Bündgens-Kosten, J. (2012). Behaviorism, constructivism, and communities of practice: How pedagogic theories help us understand game-based language learning. In H. Reinders (Ed.), *Digital games in language teaching and learning* (pp. 50–69). Palgrave Macmillan.

Gonzalez-Lloret, M., Ortega, M.-D., & Payne, S. (2020). Gaming alone or together? L2 beginner-level gaming practices. *Perspectiva, 38*(2), 1–21.

Holden, C., & Sykes, J. (2011). Leveraging mobile games for place-based language learning. *International Journal of Game-based Learning, 1*(2), 1–18.

Jabbari, N., & Eslami, Z.-R. (2019). Second language learning in the context of massively multiplayer online games: A scoping review. *ReCALL*. http://dx.doi.org/10.1017/S0958344018000058

Neville, D. (2010). Structuring narrative in 3D digital game-based learning environments to support second language acquisition. *Foreign Language Annals*, *43*(3), 446–469.

Perry, B. (2021). Gamified mobile collaborative location-based language learning. *Frontiers in Education*. http://dx.doi.org/10.3389/feduc.2021.689599

Peterson, M. (2016). The use of massively multiplayer online role-playing games in CALL: An analysis of research. *Computer Assisted Language Learning*, *29*(7), 1181–1194.

Peterson, M. (2021). Digital simulation games in CALL: A research review. *Computer Assisted Language Learning*. http://dx.doi.org/10.1080/09588221.2021.1954954

Purushotma, R. (2005). You're not studying, you're just... *Language Learning and Technology*, *9*(1), 80–96.

Purushotma, R., Thorne, S.L., & Wheatley, J. (2008). 10 key principles for designing video games for foreign language learning: Ravi Purushotma, Steven L. Thorne, and Julian Wheatley [Internet]. Version 1. lingualgames. April 15, 2009. https://lingualgames.wordpress.com/article/10-key-principles-for-designing-video-27mkxqba7b13d-2/

Reinders, H., & Wattana, S. (2012). Talk to me! Games and students' willingness to communicate. In H. Reinders (Ed.), *Digital games in language learning and teaching* (pp. 156–188). Palgrave Macmillan.

Reinhardt, J., & Sykes, J. (2012). Conceptualizing digital game-mediated L2 learning and pedagogy: Game-enhanced and game-based research and practice. In H. Reinders (Ed.), *Digital games in language learning and teaching* (pp. 32–49). Palgrave Macmillan.

Reinhardt, J., & Thorne, S. (2020). Digital games as language learning environments. In J. Plass, R. Mayer, & B. Homer (Eds.), *Handbook of Game-based Learning* (pp. 409–436). MIT Press.

Scholz, K. (2016). Encouraging free play: Extramural digital game-based language learning as a complex adaptive system. *CALICO Journal*, *34*(1), 39–57.

Shintaku, K. (2016). The interplay of game design and pedagogical mediation in game-mediated Japanese learning. *International Journal of Computer-Assisted Language Learning and Teaching*, *6*(4), 36–55.

Vazquez-Calvo, B. (2021). Guerrilla fan translation, language learning, and metalinguistic discussion in a Catalan-speaking community of gamers. *ReCALL*, *33*(3), 296–313. http://dx.doi.org/10.1017/S095834402000021X

Verified Market Research. (2022). Educational games market size and forecast. Accessed July 28, 2022, from https://www.verifiedmarketresearch.com/prod uct/educational-games-market

Warner, C., Richardson, D., & Lange, K. (2019). Realizing multiple literacies through game-enhanced pedagogies: Designing learning across discourse levels. *Journal of Gaming & Virtual Worlds, 11*(1). http://dx.doi.org/10.1386/ jgvw.11.1.9_1

Zanettin, F. (2012). Translation-Driven Corpora. Corpus Resources for Descriptive and Applied Translation Studies. Routledge.

Zheng, D., Young, M., Wagner, M., & Brewer, R. (2009). Negotiation for action: English language learning in game-based virtual worlds. *Modern Language Journal, 93*(4), 489–511.